ISBN 978-1-330-77290-4
PIBN 10103513

1 MONTH OF
FREE
READING

at

www.ForgottenBooks.com

By purchasing this book you are eligible for one month membership to ForgottenBooks.com, giving you unlimited access to our entire collection of over 1,000,000 titles via our web site and mobile apps.

To claim your free month visit:
www.forgottenbooks.com/free103513

English
Français
Deutsche
Italiano
Español
Português

www.forgottenbooks.com

Mythology Photography **Fiction**
Fishing Christianity **Art** Cooking
Essays Buddhism Freemasonry
Medicine **Biology** Music **Ancient
Egypt** Evolution Carpentry Physics
Dance Geology **Mathematics** Fitness
Shakespeare **Folklore** Yoga Marketing
Confidence Immortality Biographies
Poetry **Psychology** Witchcraft
Electronics Chemistry History **Law**
Accounting **Philosophy** Anthropology
Alchemy Drama Quantum Mechanics
Atheism Sexual Health **Ancient History**
Entrepreneurship Languages Sport
Paleontology Needlework Islam
Metaphysics Investment Archaeology
Parenting Statistics Criminology
Motivational

ARTISANS

AND

MACHINERY:

THE MORAL AND PHYSICAL CONDITION OF THE

MANUFACTURING POPULATION

CONSIDERED WITH REFERENCE TO

MECHANICAL SUBSTITUTES

FOR

HUMAN LABOUR.

BY P. GASKELL, ESQ.

SURGEON.

LONDON:

JOHN W. PARKER, WEST STRAND.

M DCCC XXXVI.

R. CLAY, PRINTER, BREAD-STREET-HILL.

PREFACE.

THE great importance of the subjects discussed in the following pages will be understood, by saying that they involve questions of the highest interest to our commercial relations, and the welfare of the entire kingdom. The declension of the most numerous class of artisans in Great Britain, from comfort, morality, independence, and loyalty, to misery, demoralization, dependence, and discontent, is the painful picture now presented by the domestic manufacturers. The hand-loom weavers, whether of cotton, linen, worsted, or silk, and the multitudes engaged in bobbin-net, lace, and other manufacturing processes, still carried on as household labour, together with all other industrious classes, on whose path steam-machinery is advancing, present a most interesting and anxious subject for examination.

The domestic labourers were at one period a most loyal and devoted body of men. " Lancashire," says an intelligent witness before the Select Committee of Hand-Loom Weavers in 1834, " was a particularly loyal county. There was a call made upon their patriotism at one time to repel the gigantic power of Buonaparte, and it was not made in vain: there were 30,000 volunteers stepped forward in the county, and upwards of 20,000 were hand-loom weavers. Durst any Government call upon the services of such a people, living upon three shillings a week ?"

Unparalleled distress, and long-continued privations, have, it is to be feared, operated prejudicially upon the minds of this large class of artisans. " I have not merited these things !" says another witness : " I am a loyal man, strongly attached to the institutions of my country. I am a friend to social order, and I never shall act upon any other principle myself; but I cannot think I ought tamely to submit to perish without a struggle; and I am confident, that, unless something be done to prevent it, any accidental cause, such as an advance of the price of provisions, or a deficiency of crops, must bring thousands of us to a premature grave. This is the exact condition of things."

Nor can any wonder be felt that men should grow discontented and dissatisfied who labour fourteen or sixteen hours daily, and earn from four to six shillings per week, and who see not the most remote probability that their condition will be improved. Upwards of a million of human beings are literally starving, and the number is constantly on the increase, hand-weaving being the only refuge for the adult labourer, since the spread of the factory system.

Irreligion and general immorality must ever attend hopeless poverty. Men thus circumstanced become reckless and dispirited, and it is painful to witness the growth of unfavourable dispositions in classes who have been driven to destitution by causes far beyond their control. The evidence given before the Committee above mentioned, both by the masters and men, is not less startling than true.

It would have been well if steam and mechanism, in breaking up a healthy, contented, and moral body of labourers, had provided another body, possessing the same excellent qualities, as men and citizens: but it has not been so. "Manufactures," says a late writer, "naturally condense a vast population within a narrow circuit; they afford every facility

for secret cabal and co-operative union among the
work people; they communicate intelligence and
energy to the vulgar mind; they supply, in their
liberal wages, the pecuniary sinews of contention,
should a spirit of revolt become general; and the
ample means of inflaming their passions and de-
praving their appetites, by sensual indulgences of
the lowest kind. [Persons not trained up in a
moral and religious nurture necessarily become,
from the evil heart of human nature, the slaves of
prejudice and vice; they can see objects only on
one side,—that which a sinister selfishness presents
to their view; they are readily moved to outrage by crafty demagogues; and they are apt to
regard their best benefactor, the enterprizing and
frugal capitalist, who employs them, with a jealous
and hostile eye."] The details contained in the following pages will show to what an extent the above
conditions have operated upon the factory artisan.

The opinions of the Author have been formed
from a long acquaintance with the classes of which
he speaks; and here he may be permitted to make a
remark respecting the Reports of the Factory Commissioners.   These Reports are highly honourable
to the gentlemen who have been severally engaged
in drawing them up; still they do not exhibit the

factory population · either as it is or as it has been; and the deductions which the Commissioners have drawn overlook many of the most important circumstances connected with the industry of the labouring classes. The evidence upon which the Reports are founded is, as will be seen in the analysis of it contained in the Appendix to the present work, of the most opposite character, and admits of being construed either one way or the other, just as the particular views, or the *personal* associations, of the observer might determine.

It is to be wished that the gentlemen who have acted as Factory Commisioners would visit the manufacturing towns as simple observers, and that they would examine into the condition of the operatives without show and official form. They have obviously taken great interest in the subject, and would find it well worth their while to pursue the inquiry. The masters have expressed, very naturally, their surprise at the Reports: a moment's consideration, however, will serve to show that the Reports are exactly such as might have been expected, from the mode in which the inquiry was conducted.

It is an approximation to absurdity to believe that any man will accuse himself or family of flagrant or even of minor crime; neither is it much further from absurdity to believe that any class, accustomed to a particular social and domestic condition, can be brought to acknowledge that it is essentially evil. A commission of inquiry, therefore, despatched to examine into these points, has little or no chance of coming at the truth, unless the parties so commissioned have a certain amount of previous information. The only way open to them is to call before them witnesses, and from these to extract whatever evidence they can give.

To show the impossibility of arriving at the truth by such means, it may be sufficient to say, that, in the majority of instances, the witnesses give the most conflicting evidence, even upon points connected with their own daily experiences. Thus to the question, " Whether the factory population were degenerated in appearance and stunted in growth?" six operatives replied. Of these, three positively say, Yes; and three as positively say, No! The same result followed other questions of an equally significant character; six speaking one way, and seven another: and, what is very remarkable, the proportions of aye and no are in many cases nearly balanced.

The fact is, that the operatives themselves cannot be supposed to judge fairly of their condition. The plan of seeking information directly was tried, very extensively, by the author, but without any satisfactory result. It is true that he accumulated a series of answers, from which he might have drawn similar deductions to those of the Factory Commisioners ; but it must be obvious that such deductions would take their tone from circumstances extraneous to the actual value of the questions. The Factory Commisioners visited the factory districts at a time when the public mind had been filled with the most fearful details of the cruelty and profligacy existing in them ; and on finding that many of these details were gross exaggerations, and that in some mills an admirable system of physical and moral discipline had been established, they have gone to the opposite side of the question, and consequently are as much in error, on points of opinion, as many of the theoretical witnesses examined before Mr. Sadler's Committee in 1833.

The truth of the Author's statements, regarding the social and domestic habits of the artisans brought under the influence of factory labour, is amply corroborated by the evidence of every resident observer, who has been placed under circumstances to make his evidence valuable. Dr. Kay, who officiated as medical attendant to a public charity, in a situation which led him into the homes of the operatives; Mr. Roberton, an acute and intelligent man, connected with the Manchester Lying-in Hospital; Mr. Ashworth, employed by some benevolent individuals to visit the residences of the lower classes; the gentlemen acting as visitors to the Provident Society; and several eminent manufacturers, who have themselves, at various times, written on these topics;—one and all speak the same language.

In speaking of the Reports of the Factory Commissioners, it must not be supposed that they are undervalued; on the contrary, they have brought to light a vast mass of highly important information, which could not have been obtained by any other means. The only error of the Commissioners, consists in their having formed conclusions, without taking into consideration the influence of several powerful agents acting upon the great body of artisans.

With the commercial economy of manufactures, the present work does not pretend to deal. The important questions connected with that economy, are handled in so far only as they bear upon the condition of the labourer.

The trains of facts and reasonings on the substitution of steam-machinery for human labour bring the Author into direct collision with many eminent writers on political economy. In entering into the contest, he is aware that he shall have to encounter much opposition; but his facts are undeniable, and his deductions are illustrated by every-day experience.

It is a new era in the history of commerce that an active and increasing trade should be the index, not to the improvement of the condition of the working classes, but to their poverty and degradation: it is an era at which Great Britain has arrived; and it behoves every man, anxious for the well-being of his country, to turn his attention to this extraordinary fact.

CHAMPION HILL,
February, 1836.

CONTENTS.

APPENDIX.

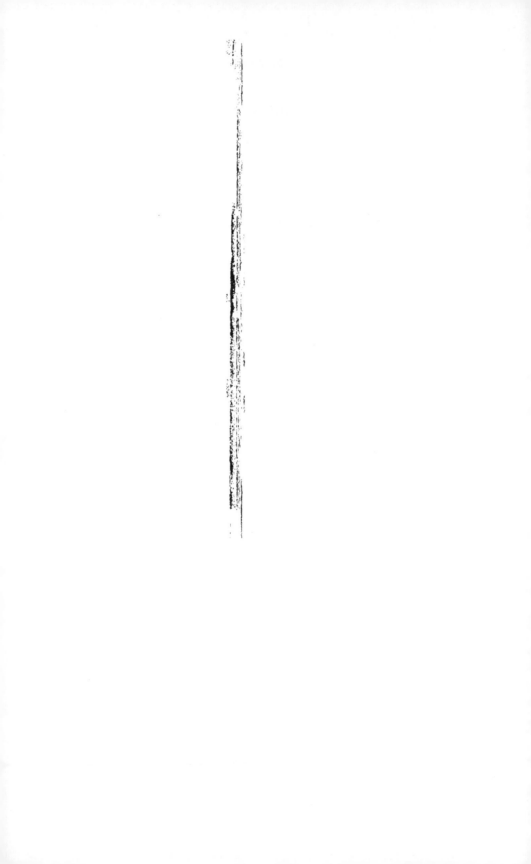

INTRODUCTION.

A work devoted exclusively to an examination of the moral, social, and physical conditions of the industrious classes connected with manufactures, has been for some time much wanted. The vast importance of the subject, and the numerous interests connected with it, renders it highly desirable that it should be carefully examined and dispassionately considered, and that a book should be the result to which all parties may look with confidence, and in which the general reader may find accurate information.*

. Committees of the House of Commons have, at different periods, examined into some of the points of this inquiry. It happens, however, unfortunately, that the evidence given before these Committees, and the

---

* The number of adult individuals alone engaged in arts, manufactures, and trade, amounts to 1,564,184, being 50 per cent. more than those employed in agriculture. This disproportion is doubled by taking into account the young persons engaged in manufactures. The number stated also is a mere approximation.

reports founded upon that evidence, are looked at suspiciously, and have in effect little weight or consideration.*   This has arisen, partly from the peculiar nature
of the evidence, which too often is tinged so strongly
with party spirit, that it subjects itself at once to doubt
or total unbelief; and partly from the want of knowledge
amongst the members of the committees, which prevented
them applying such questions and trains of reasoning
and deductions as the actual condition of the subject
demanded.   Hence, though many valuable facts have
been elicited by these inquiries, they are in such a crude
form as to be nearly valueless.

Connected in no way with manufactures, not having
any private interest in the existence or nonexistence
of any particular order of things, the Author trusts he
shall supply a desideratum in the history of his country—and at a juncture when men's minds are excited
upon a subject, which has but lately begun, to have
that attention paid it which its magnitude and overwhelming value demand.   In the prosecution of his work,
he has studiously confined himself to data, generally the
results of extensive personal research and inquiry, or
obtained from documents worthy of implicit belief.

The questions of infant labour, the effects of factory
labour in general, the physical condition and peculiar
diseases of the labourers, have been treated plainly and

---

* Witness the Committee of the House of Commons in 1832, of
which Mr. Sadler was chairman.   The mildest term which the
evidence before that Committee deserves is, that it is full of
extravagances.

succinctly, upon considerations drawn from the known constitution of the human body, and the consequences produced by various external agencies upon its healthy functions.

The moral, social, and domestic relations of the immense portion of the productive population of the kingdom, now engaged in manufactures, present a picture as strange and as deeply interesting as any in the whole circle of the history of mankind. To the philanthropist—to the man anxious for the well-being and social happiness of his species—it is one calculated to fill the mind with anxiety. It has been little attended to, and still less understood. Remedies are wanted, but before they can be efficiently applied, the disease must be studied; mere empiricism, even when founded on the purest motives, is dangerous ; and when the interest and happiness of millions are at stake, a clear and distinct understanding of their wants and failings should precede any attempt to satisfy the one or rectify the other.

In developing the existing state of things, with respect to combinations, the truck system, the cottage system, and the influence of machinery on the value of human labour, many important truths are brought into full daylight, unperverted in their bearings by the mistaken ideas, sometimes of one party, sometimes of another, which have invariably distorted, or partially concealed them, as best suited their peculiar purposes. A strenuous effort, too, has been made to demonstrate satisfactorily how much mischief is arising, and has arisen, from a division of interest, and want of mutual cooperation between the masters and the men.

In the statistical divisions of this work, the Author has done all that can be done with the subject, and he can add his mite of vexation to that of others who have been engaged in similar inquiries. The utter want of any thing approaching to correct registration is one of the severest drawbacks to those who wish to verify their positions by references to figures. All that the utmost industry can expect to attain is but an approximation to accuracy, and it may be questioned whether it is not safer to rely upon deductions drawn from other and better authenticated sources of knowledge. The difficulty in these respects, is increased a hundred-fold in manufacturing districts, the population of which is undergoing incessant changes, quite independent of the operation of natural causes, and in which too the separatists from the Established Church constitute the numerical majority. Many of these separatists keep no registries whatever; and in all so much laxity and uncertainty prevails, that they are worse than useless as documentary evidence.

The little amount of written information on all these subjects is very extraordinary, especially when it is borne in mind how large a proportion of the national wealth, and of the entire population, are involved in them. This may perhaps have arisen from the circumstance of the existing preeminence of manufactures being but the growth of a day—being as yet but a

Hercules in the cradle. It is indeed only since the introduction of steam as a power that they have acquired their paramount importance ; one generation even now is but passing away since this epoch, and what mighty alterations has it already wrought in the condition of society !—changing in many respects the very frame-work of the social confederacy, and opening into view a long vista of rapid transitions, terminating in the subjection of human power, as an agent of labour, to the gigantic and untiring energies of automatic machinery.

It is high time that the erroneous opinions currently entertained on many points connected with factory discipline and factory labour should be removed, and that the feelings of sympathy and needless commiseration, expressed by certain portions of the community, should be directed into a more legitimate and less harmful channel. One great cause of the unhappy differences which have so completely sundered the confidence of the employers and the employed, had its origin in the want of diffusion of correct knowledge. The masters have not at all times shown that their opinions were trustworthy. But it has been the men who have chiefly erred, and with the most deplorable results to themselves. They have suffered their better judgments to be warped, and their passions led astray, by heartless and designing demagogues, who have taken advantage of their ignorance, led them to the commission of crimes, ruined their comfort, and destroyed their social character, for

the purpose of battening and luxuriating upon their
miseries and degradation. The labours of the Factory
Commissioners have been of service; and the Author
finds that his views and opinions have in many important points been amply corroborated by their reports,
since the first appearance of many of the following
observations.

The causes which have led to the present declension
in the social and physical condition of the artisans, the
Author believes either to have been wholly misunderstood, or very inadequately appreciated. It is not
poverty alone—for the family of the mill labourer
earn what is sufficient to supply all their wants; it is
not factory labour, considered *per se ;* it is not the lack
of education, in the common acceptation of the word :—
no; it has arisen from the separation of families, the
breaking up of households, the disruption of all those
ties which link man's heart to the better portion of his
nature,—viz. his instincts and social affections. It is
these which render him a respectable and praiseworthy
member of society, both in his domestic relations, and in
his capacity of a citizen. The class of hand-workers have
indeed sunk beneath poverty, with its many attendant
evils!

The part of the masters in the work of reform, naturally is, and ought to be, the leading one. They are,
above all men, interested; and great responsibility rests
with them. They have within their power the capability of doing much either for good or for evil. It is their

bounden duty to examine into every thing bearing upon the subject, with the most minute care, with a spirit of strict justice, and with a disposition to ameliorate, as far as is consistent with their own private and indisputable rights. In doing this, they should endeavour so to act, that the confidence of the men may go hand in hand with them, or it will be of no avail.

The universal application of steam-power as an agent for producing motion in machinery, has closely assimilated the condition of all branches of manufacturing industry, both in their moral and physical relations. In all, it destroys domestic labour; in all, it congregates labourers into towns, or densely peopled neighbourhoods; in all, it separates families; and in all, it lessens the demand for human strength, reducing man to a mere watcher or feeder of his mighty assistant, which toils and labours with a pertinacity and unvarying continuance requiring constant and sedulous attention.

It is much to be wished, that "men in high places" would examine, somewhat more in detail, the existing condition of the manufacturers.* The conversion of a great people, in little more than half a century, from agriculturists to manufacturers, is a phenomenon worthy the attention of any statesman. It is an attention, too, which will be forced upon them, when, from their

---

* " In the recent discussions concerning our factories, no circumstance is so deserving of remark as the gross ignorance evinced by our leading legislators and economists."—*Dr. Ure's Philosophy of Manufactures*, p. 6.

want of knowledge, they will be liable to take steps
which may prove destructive to one or both of the great
divisions of national property.

The change which has recently been made in the
constitution of the House of Commons is another
important reason why information should be extended
widely and generally. The change is one characteristic of the times; and the introduction to the House
of persons of strictly commercial habits and views,
will necessarily operate very powerfully upon the
course of legislation. The change will not,[a] however,
rest here: the preponderance already acquired by
manufactures is progressing rapidly; and its represen-
tatives will, ere long, take the position afforded them
by their vantage ground. The riches of a great and
wealthy nation are pouring into the tide of manufactures, and swelling its ascendency; and it must soon
become in appearance, what it is in reality, the directing
current of commercial prosperity. From the want of
enlarged views, it is to be feared that crude and badly
digested enactments may interfere between the employer and the employed,* to the serious injury of
both parties, and to the ultimate endangering of the
present lofty pre-eminence enjoyed by Great Britain, as
the grand focus of manufacturing intelligence; and
may so hamper and obstruct the operations of capital,
as to lead, to some extent, to its abstraction.

* The fears thus expressed were amply fulfilled by the *Factory
Regulation Act*, passed by Parliament on the 29th of August,
1833.

It is above all things of importance, that the condition of the labourers should be carefully and maturely considered. Though danger may arise from legislative enactments, this is the slumbering volcano which may at any time shatter the whole fabric to atoms, and involve in one common ruin, themselves, the master, and the manufacture. The struggle carrying on between human power on the one hand, and steam, aided by machinery, which is constantly improving in construction, and increasing in applicability, is gradually approaching a crisis. The contest has hitherto been between the vast body of hand-workers, who have been forced to cling to their ancient habits, till no market is open to their labour ; but it is now commencing between another great body and machinery. The adaptation of mechanical contrivances to nearly all the processes which have as yet wanted the delicate tact of the human hand, will soon either do away with the necessity for employing it altogether, or it must be employed at a price that will enable it to compete with mechanism. Adult human labour must ever be expensive ; it cannot be carried beyond a certain point ; neither will it permit a depression in wage below what is essential for its existence.

It may indeed be doubted how far the interference of Government in questions of this nature is likely to prove beneficial, and whether the parties, the masters on the one hand, and the workmen on the other, would not act most wisely by saying as the merchants of France said to Colbert, when it was proposed to take measures to protect their interests, — "*Laissez nous faire*,"—let us alone, we shall take care of ourselves. There are many contingencies, and many interests, which must be always overlooked ; and in the endeavour to remedy one evil a path is often opened for the approach of others. The best preserving power is to be found in the balance of interest between the commercial economy of manufactures, and the social well-being of the employers and the employed.

The most important point, however, in which the subject presents itself is the rapid substitution of automatic for human labour. All the great branches of manufacture which not long ago occupied the cottage population of Great Britain are, one by one, becoming absorbed in factories, and it is to this withdrawal of domestic labour that we must attribute the wide, nay, universal distress, which has spread over the land. The old poor law has been blamed as the cause of the evil, but most erroneously ; the evil has, indeed, shewn itself through the agency of that law, but we repeat that the cause of the distress was unconnected with it, and cannot be remedied by its alteration.

MORAL, SOCIAL, AND PHYSICAL CONDITIONS

OF THE

DOMESTIC MANUFACTURERS

BFFORE AND AFTER THE

APPLICATION OF STEAM-POWER.

CHAPTER I.

Domestic Manufacturers—General union of Manufacture and
Farming, Residences and Characters of the Home Labourers—
Home Labour, its influence upon the domestic and social vir-
tues—Physical Conditions—Families—Distinction of Rank—
Squire, Yeoman, and Labourer—Comparison of the wants
and habits of past and present Manufacturers—Leasing of
Land—Peculiar Habits—Manners, &c.—State of Manufac-
tures—Limited supply of Yarn—Inadequacy of existing
Machines—Hand-loom Weaver and Farmer—Rate of Wages
—Causes which led to the abandonment of Farming as an
accessory to Weaving—Influence upon the social rank of the
Weaver—Simple hand-loom Weaver, his Condition—Spinners, their Condition, Changes, Improvement in their Machines
—Conversion of the small Freeholders into Spinners, their
Character—Effects of this upon Farming—Establishment of
Mills—Influence upon the domestic Spinner—Ruin of the class
of Yeomen—New order of Weavers—Human Power, difficulty
of managing—Present state of Hand-loom Weavers—Remedial
agents—Cultivation of wastes—Allotment system.

BEFORE the year 1760, manufactures were in a great
measure confined to the demands of the home market.*

* The annual consumption of cotton in British manufactures
barely reached four millions of pounds,† now it amounts to two
hundred and seventy millions of pounds. The export of manufactured cotton was only valued at 335,000l. in 1780. In 1833
it amounted to 18,459,000l. real value.

At this period, and down to 1800, during which interval a general impetus had been given to this branch of trade by foreign and increased home consumption—and in which, also, great improvements had taken place in the construction of the machines, all tending to facilitate and hasten production—the majority of artisans had laboured in their own houses, and in the bosoms of their families. It may be termed the period of Domestic Manufacture ; and the various mechanical contrivances were expressly framed for that purpose. The distaff, the spinning wheel, producing a single thread, and subsequently the jenny and mule, were to be found forming a part of the complement of household furniture in the majority of the cottage-homes of Great Britain, whilst every hamlet and village résounded with the clack of the hand-loom.

These were, undoubtedly, the golden times of manufactures, considered in reference to the character of the labourers. By all the processes being carried on under a man's own roof, he retained his individual respectability, he was kept apart from associations that might injure his moral worth, and he generally earned wages which were not only sufficient to live comfortably upon, but which enabled him to rent a few acres of land ; thus joining in his own person two classes which are now daily becoming more and more distinct. It cannot, indeed, be denied, that his farming was too often slovenly, and conducted at times as a subordinate occupation ; and that the land yielded but a small proportion of what, under a better system of culture, it was capable of producing. It nevertheless answered an excellent purpose. Its necessary tendence filled up the vacant hours, when he found it unnecessary to apply himself to his loom or spinning machine. It gave him employment of a healthy character, and raised him a step in the scale of society above the mere labourer. A garden was likewise an invariable adjunct to the cottage of the hand-loom weaver; and the floral tribes, fruits, and edible roots, were zealously and successfully cultivated.

The domestic manufacturers were scattered over the entire surface of the country. Themselves cultivators, and of simple habits and few wants, they rarely left their own homesteads. The yarn which they spun, and which was wanted by the weaver, was received or delivered, as the case might be, by agents, who travelled for the wholesale houses; or depôts were established in particular neighbourhoods, to which they could apply at weekly periods.*

Thus, removed from many of those causes which universally operate to the deterioration of the moral character of the labouring man, when brought into large towns—into immediate contact and communion with his fellows, and under the influence of many depressing physical agencies—the small farmer, spinner, or hand-loom weaver, presented an orderly and respectable appearance. It is true that the amount of labour gone through was but small,—that the quantity of cloth or yarn produced was but limited.—for he worked by the rule of his strength and convenience. They were, however, sufficient to clothe and feed himself and family decently, and according to their station; to lay by a penny for an evil day, and to enjoy those amusements and bodily recreations then in being. He was a re-

---

* The sedentary occupation of these primitive manufacturers gave rise to studious and reflective habits. Some of the best practical botanists of the day, and several very eminent mathematicians, were found amongst the Lancashire cotton weavers.

spectable member of society ; a good father, a good husband, and a good son.

It is not intended to paint an Arcadia—to state that the domestic manufacturer was free from the vices or failings of other men. By no means ; but he had the opportunities brought to him for being comfortable and virtuous—with a physical constitution uninjured by protracted toil in a heated and impure atmosphere, the fumes of the gin-shop, the low debauchery of the beer-house, and the miseries incident to ruined health. On the contrary, he commonly lived to a good round age, worked when necessity demanded, ceased his labour when his wants were supplied, according to his character, and if disposed to spend time or money in drinking, could do so in a house as well conducted and as orderly as his own ; for the modern weaver or spinner differs not more widely from the domestic manufacturer, than the publican of the present day differs from the Boni-face of that period, whose reputation depended upon good ale and good hours, and who, in nine cases out of ten, was a freeholder of some consequence in the neighbourhood.

The circumstance of a man's labour being conducted in the midst of his household, exercised a powerful in-fluence upon his social affections, and those of his offspring. It but rarely happened that labour was pre-maturely imposed upon children ;—a man's own earnings, aided by the domestic economy of his wife, generally sufficing to permit growth and bodily development to be to some extent completed, before any demand was made upon their physical energies. This permitted and fostered the establishment of parental authority and domestic discipline. It directed the child's thoughts and attachments to their legitimate objects, and rendered it submissive to that control which is essential to its future welfare. When it was enabled to join its exertions to those of its parent for their mutual support, it did so with no idea of separate interests, but with a free acknowledgment that the amount of its earnings was entirely at the disposal of the head of the family. Thus remaining and labouring in conjunction with, and under the eye of, its parents, till manhood and womanhood were respectively attained, it acquired habits of domestication exceedingly favourable to its subsequent progress through life; home being, to the poor man, the very temple of fortune, in which he may contrive, if his earnings are not scanty indeed, to live with comfort and independence.

In this respect, the child of the domestic manufacturer was advantageously placed. It remained under its paternal roof during the period in which puberty was developed; its passions and social instincts were properly cultivated, its bodily powers were not too early called into requisition; it had the benefit of green fields, a pure atmosphere, the cheering influences of nature, and its diet was plain and substantial. Under these auspicious circumstances it grew vigorously, acquired a healthy tone of system, the various parts of its physical organization were well compacted and arranged, and it presented an aspect fresh and blooming, denoting animal energy and vital activity.

The distinctions of rank, which are the safest guarantees for the performance of the relative duties of all classes, were at this time in full force. The ' Squire,' as the chief landed proprietor was generally termed, obtained and deserved his importance from his large possessions, low rents, and a simplicity and homeliness

of bearing which, when joined to acknowledged family
respectability, made him loved and reverenced by his
tenants and neighbours.   He mingled freely in their
sports—was the general and undisputed arbiter in all
questions of law and equity—was a considerate and generous landlord—a kind and indulgent master—and looking at him in all his bearings, a worthy and amiable
man ; tinged, it is true, with some vices, but all so coated
over with wide-spreading charity, that the historian
willingly draws the veil of forgetfulness over them.
This race of men is now nearly extinct in the manufacturing districts.   Their possessions are passed into new
hands—their descendants " pushed from their stools "
by an order of men having few or no traits in common
with them.   They indeed belonged to a race indigenous
to a peculiar grade of social advancement, no longer in
being, and with them, for they were equally a part of
the same system, the " Yeomanry of England," the
small farmers have fallen victims to the breaking up of
a condition of society, and a state of property, which
secured a flourishing rural population.

Modern Utilitarians measure man's actions, and
every thing referring to his condition, by mind.   That
state of things is, however, the best, which brings
to each man's fireside the greatest amount of domestic
comforts, though it may not be that which will enable
him to boil his pot scientifically, or calculate an abstruse
problem in mathematics.   It is not denied, neither is it
wished to conceal the fact from observation, that squire,
yeoman, and manufacturer, differed very materially in
some of these respects from the individuals occupying
a correspondent rank at the present period, and that the
latter, when looked upon in this point of view, are

infinitely superior to the former. Neither in comparing the two is there any intention of wishing that society should be again taken back to that particular level in the onward progress of civilization. The forward impulse must and will be obeyed, whatever the consequences may be to the welfare and happiness of the labouring community.

At the present time may be seen a daily spread of knowledge, joined to a gradual depression in the scale of social enjoyments; vast and incessant improvements in mechanical contrivances, all tending to overmatch and supersede human labour, and which threaten to extirpate the very demand for it; a system of toil continued unbroken by rest or relaxation for twelve or fourteen hours, in a heated mill, and an utter destruction of all social and domestic relations. At the time to which we are alluding, there was a calm and equable flow of occupation, alternating between the loom and the greensward—an intelligence seldom looking beyond the present—an ignorance of nearly every thing but the most common arts of life—a knowledge chiefly traditional—a proper station in the social arrangement—a demand for labour full as great, if not greater than the existing supply—a rate of wages quite equivalent to the simplicity and limited range of their wants—and all the social and domestic relations in full force, and properly directed.

The great question here is the measure of social and domestic happiness, for these are but synonymes of social virtue. They coexist and have an intimate dependence one upon another. Degradation in these conditions will ever be simultaneous with moral declension—a declension incompatible with the performance of a great majority of man's best and most sacred duties.

If the comfort of the poor man is to be estimated by variety of wants, by his living in an artificial state of society, surrounded by all the inventions resulting from a high degree of civilization—by having these brought to his door, and every facility afforded him for procuring them—the aboriginal and home manufacturer sinks very low when compared with the present race. If, on the contrary, comfort and domestic happiness are to be judged by the fewness of a man's wants, with the capability of securing the means for their supply, the tables are turned in favour of the domestic manufacturer.

If the comfort of these states of society is to be calculated upon another ground—namely, the nature of their separate wants and habits—it brings into light very striking contrasts. The present artisan shows a high order of intelligence, seeking his amusement in the newspaper, the club, the political union, or the lecture-room ; looking for his stimulus in the gin and beer shops ; taking for his support a limited supply of animal food, once a day, joined with copious dilution of weak tea, the almost universal concomitant of the spinner and weaver's breakfast and evening meal, in many cases indeed being nearly its sole constituent ; he is debarred from all athletic sports, not having a moment's time to seek, or a bodily vigour capable of undertaking them ; he has an active mind in a stunted and bloodless body ; there is a separation of the labourer from his family during the whole day, and a consequent disruption of all social ties ; and this too joined to a similar separation amongst the various members of his household.

The domestic artisan possessed a very limited degree of information ; his amusements were exclusively sought in bodily exercise, quoits, cricket, the dance, the chace, and numerous seasonal celebrations; he lived in utter ignorance of printed books, beyond the thumbed Bible and a few theological tracts; he sought his stimulus in home-brewed ale; he had for his support animal food occasionally, but subsisted generally upon farm produce, meal or rye bread, eggs, cheese, milk, butter, &c. the use of tea being quite unknown, or only just beginning to make its appearance; he had a sluggish mind in an active body; his labour was carried on under his own roof, or, if exchanged at intervals for farming occupation, this was going on under the eye, and with the assistance of his family; his children grew up under his immediate inspection and control; no lengthened separation taking place till they got married, and became themselves heads of families engaged in pursuits similar to his own, and in a subordinate capacity. Lastly, the same generation lived age after age on the same spot, and under the same thatched roof, which thus became a sort of heir-loom, endeared to its occupier by a long series of happy memories and home delights—being in fact looked on as an old and familiar friend; and, in the end, they crowded the same narrow tenement in the quiet and sequestered church-yard, suffered to moulder in peace beneath its fresh and verdant turf, and swept over by the free, the balmy, and the uncontaminated breath of heaven.

One circumstance exceedingly favourable to the development and continuance of industry and temperance, was the plan, now nearly, if not quite exploded, of leasing small farms for one or more lives. A man's character always aided him very materially in these arrangements with his landlord, as upon this depended the amount both of rent and fine, a respectable man, it was well known, not being likely to exhaust and impoverish the land during his interest in it. Number-less examples might be quoted in illustration of this

position, and many circumstances detailed showing
what a beneficial influence resulted from it, upon the
tone and bearing of the manners of the small farmers.
They were indeed a highly creditable body of men—
priding themselves alike on the good opinion of their
landlord, the excellent condition of their farms, and the
quality of their yarn or cloth.

The social virtues, it has been said, will be found
pari passu with social comforts. The vices that were
incident to this state of things were the result of man's
natural propensities, and depended more upon the want
of any sufficient check upon his passions, which were
kept in a state of excitement by health and bodily
vigour, than upon moral depravity springing from
intentional and reiterated wrong doing. The very fact
of these small communities (for they were generally
found congregated in petty irregular villages, containing
from ten to forty cottages) being, as it were, one great
family, prevented, except in a few extraordinary instances, any systematic course of sinning. This moral
check was indeed all-powerful in hindering the commission of crime, aided by a sense of religion very
commonly existing amongst them. In one respect
this failed, however, and it was in preventing the
indulgence of sexual appetite, in a way and at a time
which are still blots upon the rural population of many
districts.

Some surprise may be excited probably by the assertion, in those whose attention has never been directed
to the subject, but it is not the less true, that sexual
intercourse was almost universal prior to marriage in
the agricultural districts. This intercourse must not
be confounded with that promiscuous and indecent
concourse of the sexes which is so prevalent in towns,

and which is ruinous alike to health and to moráls : it
existed only between parties where a tacit understanding
had all the weight of an obligation,—and this was that
marriage should be the result. In nineteen cases out
of twenty this took place sooner or later ; but still the
prevalence of such a course of indulgence was, in some
respect, decidedly injurious to the character and habits
of both individuals, weakening, as it inevitably did, thát
confidence which ought to exist between unmarried
parties, and divesting woman of that chaste and pure
influence which is capable of keeping in check man's
coarser and more vehement passions. Many of the
sports of the period, amongst the young of both sexes,
were obviously intended to facilitate and give opportunities for familiarities of the closest kind, and were
carried on under the guidance of some old crone, whose
directions governed the apparent conduct of the females
upon these singular occasions. Some curious laws are
still in being orally, which throw strong light on the
social habits of these children of nature down to a very
recent period.

---

* Poor Laws commission. — " I appeal to the experience of all
overseers in rural districts, whether instances ' of marriage
taking place among the labouring classes are not so very rare as
to constitute no exception to the general assertion, that ' pregnancy precedes marriage.' "—*Extract from Mr. Cowell's Report.*
It is much to be deplored that the depression in the condition
of the agricultural portion of the population should have led to
the demoralization which this report exhibits in such decided characters. Unhappily badly administered poor laws and bastard laws
heretofore held out a premium for moral depravity : as the report
very correctly says,—" It would be impossible for the heart of
man or demon to devise a more effective instrument for extinguishing every noble feeling in the female heart, for blighting the
sweetest domestic affections, and for degrading ·the males and

The moralist, though he may condemn and declaim against this state of things, will, if just, attach no farther blame than by saying, it was the error of a system belonging to one stage of civilization. But the philan‑ thropist, the man who, free from morbid sensibilities, views and judges the manners and customs of states in relation only to the happiness of the existing race, will lament, that intellectual excellence should be still at‑ tended by similar evils, in an aggravated and more vicious form, hid though they may be to some extent, by outward refinement; whilst he will detect and deplore the absence of all that warm-heartedness, that devotion to home and domestic duties, which in no small degree served as their atonements.

There can be no question, and the more widely inqui‑ ries are extended, the more obvious becomes the fact, that the domestic artisan, as a moral and social being, was infinitely superior to the manufacturer of a later date. He was much more advantageously placed in all points, and his condition gave ample evidence of this. That he was inferior in some respects is not denied: he could seldom read freely, or write at all, but he went to church or chapel with exemplary punc‑ tuality ; he produced, comparatively speaking, but little work, but he was well clothed and well fed ; he knew nothing of clubs for raving politicians, or combinations which could place him in opposition to his employer,

females of that portion of the community connected with the receipt of parish relief, than this truly diabolical institution." Again, " the English law has abolished female chastity, self-respect, proper pride, and all the charities of domestic life, connected with its existence. It has destroyed likewise the beneficial influence which this virtue in woman reflects on the character of man."— *Vide Report—passim.*

but he was respectful and attentive to his superiors, and fulfilled his contracts to the letter. He had never heard of mechanic institutes, Sunday schools, or tract societies, but he listened devoutly to the reading of his Bible ; he had no gin or beer-shop orgies, but he spent his hours in rude sports, in the highest degree conducive to health : he followed, in short, that art mentioned by Cicero— "Hanc amplissimam omnium artium bene vivendi disciplinam, vità magis quàm litteris persequunti sunt."

 Various circumstances had been for a considerable period producing important modifications in the condition of the domestic manufacturer, prior to the introduction of steam as an antagonist to human power ; and a brief review of these will form an interesting and curious feature in the history of the manufacturing population, and illustrate the great changes which the last forty years have sufficed to operate in their circumstances and characters.

The distaff and spinning-wheel, producing a single thread, were for a long time the only methods of spinning. About the middle of the last century the demand for cloth was so much increased, that the inventive faculties of those interested in it were called into activity, and improved machines for spinning were very soon the result. Some of the contrivers of the most important improvements failed to demonstrate for a while the value of their discoveries ; others were driven, by a cruel and ill-judged persecution, to carry their knowledge to other countries. A narrow and prejudiced view was taken by the public at large, and little encouragement given, for a time, to those who have in the end proved themselves the greatest benefactors to the commerce of their country. In the teeth of all these impediments the pressing demand for cloth gradually forced the domestic manufacturer to the adoption of improved modes of spinning; for the difficulty had always lain in producing an adequate supply of materials in a state fit for the loom. One half the weaver's time had generally to be spent in waiting for work. This state of things was however remedied by the mule and the jenny, both of which enabled the spinner to produce a greatly increased quantity of yarn, when compared to that formerly supplied by the wheel.

The hand-loom weaver was of course greatly benefited by all these improvements, without any extra outlay of capital,—the loom which sufficed to weave a small amount being of equal efficiency to turn out a greater. The call for more cloth, and the facilities given in the first processes, removed him from the vacillating and uncertain condition in which he was before placed.*

A family of four adult persons, with two children as winders, earned, at the end of the last and at the commencement of the present century, 4l. per week, when working ten hours per day; when work was pressed they could of course earn more—a single weaver having been known to earn upwards of two pounds per week. This however required great industry, and was by no means common; weaving, too, when thus exercised, is not easy labour; the position in which the weaver sits is not the best for muscular exertion, as he has no firm support for his feet, which are alternately raised and depressed in working the treddles. He has thus to depend for a fulcrum chiefly on the muscles of his back, which are kept in constant and vigorous action, while one order of muscles is employed with little power of variation, in moving the shuttle and beam. These processes, when carried on for many successive hours, are very wearying, and the exertion required becomes, after

* *Vide* Appendix, (Note A,) on the changes above-mentioned.

a while, laborious. The weaver who worked hard, therefore, actually toiled—a condition widely different from that of the steam-loom weaver.

One of the first effects of the constant demand upon the labour of the weaver, resulting from a more extensive and permanent supply of yarn, was the gradual abandonment of farming as an accessory, which had been very common with the more respectable portion of the weavers. His labour, when employed on his loom, was more profitable, and more immediate in its return, than when devoted to agricultural pursuits. This necessarily led to the introduction of a new order of farm tenants, men who devoted themselves exclusively to the cultivation of the soil, who looked to its produce as their only mode of acquiring the means of support, and who, in nine cases out of ten, were mere holders at will—a lowering in respectability, which it is probable will be scarcely understood, by those who are not familiar, with the feeling and grades of rank in this class of labourers.

This change in the weaver's occupation produced very considerable influence upon him in a social point of view. It tended decidedly to lower his rank and character, by making him a simple labourer, and by removing him from that, which did then, and which still does, confer rural distinction—the holding or possessing land. This had formerly brought himself and children partially upon the same level with the small freeholder or yeoman, properly so called. It had also brought him into contact with this order of men on many occasions;—and remotely, it is true, but still near enough to benefit him, it had assimilated his condition with that of the gentry of the neighbourhood : it gave him an honest pride in his capacity, heightened the tone of his general character, and was thus morally beneficial to him.

The great body of hand-loom weavers had indeed at all periods been divided, by a well-defined line of demar- cation, into two very distinct classes. This division arose from the circumstance of their being landholders, or entirely dependant upon weaving for their support. It has been seen that the weaver, who was also a small farmer, lost something by the increase in the demand for cloth, while, from the same cause, the simple weaver, who had all along depended upon that demand, gained a step in advance, and now found himself on an equality with those who had hitherto been his superiors.

The secondary, or inferior class of artisans, had at all times been sufferers from the impossibility of sup- plying themselves with materials for their labour. Considerable vacations were frequently occurring in this respect, and at these periods they underwent some privations. This irregularity had produced its usual effects upon their industrial character, rendering them improvident, devoid of forethought, and careless in their expenditure. Not being able to calculate, had they been so disposed, upon the certainty that their exertions would be invariably called for, they became indifferent, enjoyed the good whilst it lasted, and starved through the interval as they best might.*

* It is an indisputable fact, that irregularity in the demand for labour, from whatever cause it may arise, by occasionally throwing the workmen out of employ, and generating idle habits, is one of the most disorganizing and degrading influences which can be brought to bear upon their character. Independently of the diminished rate of wages, and the acrimonious and suspicious feel- ings which, of late years, have sprung up between the masters and men, the stoppages which have taken place in nearly all the mills in rotation, for periods more or less protracted, sometimes from the fault of one party, sometimes of another, have been full as injurious to the moral dispositions of the men as the other two put together.

The class of poor weavers were thus instantaneously elevated very considerably in worldly consideration. They were freed from one great cause of depression, which had hitherto prevented all chance of improvement. They now took their stand upon the same ground with the weaver who had hitherto been a small farmer, and who had come down one degree in the social scale, in consequence of giving up his land for the purpose of devoting himself to the more profitable business of the loom. This amalgamation of the two divisions which had heretofore existed amongst domestic manufacturers, raised on the whole their general character as a body, rendered them more united, and by diffusing one species of labour universally over the entire class, gave them a community of interests and feelings which bound them together.

A very material improvement, therefore, had been gradually operating in both classes of weavers during the half century immediately preceding the application of steam power. This improvement had not arisen so much from any increase in the rate of payment for labour, as from a market generally understocked, and a constantly increasing production for yarn, which enabled them to work full hours, and consequently to throw off a regular and sufficient quantity of cloth.

The wages earned when the supply of yarn became regular, were amply sufficient to supply all the wants of the weavers, and to furnish them with many luxuries and comforts proper to their condition. Even after these had been supplied a surplus remained, which, if properly husbanded, would have saved them from the miseries which burst over them at a subsequent period. There seems to be, however, something about the operatives generally unfavourable to the accumulation

of money, even when placed under circumstances
where it might fairly be supposed that they had
an opportunity given them for the purpose. Their
savings rarely exceeded a very small sum. It is true,
they lived better; in fact, they lived too well; they
clothed better, and they did not contemplate the change
which was impending over them, and consequently did
not "set their houses in order," but rather looked forwards to a continuance of their prosperity, and pleased
themselves with the anticipations of still farther additions to their present comforts. It can excite no wonder
therefore, that they, with their limited intelligence,
strenuously opposed the steam-looms, which they looked
upon as usurping what they imagined to be the
rights of their industry; nay, pushed the principle still
further, and appeared to believe that they had a pre-
scriptive and just claim to a monopoly of this labour.

In the mean time, the condition of the spinners, or as
they may well be termed during the prosperous days
of hand-manufacture, the aristocracy of artisans, was
undergoing changes still greater and more rapid than
that of the weavers, and passing through a revolution
which modified the whole body, and terminated finally
in the ruin of the greater portion.

In the early times of manufacturing, the spinner and
the weaver were to some extent synonymous,—so far
indeed, that the processes were carried on under the
same roof, and by the same individuals ; the distaff, the
wheel, and the loom being all called into requisition by
a single family.

At a later period, when improvements in machinery
progressed rapidly, stimulated as they were by the
inability constantly felt to supply the demand for yarn;
and as these improved machines at each step became

more bulky, more complicated, and consequently more expensive, a division began to shew itself between the weaver and the spinner, the latter throwing aside his wheel and devoting himself to the loom, trusting to external sources for his yarn, from a growing inability to purchase such machinery as would enable him to spin profitably,—and the former deserting the loom, and applying his funds to procure the best and most recent contrivances for spinning, knowing as he did that a market was always open to his produce.

At this period, that is, at the time when spinning was become a separate branch, and when the division between the two bodies was well defined, the spinners were joined by another class of persons, who had heretofore held aloof from manufacture; these were the yeomen—the small freeholders, now nearly extinct, as a part of the social confederacy.

The yeoman had lived generation after generation upon his patrimonial acres, rarely increasing their extent, and quite as rarely lessening them. He had, however, failed to keep pace with the onward march of events—had confined himself to cultivating his land precisely in the same way in which it had been cultivated by his forefathers—viewed all innovations as rank heresy, vegetated upon his natal soil, profiting either it or the world but little, yet having, notwithstanding, many points about him of real value. He was strictly honest in all his dealings, though almost universally improvident, more, however, from want of mental energy and forethought, than from actual extravagance; contented with his lot, and a kind and hearty neighbour, but utterly unable to cope with the crisis which was opening upon him. He had hitherto been surrounded by petty farmers, who had generally eked out their land cultivation by being weavers, and who had served him as bulwarks or break-waters against the impending storm. These were one by one removed, and their places immediately occupied by a race of men who gave a considerably increased rent, and who, by improved modes of husbandry, and by wringing from the soil all it could possibly yield, soon drove the small proprietor from the markets which he had so long supplied. Thus pressed upon by superior industry, and an activity with which he could not compete, the yeoman was driven to embark some portion of his means in the purchase of spinning machines, and, before very long, great quantities of yarn were produced by the inmates of old farm-houses, in which previously the most sluggish inertness had prevailed.

Nothing can more clearly shew how very imperfectly this class had used its resources than the fact, that five-sevenths of those who purchased these machines were obliged to have recourse to a loan, generally a mortgage, to raise the money.

The price of the more complicated spinning machines was very considerable, and it has been seen removed them out of the reach of the inferior class of weavers. At the same time monied men began to fix their attention on a branch of trade, the returns from which were very rapid. This brought a farther accession of capital into it, and led to the erection of mills, containing a greater or less number of spinning machines, propelled by water power; with the assistance of human labour. These mills were built in places at some distance from the towns, though as near as circumstances would permit for the convenience of markets, and readiness of transport for the raw and manufactured material. Their site, in other respects, was chosen with regard to two necessary things,—one, the existence of a stream of sufficient

volume and permanence,—and the other the neighbourhood of suitable workmen.

These mills were exclusively devoted to the first processes of manufacture, namely, carding and spinning.
Their gradual increase very soon influenced the prosperity of the domestic manufacturer—his profits quickly
fell, workmen being readily found to superintend the
mill labour, at a rate of wages high it is true, but yet
comparatively much lower than the estimated value of
home labour.

Another cause which tended to injure the private
spinner was the incessant and expensive improvements
in the construction of machines.* Thus the man who one
year laid out a considerable sum in the purchase of a
jenny of the best and most approved make, found himself, in the course of the year following, so much behind-
hand, that with his utmost industry he could barely turn
out a sufficient quantity of yarn to repay him for his
present labour, in consequence of alterations which threw
the productive power of his machine into the back-
ground. The price of yarn became of necessity depreciated
in proportion to the quantity produced, which was now
more than sufficient to supply the home demand. Finding his efforts futile to keep pace with improved machinery, he was compelled either to dispose of his
jenny, and this at an immense sacrifice, often indeed at
a merely nominal price, or make an arrangement with
the maker for an exchange at a rate almost equally
ruinous. The number of machines which at this period
were thrown back into the market, gave a strong impulse
to the growth of the mills; a machine which was not suf-

* Precisely the same cause of distress is now operating upon the
woollen and bobbin-net manufactures at the present moment.

ficiently perfect for the purpose of domestic manufacture
doing well enough in a mill in conjunction with others,
worked at a less rate of wages, and assisted by water
power, when its use was valueless to its original owner;
he was consequently left in many cases in a worse
condition, in a pecuniary point of view, than when he
commenced his new vocation, no time having been given
him to cover its first cost.

This necessarily led to great difficulties and to em-
barrassments of no ordinary kind, and was the first
step towards the abolition of the small freeholders, or
yeomen, in many districts. Their long course of inactivity, and the little diffusion of intelligence amongst
them, rendered them incapable of maintaining the struggle with men who had been accustomed to the variations
of trade, and whose forethought enabled them to apply
remedies, and take such precautionary and anticipative
measures as screened them from loss. Their little
estates became in the course of a few years so encum-
bered, as to be utterly worthless to them, and a very
rapid and very extensive change took place in landed
proprietorship from 1790 to 1810, the period when this
transition was in progress.

This declension, though nearly, was not quite universal. The apathy which had so long oppressed and
hidden the energies of their character, had failed in quite
extinguishing them; and a few of these men, shaking
off their slothful habits, both of body and mind, devoted
themselves to remedying their condition with a perseverance certain to be successful. Joining to this
determination a practical acquaintance with the details
of manufactures, personal superintendence and industry,
several of the most eminently successful steam-manu-
facturers have sprung from this class of people, and have

long since become the most opulent of a wealthy community.*

There is a singularity attending the rise of some of these individuals, showing very strongly how infinitely superior is personal endeavour, to accumulated wealth, when devoted to the same purposes. Few of the men who entered the trade rich were successful. They trusted too much to others—too little to themselves; whilst, on the ·contrary, the men who prospered were raised by their own efforts—commencing in a very humble way, generally from exercising some handicraft, as clock-making, hatting, &c. and pushing their advance by a series of unceasing exertions, having a very limited capital to begin with, or even none at all save their own labour.

The time was now arrived when another great change took place in the relative situations of the two divisions of manufacturers.† The improved machines, their increased number, the establishment of mills, the accession of capital—one and all produced a much greater quantity of yarn than could by any possibility be converted into cloth by the then hand-loom weavers. A surplus of course remained, which was either sent to the foreign market, or remained as a dead weight upon the maker. The demand for cloth was however still unsupplied, and it became necessary to introduce great numbers of new hands as weavers. So long as the supply of yarn had been limited, or beneath, or just equal to the demand, the weavers had felt but little competition; their wages had consequently remained steady. Now, however,

* Witness the Peels, the Strutts, and others. Mr. Peel, the grandfather of Sir Robert Peel, Bart. was originally a yeoman, farming his own small estate at Cross, near Bolton.

† The whole of these series of changes were operated from the invention of the fly shuttle by John Kay, in 1738, to somewhere about 1800.

D

when the outcry for cloth continued, and yarn was abundant, a large body of weavers immigrated into the manufacturing districts : great numbers of agricultural labourers deserted their occupations, and a new race of hand-loom weavers, which had undergone none of the transitions of the primitive manufacturers, were the product of the existing state of things.

This body of men was of a still lower grade in the social scale than the original weavers, had been earning a much less amount of wages, and had been accustomed to be mere labourers. The master spinners, therefore, found them ready to work at an inferior price, and thus discovered an outlet for their extra quantity of yarn. This at once led to a great depreciation in the price of hand-loom labour, and was the beginning of that train of disasters which has finally terminated in reducing those who have kept to it to a state of starvation.

Human power is urged beyond a certain point with great difficulty ; and, what is still worse, when great numbers of individuals are in exclusive possession of one particular occupation, it is a power difficult to manage, and still more difficult to be depended upon. Nor are these the only unpleasantnesses connected with it ; men are apt to acquire notions of exclusive possession, and to hold an opinion that improvements in machinery, which lessen the value of their labour, are wrongs inflicted upon them—are infringements upon their peculiar domain. These things were keenly felt by the early manufacturers, who had to trust entirely to hand labour. They were subjected periodically to severe immediate losses, and to the chance of still greater ulterior ones, by the refractory spirit of their hands, who timed their opportunity, when the markets were particularly pressing, to urge their claims. They had indeed but little alternative, and it is quite certain that a crisis was rapidly approaching which would have checked the progress of manufactures, when steam, and its application to machinery,* at once turned the current against the men, and has been since steadily, but securely sweeping their opposition to the dust, all their efforts to free themselves from its subjection having been totally un-, availing, and worse than useless.

From the time of the introduction of steam power, a most extraordinary and painful change has been wrought in the condition of the hand-loom weavers, and their labour may fairly be said to have been crushed beneath the steam engine. They constitute the bulk of our present domestic manufacturers. We have traced them from comparative wealth, through various changes, and it now remains to examine their present condition.

It may perhaps excite surprise that any large body of men should be found adhering to domestic manufacture; and the question has often been asked—why did not the operatives already engaged in manufacturing processes, become the first workers on steam looms, and in other factory labours? This, on a *prima facie* view of the question, would appear to have been the most natural order of things. We have already said that the introduction of steam looms, and the use of machinery in general, was viewed suspiciously, and treated with hostility by those who supposed that this was an infringe-

*. The first steam engine applied to cotton spinning was erected in 1783. Sir R. Arkwright's first use of this power was in 1790. In 1800 there were about 32 steam engines in Manchester, according to Mr. Farey. The steam looms were introduced from 1800 to 1806, and followed by serious riots, and breaking and destroying of machinery.

ment upon their proper domain of industry. This feeling naturally kept the hand-loom weavers aloof from the first spinning and weaving mills ; so that these were furnished with their complement of hands from other sources.

The majority of workers, however, in the early spinning establishments, were children ; partly on account of the machines being small, and partly from a difficulty of procuring adult labour. But farther than this : machinery improved with great rapidity, and to quote Dr. Ure,— " The effect of improvements in machinery supersedes the necessity for the employment of the same quantity of adult labour as before, in order to produce a given result ; and in substituting one description of human labour for another, it is the less skilled for the. more skilled, juvenile for adult, female for male." In this inevitable and unvarying result of the adaptation of scientific discoveries to manufactures, is to be found one great cause of the number of hand-loom weavers having undergone little or no diminution, although their particular branch of industry has been reduced to the most wretched and worst paid condition of labour of any at present in existence.

Those who have made it a reproach to the hand-loom weavers, that they have obstinately clung to their employment in place of taking advantage of the factories, completely overlook the facts of their case. It is well known that steam looms do not require an adult labourer, but that they are supplied entirely by young women and girls ; and that, notwithstanding the vast extension of the factory manufacture, it is more than kept pace with by mechanical inventions, and in place of demanding more, and adult labourers, it could at this moment very readily discharge a multitude of operatives.* There is no room for the male hand-loom weaver—the factories are closed against him by the sternest necessity.

In this state, and since the deplorable condition to which they have been reduced has drawn them to the verge of desperation, and forced them to make their sufferings known, and to endeavour to find some means of relief, it has become common, amongst a certain class of writers, to brand the unfortunate weavers as a set of idle, dissolute, and thieving people, unworthy of the so-called blessings of being *engaged* in factory labour. The gross injustice of this charge is made apparent by the slightest examination.

Families, comprising nearly one million of human beings, dependent on hand-loom weaving, have been living in the lowest depths of poverty for years : the father, aided by his grown-up children, toiling for fourteen hours per day, and condemned to find his wages falling from time to time, till they have been reduced to a miserable pittance, not sufficient to furnish the simplest necessaries of life. The prices paid for weaving a particular kind of cloth, as shewn in the following table, will exhibit the extraordinary depreciation which has taken place in the value of this species of labour :—

	s.	d.
1795	39	9
1800	25	0
1810	15	0
1820	8	0
1830	5	0

From this latter sum has to be deducted 1s. 3d. for

* *Vide* " Philosophy of Manufactures," p. 326.—Minutes of Evidence of the Select Committee on Hand-loom Weavers, 1834. —.P. 194, 200, 428.

necessary disbursements, and the net wage is thus reduced to 3s. 9d. in this particular case. This is not a solitary instance; it is an example of the entire labour connected with hand-loom manufacture.*

According to Mr. Felkin, in the Factory Commission Report, the net weekly earnings of the hands engaged in the cotton stocking trade are from 4s. to 7s. The misery suffered by this large and industrious class of operatives is dreadful, and is followed by many evils, physical as well as moral. Upon the sum above mentioned, a man, his wife, and their children, have to be supported; the consequence is, that they are half starved, half clad, and utterly destitute of the most common comforts.

Another large and interesting class of domestic manufacturers is that connected with the bobbin-net trade. Not far from two hundred thousand young women earn a scanty livelihood by embroidering this material in Great Britain. Mr. Power, in his Report on Nottingham, remarks: "Almost the youngest of them is able to speak with regret of a better state of earnings, and a period of less necessity for constant labour. They begin early and work late, and during this long daily period their bodies are constantly bent over the frame on which the lace is extended, the head being usually kept within five or six inches of the frame, the edge of which presses against the lower part of the chest. One effect universally produced is short-sightedness, and often a general weakness of the eyes, with consumptive tendency, distortion of the limbs, and general debility, from the confinement and the posture."

---

* *Vide* Appendix, Note B, for tables of wages, price of provisions, &c. &c. at different periods.

In reference to this statement, it is remarked by Dr. Ure, and we regret that many extracts might be made of a similar tendency : " Aversion to the control and continuity of factory labour, and the pride of spurious gentility or affectation of lady-rank, are among the reasons why young women so frequently sacrifice their comfort and health to lace-embroidery at home. One girl, in her examination, states, ' I like it better than the factory, though we can't get so much. We have our liberty at home, and get our meals comfortable, such as they are.' " Surely this is language not calling for reprobation, but expresses feelings worthy of encouragement, and deserving our warmest sympathy. It is the love of home, the duties of the social hearth, the very field in which woman ought to move, that is pictured in the simple language of the lace-girl. Would to God the same feelings prevailed in the cotton manufacturing districts amongst the sex !

Mr. Baines, in his work on the cotton manufactures, goes one step farther than Dr. Ure, and says : " The second cause of the low rate of wages amongst the hand-loom weavers is, that their employment is in some respects more agreeable, as laying them under less restraint than factory labour ; being carried on in their own cottages, their time is at their own command ; they may begin and leave off work at their pleasure ; they are not bound punctually to obey the summons of the factory bell ; if they are so disposed they can quit their loom for the public house, or to lounge in the street, or to accept some other job ; and when urged by necessity, they make up for lost time by great exertion ; in short, they are more independent than factory operatives ; they are their own masters, and they have the power, in case of urgent necessity or strong temptation, to embezzle a

few cops of the employer's weft in order to buy bread or
ale, which is a very common occurrence. All this
makes the weaver's occupation more seductive to men
of idle, irregular, and dissipated habits, than other
occupations. *It is a dear-bought miserable liberty, but
like poaching or smuggling,* it is more congenial to
some tastes than working under precise restrictions for
twice the remuneration." These observations are most
unjust towards the hand-loom weavers.

The following, out of many cases, are related by Sir
David Barry, and they shew in the strongest light the
falsehood of .Mr. E. Baines's statement, and the unfair-
ness of Dr. Ure's remarks, qualified even as the latter are.

" John Harrop works in a back damp earthen-floored
shop, and sleeps in a miserable dirty garret in the same
building : no bedstead—scarcely any furniture. Earns
on an average 6*s.* per week ; out of which he pays all his
loom expenses, more than 1*s.* per week. He is twenty-five
years of age, his wife twenty-one ; one child, and likely
soon to have another. He is thin, pale, hollow-cheeked,
and looks half-starved. *He works from five in the morning
till nine at night now (sixteen hours), and often longer in
winter. Solemnly assures me that he never takes thirty
minutes to all his meals during working hours. Would
like exceedingly to become a power-loom dresser, but it
requires great interest to get such a birth."*

Does this case require one word of comment ? It is
one of multitudes.

" Thomas Smith. Two elder daughters, now weaving,
would go to power-looms if they could get places."*

We again repeat, that these instances are examples
bearing upon the entire class of hand-loom weavers.
There is no indisposition to work ; but, on the con-

* Factory Commission Report, Part II. p. 42. Glasgow.

trary, they endure a kind of slavery unmatched in any quarter of the globe. And what is the actual condition of these poor men ?—

"It is, I conceive, unnecessary to specify the miserable domestic circumstances of each hand-loom weaver's family that I have visited (in Glasgow, &c.) They are all reduced to the most squalid poverty. Compelled by competition to sell their labour so cheaply that the very utmost quantity which an individual čan furnish is barely sufficient to procure for him in exchange the coarsest raiment, the meanest dwelling, and but a stinted allowance of the cheapest food. There is no combination among these poor men. They work in damp detached cellars as long as they can see. Each brings his individual labour to the proprietor of the material, who will, of course, accept of the cheapest offer."*

"The hand-loom weavers (of Manchester) labour fourteen hours and upwards daily, and earn only from 5s. to 7s. per week. They are ill-fed, ill-clothed, half-sheltered, and ignorant, weaving in close damp cellars, or crowded in ill-ventilated workshops ; and it only remains that they should become, as is too frequently the case, demoralized and reckless, to render perfect the portraiture of savage life." Such is the language of Dr. Kay, in a small work, got up from materials furnished by the Board of Health, during the Cholera of 1831.†

These are statements applicable to the woollen weavers of Yorkshire, and the cotton-weavers of Lancashire, Nottinghamshire, and Derbyshire. The darkest part of the

---

* Sir David Barry, *in eodem.*

† *Vide* Appendix, Note C, containing a most touching piece of evidence, comprising the life and experiences of a hand-loom weaver.

picture refers chiefly to the hand-loom weavers congregated in large towns. The bulk of this class of labourers, however, is scattered in the neighbourhoods of the manufacturing towns; and, notwithstanding the extreme depression of their wages, and their consequent abject poverty, a more patient, sober, and industrious set of men does not exist. The privations which they have suffered, and the multitude of adult labourers compelled to cling to this branch of industry, are surely sufficient arguments to prove that some remedial measures are imperatively demanded; and surely more than sufficient to demonstrate, that machinery impelled by steam, before the gigantic march of which they have sunk, has, notwithstanding the vast additions which it has already made, and is still making to our national resources, been tracked by woe and suffering to a large and deserving class of operatives.

The condition in which machinery found the domestic manufacturers has been clearly and fully explained; and the condition to which they are now reduced, by prolific production, with which it is impossible for human labour to compete, presents a most unhappy contrast.* There is no hope,—no ground of retreat for them in manufactures;—day after day adaptations of mechanical science are developed, which compel those already engaged in factory labour to exercise the most vigilant care to prevent themselves being thrown out of employ. " The spinners and power-loom dressers (of Glasgow), who have been all hand-loom weavers, now prevent any more of their former companions from being employed in

---

* Not only has this facility of production ruined hundreds of thousands of our own cottage manufacturers, but it has also ruined 2,000,000 of East Indian hand-weavers. This fact will be noticed more at length in a subsequent chapter.

their present business. They are united into close exclusive societies, and absolutely possess a monopoly of well - paid cotton labour. They keep up their prices, and keep down their numbers. They can stop every factory in Glasgow whenever they please, and their means would enable them to hold out some time : but a strike of a month would starve more than three-fourths of the hand-loom weavers, even supposing that they could bring about a strike, which, under their circumstances, would be impracticable." This is the language held by Sir David Barry, in the Factory Commission Report. Does it appear, from this, that the hand-loom weavers have an opportunity for changing their industrial condition, and that they are withheld from doing so by their own negligent, idle, and dissolute habits ?

" In cotton spinning it would now be possible to reduce the wages of labour, because, since the mules have been enlarged, there is always a sufficiency of hands ; but it has never been the policy of the masters to do so, unless when absolutely compelled by the want of profits, knowing that the lower the work-people are reduced in circumstances, the less dependance can be placed on their labour. The operative spinners, aware that a great excess of hands would have the effect of reducing their wages, combine to pay the expense of sending their unemployed comrades away to America. Mr. H. Houldsworth, of Glasgow, states that he knows this fact from the individuals themselves, and from their wives, and has occasionally been solicited to aid the families in their emigration, and to forward them sums contributed by the Union for their temporary support. " Within the last three years there have been not less than eighty or one hundred spinners, shipped from Glasgow, which is perhaps one-eighth of the whole."*

In the face of evidence of this nature, given for very different purposes from that for which it is here used, can it be maintained that the hand-loom weaver is a voluntary sufferer, or a victim to his own idleness and dislike for factory labour? It is the spinning and dressing departments which could alone employ him, steam weaving being superintended by young women only. There is no outlet for his labour; he must either adhere to his loom, or he must perish of want. The circumstance of so many thousand families being dependent on hand weaving, is the strongest proof that can possibly be adduced, of the undying aptitude for labour, of the passive courage and unwearying industry, of a large portion of our population. In their struggles with want they have not sunk down into pauperism; and fathers of families with earnings barely averging 5s. per week, have nobly toiled on, in the midst of starvation, rarely having recourse to the poor-rate. Although famine and cold, and supplications for bread from the mouths of his children — although feebleness and hunger, and over-strained exertion—have been the lot of the hand-loom weaver, it is of late only that he has began to feel that he was reduced to extremity; that his contest with steam production was a vain one; that it had ground him to the dust, and must ultimately either starve him into outrage, or force him to quit his country. It is only of late, we repeat, that this feeling has developed itself; the wonder is, that it has been so long delayed, for the minimum rate of wages has been passed long ago. The appearance and daily experiences of the hand-loom weaver will satisfy every inquirer, that he is exchanging his labour for a

* Report on Manufactures, p. 311.

price utterly inadequate to supply the commonest wants of humanity.

The causes assigned by the hand-loom weavers for the present depressed condition, are in the main correct; yet the remedies they propose, however just they may be in the abstract, are to some considerable extent inexpedient, nay, impracticable.* Local boards for the regulation of wages would be useless; wide alterations in taxation are nearly, if not altogether, impossible; taxing steam power, when applied to manufacture, would derange the entire commerce of the kingdom, and would be attended with other difficulties, which would press rather upon the operatives than upon capital, but it would never restore hand-loom weaving. Greatly as we deplore the condition of this body of men, we would urge known and possible modes of amelioration, and not lead them to further murmuring and discontent by holding out any hope of benefit from interference with the commercial policy of manufacture.

The most practicable of the proposed plans is the taxing of machinery, or, what would be equivalent to it, shortening the hours of labour. Both would limit production, and raise its value, and hence hand-labour would be benefited. The benefit would, however, be temporary—the restriction would stimulate mechanical ingenuity—and the crisis between human and automatic industry would be accelerated. A moment's examination of the consequences of "strikes" would shew the hand-loom weaver that restriction injures the operative.†

One remedial agent, of great value to the wretchedly

* *Vide* Appendix D. for resolutions of the hand-loom weavers.
† *Vide* Chapter on the Influence of Machinery on the value of Human Labour, &c.

paid operative, would be the cultivation of "waste lands." According to a very able report drawn up by Mr. Cowling, it would appear that there are fifteen million acres of waste land, capable of improvement, in Great Britain and Ireland, and somewhere about sixteen million acres incapable of being turned to profitable account. There can be little doubt, however, that this quantity of waste land is rather founded upon conjectural data than upon actual survey. Admitting this, there can be no question but that there are many millions of acres of uncultivated soil which would, under a proper system of tillage, yield a more than equal return for a proper outlay expended upon it. But this return would not be immediate; and many of the most extensive tracts are so far removed from available markets, for the sale of their produce, that there is little room to hope for their being called into useful cultivation. No capitalist will embark money upon the speculation of reclaiming waste; for, as Mr. Cowling very justly remarks, " such an enterprise would undoubtedly be attended with considerable loss in the first instance; but," he continues, " you have a surplus of labourers, whose maintenance imposes upon the poor-rates a burden of 2,000,000l. per annum : if you employ these labourers on the improvement of your wastes, you will be losers to the amount of one million per annum by the undertaking; but as the poor-rates will be lessened two millions in amount, the public will be a gainer of one million by the undertaking." In an able work are the following remarks on waste lands and their cultivation :—" It is argued that waste lands remain uncultivated because they are barren— because their cultivation would not yield an adequate return for the outlay required for their tillage. We cannot accede to this opinion ; we contend, on the contrary, that each division of the British dominions contains extensive and valuable tracts of waste lands, which are not naturally barren,—which in their present state are comparatively unproductive, because they are not tilled,—which require nothing but tillage to render them productive, and which would make an adequate return for any outlay which a judicious and industrious occupier might think it necessary to expend in reclaiming and cultivating them." Mr. Jacobs, in his very excellent work on the Cultivation of Poor Soils, remarks :—" Every man who has been far from home must have observed, on every barren heath, some spots surrounding cottages, which exhibit marks of productiveness forming a striking contrast with the sterility that surrounds them. If inquiry has been made, it has been found that at one period all was alike barren ; that the difference has been created solely by the application of human labour ;" and further, ·" the practicability of achieving the object of bringing our waste lands to a degree of highly productive cultivation, and with an enduring profit after a course of years of perseverance, may be inferred from what has been performed in other countries, at no great distance from our own. In the Netherlands, the district called Maesland, between Ghent and Antwerp, is a mere agricultural country. It is better peopled, better cultivated, and more productive, than any other spot in Europe of similar extent. It was, in the time of the civil wars in Flanders, a mere sandy heath, without inhabitants, without cultivation, and without live-stock. The change has been effected by persevering labour through many generations ; and the results of that labour are most strikingly exhibited in the fruitful fields, the beautiful cattle, the healthful and cleanly population, .the comfortable residences, and all the other visible marks of rural prosperity."

It can admit of no dispute, therefore, that there are
numerous tracts of waste ground capable of being sufficiently fertilized for useful and profitable purposes. It
is, however, somewhat fallacious to assume that all waste
land is capable of profitable cultivation, or that at some
period the whole country was barren, and presented an
aspect similar to that now seen on our heaths and commons.   The mere existence of a piece of waste ground,
in the midst of a highly cultivated district where land is
valuable, is a proof, *de facto*, of the inferiority, generally
speaking, of such ground;   not that it is absolutely
barren,—for there is no soil, however sterile, but tillage
and manure will make something of it,—but that the
space is not worth the outlay for its subjection.   And
again, it must be borne in mind that our poor soils and
waste lands belong to somebody : they are not waifs on
which any man may seize and appropriate ; freehold and
manorial rights meet us at every step, and great difficulties are often experienced in securing a good title ; and
these, when added to the natural disadvantages of the
soil, prevent capital from locating itself upon it.

A case in illustration occurred some years ago.
Several gentlemen were anxious to rescue a large body
of hand-loom weavers, in the neighbourhood of Manchester, from a state of miserable poverty.   Eleemosynary relief would have been useless; and it was
found that, with a very praiseworthy spirit, they had
abstained from making application for parochial relief,
except in cases of sickness.   It was clear that these
men, who exhibited the most unequivocal marks of
industrious and sober lives, were the victims of their
gigantic antagonist, steam ; and that all which was required to render them comfortable was a means by which
their labour might be made available.   Funds were

provided to enable them to emigrate; but objections were raised to this, as we could see no substantial cause for robbing ourselves of upwards of one hundred valuable families. In the case of a few inferior cottage tenants, the most admirable effects had resulted from attaching small plots of ground to their cottages, and satisfied, that if men are furnished with means for being useful to themselves and to others, they will never fail to be so, it was resolved to give these poverty-stricken weavers small garden-plots, on the cultivation of which their idle and now useless time might be spent. In pursuance of this determination suitable ground was sought; but the excessive price demanded in the immediate outskirts of the town was a complete prohibition. A rough and sandy waste, as irreclaimable in appearance as could well be imagined, was, however, at length fixed upon. But here again a price, and that not a small one, was demanded; and this, joined to the conveyance, the outlay necessary for fencing, the first coating of manure, and other additamenta, clearly showed that upwards of twenty years must elapse before even interest of money could be expected; all things, too, supposed to proceed favourably. The plan was, in a great measure, abandoned, because private capital will not submit to this delay, and probable prospective loss.

The cultivation of waste land ought to be a national work; and the funds of the country could not be better employed. Twenty millions have been voted as the redemption money of the West Indian slaves: the condition of the domestic manufacturers is beyond comparison inferior to that of the late slave population of the colonies.

In considering waste lands, therefore, as being beneficial agents in reference to the depressed artisan, something more should be taken into account than the mere existence of wastes, and their capability of being cultivated.

Home colonization, which has been partially tried, is the locating a body of labourers on some particular district, and there converting them into small farmers. *If* the speculation should answer,—*if* the promoters of it should continue to watch carefully over the interests of their colonists,—*if* enlightened and generous rules are laid down for the internal government of these colonies,—they may succeed, but not unless. *The scheme goes too far: it changes the character of the labourer—it makes him a small farmer without capital*, and thus leaves him exposed to ruin from a single bad season, or from depressions in the markets. The examples of the Dutch colonies do not apply with sufficient correctness to Great Britain.

The weavers have themselves answered the question of emigration as a means of ameliorating their condition;* and till every means have been tried at home, the wholesale exportation of our labouring population is a scheme to be decried. New countries require emigrants, not from the class of pauperised artisans, but men with small capital, sufficient to carry them through the first stages of colonization. In this way Canada has been enriched by many thousands of our most valuable citizens, and many millions of our wealth. We have not the slightest hesitation in affirming, that we have space enough, and more than enough, for the absorption of every half-fed and half-paid labourer now pining in want and in despair. If emigration be encouraged as a means

* *Vide* Appendix—Opinions of the Hand-loom Weavers.

of peopling new states, let the recommendation rest upon
that basis; but we protest against emigration being encouraged as a means of ridding us of our surplus labourers,
upon the ground that Great Britain has no resource
within herself for employing her sons. If the thousands of pounds which are annually wasted by parishes
to assist emigrants,—if the thousands that are annually
carried from our shores to the United States and to
Canada,—if the thousands that are spent by different
land-companies,—if all these thousands were devoted to
their legitimate uses, we should hear no more of in-
curable distress. And has this enormous waste of
wealth and labour eased by one tittle the pressure upon
the labouring community? Not one: for so universal
is this pressure, of such wide operation are the causes
leading to it, that every hiatus, every gap made by these
removals, is at once filled up. We cannot cure an universal disease in the social body by such local and partial
remedies, or rather by no remedies whatever; for emigration, employed for such a purpose, is merely lopping away
the system inch by inch, without any sanative result.
An eloquent writer, in speaking of the condition of the
poor, has forcibly and truly said—"Well may the cheek
of the patriot glow when he stands upon the quays of
Liverpool or Glasgow, and sees thousands and tens of
thousands of his countrymen proceeding into voluntary,
exile, in order to escape from the pressure of home
misery! Well may his heart burn within him when he
recognises in these pilgrim-bands the very essence and
sinews of a nation's strength,—the provident and thrifty
labourer and his family, who is carrying his industry
and his hard-won earnings to some land where poor
laws and corn laws, where taxes upon every article of
production and consumption, have no existence, and

where he hopes to find a field for his labour, as this is all
that he wants ; and this merry England denies to him !"

The *status* of the labourer should, in no respect, be
altered : he is, in his natural position, a man exchanging his labour for the means of subsistence,—in the
character of an hired servant, and aiding, by private industry, his daily wage. This is the position he ought
to hold, and, if removed from it, he is decidedly injured.
As he now stands, he has lost, in a great measure, all
self-support—in the agricultural districts, partly by the
prevalence of large farms, a system which has been
carried so far, that in eight counties, during the last
century, a diminution of not less than 20,000 cottages
has taken place, partly by being deprived of home
manufacture, and partly by the desuetude of plot and
garden cultivation ; and in the manufacturing districts by
hand-labour being ruined by steam machinery. Which
of these can be restored to him ? We cannot break up the
large farm system, neither can we bring back his home
manufacture in its original state, nor interfere largely
with machinery ; *but we can restore to him his land, and
by so doing, find him a means of supporting his family,
without at all infringing upon his character as a labourer.*
This is not a theoretical scheme,—it does not innovate
upon the industrial character of the labourer,—it does
not make his degradation a source of speculative experiment : no ! it would replace him as he has been. The
transition of property and industry has literally overwhelmed him, because *his interests* have never been
recognised.

In providing land for the poor man, the argument is
used, where is it to be found, and how is he to pay for
it ?—he is poor, he is reckless, and has neither means
nor inclination for becoming a tenant. It is lamentable

that such language should be commonly heard. It seems to proceed from a belief that the poor man is without the nobler feelings of independence and pride of self. But he is not so: he has within him all the better and higher elements of humanity, and, in his struggles with poverty and toil, he often exhibits a moral heroism, and a pure sense of religion, which ought to make him a subject for our admiration. Stretch out to him the hand of fellowship, show sympathy for his condition, enable him to exercise his energies, and the labouring man will prove himself worthy of encouragement. To assert that he is careless or indifferent is to assert a positive falsehood. Every man familiar with his feelings and disposition is aware what value the labourer attaches " to a bit of land," with what pride it is cultivated, and what a degree of independence and personal respect it gives him for himself. And this is the pivot upon which every plan for regenerating the poor should turn. Give a moral stimulus, and the battle is won.

But where is the land to be found? Every where. A superficies of many thousands of acres might be pointed out, which, during the late calamitous depression, has gone nearly out of cultivation, and which it has been impossible to let upon any terms. Again, notwithstanding the millions of acres which have been inclosed during the last century, there are still millions of waste fit for cultivation scattered over every part of the country. It must be borne in mind, that our labourers should be a fixed population; and the more closely they can be bound by local ties, the better men, and the better citizens will they be.

There can, therefore, be no difficulty in finding land, as the " waste lands of the kingdom ought to be treated as a national domain, to be divided and allotted as the demands of society for space and employment happen to

increase." The community is entitled to address the proprietors of such lands in the following terms :—
" Thousands of your fellow-countrymen are destitute of employment and food ; you own thousands of acres of waste, which yield very little profit to you, but on which labour might enable them to raise the necessaries of life which they require. If you choose, yourselves, to undertake the cultivation of these neglected lands, well and good; this will create an extra demand for labour, and afford to those persons the employment of which they are now destitute ; but if you decline this task, which is become necessary on public grounds, the general good requires that the state should step in, and take from you this source of employment and wealth, which you think proper to overlook, giving you, at the same time, the most ample compensation for the rights and advantages which you are called upon to relinquish." This would be perfectly just, and would open an immense field for improvement.

It has been urged farther, that many of the enclosures of wastes have failed as profitable speculations—and that much poor land is thus lying useless. Very true ; but why have these enclosures failed as sources of profit? —From a want of due understanding of the nature of the soil, and of the means necessary to reclaim it. It is amongst the large allotments *only* in these enclosures that failure can be instanced. The cottage allotments, varying from half an acre to an acre and a half, have been invariably successful ; witness, amongst multitudes of other examples, Knaresborough Forest and the wastes of Christchurch.*

* A body of valuable facts on the allotment system, will be found in the " Labourer's Friend," published under the direction of the Labourer's Friend Society, 20, Exeter Hall.

Waste lands have been expatiated upon at some length, because they are valuable accessories, and they occur in all places: but they are accessories only. There is abundance of land already in cultivation, which, by being divided into small allotments in the immediate neighbourhood of villages and detached cottages, would pay a vastly increased rent, and by spade husbandry produce threefold its present returns. What happens where this plan is in existence? " The cottagers in Lincolnshire and Rutlandshire hold their little tenements, *not from the farmer*, but directly from the owner; and this rescues them from all slavish and injurious dependence. The management of this little demesne never, we believe, for one hour interferes with the necessary occupations of the labourer ; it is managed principally by his wife and younger children. The labourer himself, no doubt, bestows upon his little tenement some extra labour after his daily toil is over, or occasionally the labour of a few whole days, whenever he can be spared with the least inconvenience from the work of his regular employer. The effect is all that the most benevolent heart could desire—a more comfortable, contented, and moral peasantry does not, we believe, exist on the face of the globe."

" In the year 1806, an enclosure was proposed in the parish of Broad Somerford, and a very liberal offer made to the rector for an allotment of land in lieu of tithe ; but he considered it his duty to attend to the interests of his poor parishioners, and did not consent till he had obtained the following conditions for them :—Every poor man, whose cottage was situated on the commons and waste lands, should have his garden, orchard, or little enclosure taken from the waste, within twenty years confirmed to him ; and that in case the same did not amount to half an

acre, it should be increased to that quantity. In addition
to this, eight acres were allotted to the rector, church-
warden, &c. adjoining the village, for the benefit of the
poor inhabitants, to be annually allowed them, according
to the number of their respective families; and thus
every man, who had three or four children, was sure of
his quarter of an acre at least. Very great benefit has
been derived from these provisions, and they in no way
interfere with the poor man's labour for the farmer.
Spade husbandry, and the constant and minute attention
of himself and family, secured him abundant crops even
when the farmer's failed. The profits upon every acre,
after paying a rent of 2*l.*, was 7*l.* 6*s.* 4*d.* So great was
the success attendant upon this plan, that in 1829, a
farmer made application to the rector to remit him half
his rent of 60*l.* for a farm of eighty acres, stating that
the crops would hardly repay his labour. The rector
divided it into suitable lots, and offered it to the surrounding cottagers: they were eagerly taken, and, at
Michaelmas day, 80*l.* were paid to a sixpence, for land
which had the year before been thrown up at 60*l.* "

It is to the soil we must look as the means for regenerating our labourers,—for again making them happy
and peaceable,—for again making them large consumers
of our home and colonial produce,—and, above all, for
again making them moral and independent members of
the community, and devoted adherents of their country
and her institutions.

In thus urging the restoration of the domestic manufacturers to an improved industrial status, by making
their labour available to themselves, and, in equal ratio,
beneficial to the state, it must not be supposed that
this being done all is done: but it is the first grand
step. It would be indeed vain to lessen the burden of a

man's taxation; it will be in vain to lower the price
of his bread, whether by unshackling the corn trade, or
changing our monetary standard; unless at the same time
we afford to the poor man a means of employing himself.
Adult labour is becoming daily of less value, since the
gigantic and plastic power of steam has been applied to
the arts; and hence man is condemned to the hand-loom, or
left dependent upon the exertion of his wife and children.
Open a path for his labour, and unfetter capital, which
may be beneficially employed in calling forth its energies,
and directing its efforts to a multitude of purposes, still
waiting for enterprise to become important addenda to
our national resources, and he will be saved. But if the
labourers are permitted to sink,—if they are to be
overwhelmed by the progress of scientific discovery,—
if the adaptation of mechanical contrivances is to thrust
them back into idleness,—if pauperism is to spread its
influence still deeper and deeper,—if workhouses are to
be their future homes,—then is the sun of England's
prosperity on the decline : her enormous capital, the
skill of her artisans, the enterprise of her merchants, her
unrivalled resources, her wise institutions,—none can
save her. She may go on manufacturing, she may accumulate wealth, but if large bodies of the community are
permitted to degenerate, at a pace equal to that with
which they have gone down during the last half century,
most disastrous results must speedily develop themselves.

Our artisans are yielding step by step before mechanism, whilst, at the same time, an universal pressure,
caused principally by the absorption of domestic manufacture into factories, is forcing immigration towards the
manufacturing districts, and by this means adding to the
obstructions in the labour market. And yet nothing is

done :—the only answer given by Government to the hand-loom weavers is, that it is better to work for a pittance however small, than to starve ; and the only remedial agent, as yet proposed, is one certain to be attended with great immediate suffering. The Poor Law Amendment Act does nothing whatever towards remedying the *distress*,* which has come upon the labouring population ; and it is from this that the heavy pressure on the poor-rate has arisen. It can benefit industry only by shutting up the surplus labourers in poor houses, and these, we humbly conceive, are dreadful substitutes for the cottage-homes of England.

We would, on the contrary, say to our suffering operatives, who, be it ever remembered, are the victims of agencies far beyond their influence, " We know you to be distressed ; we know, too, that this distress has arisen from a variety of causes, over which you have had no control—namely, loss of home manufacture, restrictions and trade monopolies, oppressive taxation, changes in the currency, destruction of small farming, and the loss of your proper position. To the last to some extent we can restore you ; for the rest, so many conflicting interests are at stake, that time is required for their proper adjustment."

* *Vide* Chapter on the Influence of Machinery on Human Labour.

CHAPTER II.

IT has truly been remarked by Bacon, that "the
culture and manurance of mind in youth hath such a
forcible though unseen operation, as hardly any length
of time or contention of labour can countervail its
influence."

The domestic manufacturer possessed the great
advantage, as we have already said, of carrying on
his occupation beneath the roof of his own cottage, and
in the midst of his family : here his children grew up
under his own eye and around his fire-side, and retained
for him the respect due to parental authority, by remaining members of one home and under the direction
of one head. By keeping up this natural and proper

order of things, he secured one means of making his offspring domestic in their habits, and it was his own fault
if their social character was not what it ought to be.

So long as families were thus bound together by the
strong link of interest and affection, each member in its
turn, as it attained an age fitted for the loom, joined
its labour to the general stock, its earnings forming part
'of a fund, the whole of which was placed at the disposal
of the father or mother, as the case might be ; and each
individual looked to him or to her for the adequate
supply of its wants. No separate or distinct interests
were ever acknowledged or dreamt of. If any one, by
superior industry or skill, earned more in proportion
than another, no claim was made for such excess on
the part of that individual; on the contrary, it was
looked upon equally as a part of the wages of the family
—perhaps gratefully and affectionately acknowledged,
but leading to no other result.

The family compact, of course, existed no longer than
the usual period when parental control yields before the
maturity of offspring. This was rarely before twenty-
two or twenty-three years of age, and often much later.
Grown up, as each member had, as part and parcel of a
little community, these divisions seldom took place
before marriage opened a series of new cares and new
prospects to son or daughter, which in consequence,
seceded, or, as was frequently the case, brought a wife
or husband to be joined to the family union. Generally,
however, at this period an offset or branching took place,
which was best for all parties.

This natural arrangement preserved in all their vigour
the moral obligations of father and mother, brother and
sister, son and daughter, till a time of life was gained
which had given abundant opportunity for the formation

of character—a character most assuredly the best calculated to render the labouring man happy and virtuous,
viz. a domestic one; without which, no adventitious
aid can ever secure him its possession.

The greatest misfortune — the most unfavourable
change which has resulted from factory labour—is the
breaking up of these family ties, the consequent abolition of the domestic circle, and the perversion of all the
social obligations which should exist between parent and
child on the one hand, and between children themselves
on the other.

The age at which a child became useful to its parents
so long as the great mass of manufactures was manual
and confined to private dwelling-houses, was from fourteen to sixteen. At an earlier age it was useful in a
minor degree, but that was the period at which it became
an auxiliary to the incomings of the family by regular
working.

Before this it was a mere child, entirely dependent
upon the exertions of its parents or older brothers and
sisters for support. During this time it was taught, by
daily experience, habits of subordination to its seniors.
The period at which it ranked itself by the side of the
efficient portions of the household was a happy medium
between too early an application and too late a procras-
tination of its physical energies, for the child was
sufficiently matured, in its material organization, to bear
without injury moderate and continued exertion; and
no time had, as yet, been allowed for the acquirement of
slothful habits. It came, too, at a time when the first impulses of puberty were beginning to stir new associations
in his mind. These it checked by keeping him occupied,
while he was removed from the influence of bad example,
and laboured in an open workshop, free from the stimulus

of warmth, and in the presence of his sisters, brothers, and parents, the very best anodyne for allaying and keeping in due restraint his nascent passions, whilst his moral and social instincts were under a process of incessant cultivation.

The same observations apply with still greater force to the females of the family. With them labour commenced at a somewhat earlier period, or they supplied the place of their mother in the household offices, leaving her at liberty to work for their sustenance, if such a course of proceeding was deemed necessary, or forced upon them by the pressure of circumstances. Whichever it was, she was kept from promiscuous intercourse with the other sex, at an age when it was of the utmost importance, her young sensibilities rendering her peculiarly liable to powerful and irresistible impressions. It is true that the sports of her own sex were to some extent libidinous, but to these she was not admitted till a much later period; and these, though coarse and highly objectionable, rarely ended in mischief, being considered as a sort of prelude to marriage, a custom certainly " more honoured in the breach than in the observance."

. Her occupations and feelings were therefore exclusively home-bred, and no idea existed that distinct or detached interests could intervene betwixt her parents and herself.

It is in these respects that the family of the factory labourer offers such strong contrasts and unhappy differences to their precursors in manufacturing industry.

. In the first place, there is no home labour. Home becomes therefore a mere shelter, in which their meals are hastily swallowed, and which offers them repose for the night. It has no endearing recollections which bind it on their memories—no hold upon their imaginations.

In the next place, the various members not only do not labour under their own roof, but they do not labour in common, nor in one mill; or if in one mill, so separated, that they have no opportunity of exchanging a single glance or a word throughout the long hours they are engaged there. Children are thus entirely removed from parental guardianship; and not only so, but they are brought into immediate contact with parties, generally of their own age, equally removed with themselves from inspection, and equally unchecked by a consciousness that the eye of a brother, sister, or parent may be fixed upon them. They are placed, too, under the control of an overlooker or spinner, who, from a sense of duty to his employer or himself, if moved by no baser feeling, treats them frequently with harshness,* making no allowance for childish simplicity, bashfulness, delicacy, or female failings; and this is most fatal to self-esteem, which nothing so soon injures or destroys as unworthy treatment, suffered in themselves or witnessed in others, without the power of redress, or even of appeal.

Again, they are subjected on all sides to the influence of vicious examples—are placed in a heated atmosphere, and have no occupation, save watching the passage of a thread or the revolution of a spindle. The mind is but little engaged,—there is no variety for it to feed upon, and it has none of the pure excitements which home affords. It becomes crowded with images of the very opposite

---

* The extraordinary charges made against the factories in this respect are gross exaggerations. Cruelty has existed, and does exist amongst the spinners, but by no means in the shape generally supposed.

quality, and no opportunity is given for the growth of
modesty, on the one hand, or of the social obligations of
brother, sister, or child, on the other.

The next evil which removes factory labour another
step still more widely apart from the condition of
domestic manufacture is, that the wages of children have.
become, either by universal consent, or by the growth of,
disobedience, payable to the person earning them. This
has led to another crying and grievous misfortune,
namely, that each child ceases to view itself as a subordinate agent in the household;* so far indeed loses the
character and bearing of a child, that it pays over to its
natural protector a stated sum for food and lodging;
thus detaching itself from parental subjection and control. The members, therefore, of a spinner's or weaver's
family become a body of distinct individuals, occupying
occasionally, but by no means universally, the same
home, each paying its quota to the joint expenses, and
considering themselves as lodgers merely, and appro-
priating any surplus which may remain of their wages
to their own private purposes, accountable to no one for
the mode in which it happens to be used or wasted.

It is to be feared, that the mischiefs resulting from
such an unnatural arrangement must, in the first instance, be saddled upon the errors of parents—such a
dereliction from filial duty being hardly likely to happen
spontaneously on the side of the children; and that a
plan originally adopted in a few cases by the family of
idle and depraved parents,†—and many such are to be

* *Vide* Minutes of Evidence taken before the Select Committee
on Hand-loom Weavers, p. 41, qsn. 671.

† " Too frequently the father, enjoying perfect health, and ample
opportunities of employment, is supported in idleness on the earnings of his oppressed children."—*The Moral and Physical Conditions
of the Working Classes, &c.* p. 64.

found, who would willingly live upon the toil of their children,—has become general, in consequence of the lowering in the reciprocal confidence and affection which ought to exist between parent and child.

In numerous examples, then, at the present day, parents are become the keepers of lodging-houses for their offspring, between whom little intercourse exists beyond that relating to pecuniary profit and loss. In a vast number of others, children have been entirely driven away from their homes, either by unnatural treatment, or they have voluntarily deserted them, and taken up their abode in other asylums, for the sake of saving a small sum, in the amount of payment required for food and house-room.

This disruption of all the ties of home is one of the most fatal consequences of the factory system. The social relations which should distinguish the members of the same family are destroyed. The domestic virtues, man's natural instincts, and the affections of the heart, are deadened and lost. The feelings and actions which should be the charm of the fire-side—which should prepare young men and young women for fulfilling the duties of parents—are displaced by a selfishness utterly repugnant to all such sacred obligations. Tenderness of manner—solicitude during sickness—the foregoing of personal gratification for the sake of others—submission to home restraint—these are partially lost, and their place occupied by individual independence—private avarice—the withholding assistance,* however slight, from those around them, who have a natural claim upon their gene-

* " When age and decrepitude cripple the energies of the parents, their adult children abandon them to the scanty maintenance derived from parochial relief."—*Moral and Physical Condition of the Working Classes, &c.* p. 64.

F

rosity—calculations and arrangements, based solely upon sordid motives,—with a gradual extinction of those sympathies and feelings, which are alone fitted to afford happiness—a wearing away of the more delicate shades of character, leaving nothing but attention to the simple wants of nature, in addition to the depraved appetites which are the result of other circumstances connected with their condition ;—and in the end reducing them, as a mass, to a heartless assemblage of separate and conflicting individuals, each striving for their " own hand," uninfluenced by the more gentle, the more noble, and the more humanized cares, aspirations, and feelings, which could alone render them estimable as fathers, mothers, brothers and sisters.

When it is borne in mind, at what an early period of life this separation of families takes place, its effects will be better and more correctly appreciated, and the permanence of the injurious impression produced by it will be more clearly comprehended.

Factory labour, in many of its processes, requires little else but manual dexterity, and no physical strength ; neither is there any thing for the mind to do in it ; so that children, whose fingers are taught to move with great facility and rapidity, have all the requisites for it. Hence one reason for introducing mere infants into mills,* though this is by no means the only one ; and were the hours, of labour sufficiently limited, and under proper regulation, when the present habits of their parents are considered, the evil—great in some respects as it is— would almost cease to be one. Children from nine to twelve years of age are now become part of the staple

* Considerably more than one-fourth of the entire workers in factories are under fourteen, a large proportion not being ten years old, and of all engaged under eighteen more than one-half are girls.

hands, and are consequently subjected at this tender period to all the mischiefs incident to the condition of the older work-people.*

It may be urged that the mind of a child at this age cannot, from its very structure and previous impressions, be susceptible of the more vicious and immoral parts of the system; and that its previous education, which it is presumed must have been conducted at home, will, to some extent, guard it against evil communications.

It has been truly observed, and not less beautifully than truly, that "heaven is around us in our infancy." This might have been extended, and said, that "heaven is around and within us in our infancy;" for the happiness of childhood springs full as much from an internal consciousness of delight, as from the novelty of its impressions from without. Its mind, providing the passions are properly guided, is indeed a fountain of all that is beautiful—all that is amiable—overflowing with joy and tenderness; and its young heart is a living laboratory of love, formed to be profusely scattered on all around it.

The very copiousness of its sensations, however, prevents stability in their direction, if not carefully tended; and if its heart and mind have capabilities for exhibiting and lavishing the treasures of their awakening energies, they are, from their very immaturity, more easily warped and misdirected. The hacknied quotation, "just as the twig is bent," &c. is not the less true for being hacknied. Most unhappily, every thing which goes on before the eyes of the unfortunate factory children, is but

* The "Factories Regulation Act" has caused multitudes of these children to be dismissed, but it has only increased the evils it was intended to remedy, and must of necessity be repealed.

too well calculated to nip in the bud—to wither in the spring-time of its growth—the flower which was springing up within them, to adorn and beautify their future existence.

There is no home education, and the independence assumed by older brothers and sisters, the total inattention to parental remonstrance or wishes, soon produce their influence upon a child, which is quite as ready to learn evil as good. Then, driven at the early age it is into the mill, and at once placed amongst crowds of children similarly circumstanced with itself, the impressions made upon it at home soon become permanent. The subsequent possession of money, with the bickerings that arise therefrom, alienate any spark of affection which might still be lingering in its breast for its parents, and when a mere infant, it establishes itself either as an independent inmate of its paternal dwelling, or seeks out a lodging with other parties, as the case may happen to be.

The existence of a divided interest in a household, whether the division is between man and wife, or between parent and child, is alike fatal to its best interests. No home can ever be what it ought without proper government, or where all the inmates are on such terms of equality as to give to each an equal right to the direction of the whole; and even a household so constituted will not hang long together. In the homes of the manufacturing population, the divisions between parents and children, arising from the assumption of managing their own earnings, so generally acknowledged amongst them, deprives them of the most valuable portion of their influence.

Thus, whether at home or abroad, unfettered by wholesome restraints, the factory child grows up, acquiring many vices, and utterly losing all that might render its condition one of respectability and comfort— the social and domestic virtues. Year after year rolls on, unfitting it more and more for the best purposes of life.; and if it should become a parent, it transmits to its offspring the evils of a system of which it has been the victim.

. .The entire breaking up of households, which is an inevitable consequence of mill-labour, as it now exists, is one which may be regarded as the most powerfully demoralizing agent connected with it. This is, however, aided by many other causes, some of which have been already described, and others will be noticed in the course of the work. The domestic affections, if they are to assume strength, must be steadily cultivated, and cultivated, too, in the only way of which they are capable. This is by parental kindness in the first place, which, by rendering home pleasant, and weaving its delightful associations in the young imagination, forms one of the most sacred, most delightful, and most permanent feel- ings of the human heart. In the next place, the example of proper household subordination, for without this the first will be destroyed, or so weakened as to be ineffi- cient and inoperative. Neither of these agents are brought to bear actively and properly upon the factory child. From its birth it sees nothing around it but dis- sension, and its infant cries are not hushed by maternal tenderness.* In thousands of cases it is abandoned throughout the day by its parents, both of whom are

* "The infant has not lived long ere it is abandoned to the care of a hireling or neighbour, while its mother pursues her accus- tomed toil. Thus abandoned to one whose sympathies are not interested in its welfare," &c. &c. — *Moral and Physical Condition of the Working Classes, &c.* p. 69.

engaged in the mill, and left to the care of a stranger
or a mere child—badly used—badly fed—its little heart
hardened by harshness even in the cradle; then badly
clothed—unattended during its growth by regular and
systematic kindness—constantly hearing much that is
improper—seeing on all sides strife, drunkenness, and
immorality; and finally sent into the mill, to swell the
hordes of children which have been similarly educated,
and similarly abandoned to their own resources.

It may be said, that the agricultural labourer is subjected to a separation from his family, and that the
members of his family are also, after a time, separated
from home.   This is granted, and that thus, *primâ facie*,
he appears circumstanced in these respects like the
factory labourer. Nothing can, however, be more dissimilar than the two cases, when looked at in their.true
bearings.

The agricultural labourer, it is true, pursues his occupatiou from home—but he pursues it in nine cases out
of ten solitarily, or if he works in company, it is in small
gangs; he works too in an atmosphere natural in its
temperature, and favourable to bodily health, saying
nothing of the moral influences of the sights and sounds
which are his familiar companions; his labour is physically severe, and is just sufficient to require what intellectual capacity he generally possesses ; his diet is plain
and wholesome; he is freed from the example of many
vices, by his situation, to which the factory labourer is
exposed, and his habits and modes of life are simpler
and purer.   His family, separated from each other, and
from home after a time, remain long enough under the
paternal roof to have acquired some notion of domestic
discipline, and that too under the best of all possible
teachers—a mother, whose avocations are exclusively

household. The labour of the sons, when old enough to pursue it, which is not till sixteen years of age, is that of the father, under similar circumstances. The daughters become household servants, either to persons of their own class, or, what is more general, in the houses of respectable families in the neighbourhood, or seek service in the surrounding towns and villages ; * their family interest thus, of course, merging in that of their employers. In all these cases a strict watch is kept over their morals. No point of similarity exists then between them, except in the single one of separation of families, and that too at a period and in a way to be as little injurious as possible to the moral character of the parties.

The agricultural labourer has other moral advantages over those possessed by the manufacturing one. He is frequently under the direct inspection of his employer, in the middle class of land proprietors, or respectable land-holders ; and in the inferior order of both these, he is the personal assistant, and works in conjunction with it. In the highest order, he has the reflected benefit of hereditary rank and wealth, circumstances of more importance than the superficial observer is aware of, but which are rendered sufficiently apparent by examining into the condition of the cottagers and labourers upon those estates which are benefited by the residence of their proprietors.

These are a few of the moral advantages which he possesses still, to some extent, over the factory labourer.

* Nine-tenths of domestic female servants, both in the metropolis and in all large towns, come from agricultural districts. So strong is the prejudice existing against town-bred servants, that many families absolutely refuse to take them under any circumstances.

Of late years, indeed, the breaking up of small farms, the loss of home manufacture, and other causes, have brought into operation upon him the demoralizing agency of poverty and want of employment, and its influence has done much to deprive him of many of the benefits he once enjoyed.

In addition to the enumeration already given of the evils which result from the division of families, and the early age at which children are impressed into earning their own support, with the moral degradation which is their universal effect, another misfortune, of a very prominent character, attends upon the female division of the manufacturing population. This is, the entire want of instruction or example in learning the plainest elements of domestic economy ; and this single circumstance goes far to explain many of the improvident habits which form a chief part of the curse upon their social condition. No earnings, however liberal, can compensate for this. It at once robs the home of the labouring man of every chance of being rightly or even decently conducted. If minute economy, which is the only true economy, is to be of service, it must be carefully taught, with the best means of furnishing the supplies of a family, and making these supplies go to their utmost length. Of all these essentials to the head of a household, the factory girl is utterly ignorant, and her arrangements, if arrangements they can be called, where every thing is left to chance, are characterized by sluttish waste, negligence, carelessness as to the quality of food, and indifference as to the mode of cooking, and an absence of all that tidiness, cleanliness, and forethought which are requisite to a good housewife.

So complete is the separation of families, and so entirely are all their members absorbed by mill labour,

that it very frequently happens that man and wife do
not meet during the day at all.* Working at different
mills, or at different trades, perhaps at opposite sides of
the town, their various meals are procured at some lodg-
ing-house in the immediate neighbourhood; thus adding
another evil—another cause of the dissolution of the
domestic links—to the long list already brought under
review.

The evidence given before the factory commissioners
fully bears out the statements made in this chapter.
Factory girls were found to be almost universally ignorant of domestic duties; why they are so has been
sufficiently explained. It is said, indeed, that they
make good wives to factory men, and, as such, are
generally preferred by them; but this does not make
them good wives; they are preferred because they are
engaged in the mills, and marriage for a time makes no
difference in this respect. One of the witnesses examined
before the commissioners expressed an opinion little in
unison with our own, and we quote it because it exhibits
the *fact* of the separation of families in a different light.
In answer to the question:—

" What is your opinion of the moral habits which are
contracted by boys and girls in the occupation you have
just described?"

" I would say, first of all, that where they work at
home, they are shut up all day long with their parents,
and have scarcely any acquaintance with others, and with
the feelings of their neighbours. The whole of the
feelings they thus imbibe *may be selfish*, and as their

* It has been said that few married women work in factories.
This is at variance with truth and with multitudes of cases which
have come under the author's personal notice. Some observations
will be found, when speaking of female labour, on this subject.

mode of working does not throw them out of the circle of their own house, or lead them to form any connexion with their neighbours, whatever connexions they *do* form arise from other circumstances than those of work."

It has been urged, by those who extol factory labour, that the evils flowing from separation of families are, to some extent, counteracted by the young workers being engaged under the eye of their parents or friends. Children are employed chiefly in the spinning depart-ment; acting as assistants and servants, in fact, of the spinner. This, as far as it goes, is well; it goes however but a little way.   The spinner, an adult male, is other-wise occupied than in watching attentively the conduct of his juvenile servitors.   In those mills where the pro-prietors are themselves men of high moral principle, and who pay strict attention to their work-people, some of the mischief attendant on the breaking up of families are mitigated by religious instruction; but these cases rarely are found in towns.   Some details will appear in subsequent chapters, on the benefits arising to the labourer when the mills are detached from towns, and well regulated.

CHAPTER III.

THE inquirer into the progress of the civilisation of
man has learnt the following series of facts. He
finds that as man removes from utter barbarism, from
a state elevated but one remove above the brute
creation, he raises himself a habitation, more or less
comfortable, as a shelter against the vicissitudes of the
seasons, and as a place of refuge; that, in his primeval
condition, he contented himself with the shelter of a tree,
and the protection of the natural caves or strong-holds
around him; that, at this period, he lives upon aliment
chiefly of a vegetable nature, or picks up a scanty and
precarious subsistence by fishing, or devouring the

minuter forms of animal life; that in his first advance
in social improvement, he erects himself a rude hut of
wood, or sods, or stone, as his particular locality may
point out to him, badly built, badly covered in, admitting little light, but freely open to the winds of heaven;
that he now becomes a hunter, and tills imperfectly a
small patch of ground for the production of those escu-
lent roots or seeds which experience has taught him are
fit for the support of life; that, in his next advance, he
improves his hut, forms a communion with his fellows
under an acknowledged superior, joins his labours,
whether of the chase or of cultivation, with those of
others—shows some tokens of religion, however barbarous and superstitious—selects a woman as a companion, and lays the foundation for the relations of husband
and wife; that, in his continued advance, his cottage
becomes to him more than a place of mere shelter; that
its walls are now covered with the products of war or
the chase; that it has other inmates—a family of children;
that his moral attributes slowly and imperfectly develop
themselves; that his labour or sport has for its aim the
maintenance of his family; or that his wife, not yet
freed from savage thraldrom, is the principal agent in the
production of food; that as he still progresses, his home
is better built, and assumes a different aspect; its interior
having many simple decorations, and is neat and clean,
whilst its outside bears marks of attention being paid to
effect; that he now surrounds it with a patch of ground,
over which he claims a right of exclusive possession;
that his wife now becomes to him more than a creature
retained solely for the gratification of his appetites, and
that his children are looked upon as beings in whose
welfare he is deeply and sensitively interested; that he
submits to codes of laws, or municipal regulations, which

although they may interfere with his individual liberty or particular rights of property, are yet obviously beneficial to the interests of the community of which he forms a member; that he is now stationary, has lost his preda-tory habits, and has assumed his rank as a social and moral being; that in his further advances he still improves his habitation, builds his house in a more durable manner, and with better materials; divides it into distinct compartments, and separates the sexes; that his wife is no longer an instrument of labour, but depends upon him for support; that promiscuous intercouse between the sexes is condemned and prohibited as injurious to the marriage contract; and that thus, step after step, he goes on to the maximum of civilisation and excellence of social confederation, exhibiting, in habitation, dress, and manners, a congruity, an homogeneousness of improvement, shewing how intimately all these separate conditions are essential to the perfection of the whole system.

If the progress of civilisation is thus clearly marked by these various gradations from the simple animal existence of man in his primeval state, his lapse may be truly said to be indicated by data of a similar character. Taking the extent of refinement and the perfection of social communion as they are displayed by the middle class of society—neither placing it too high nor too low —the degree to which the inferior classes in the manufacturing towns and districts have retrograded, or remained behind in the march of improvement, is very apparent. Judging them by the same rules which have been applied to mark the advancement of man from a savage state, they have made but few steps forward; and though their primitive nature is disguised and modified by the force of external circumstances, they differ but little in inherent qualities from the uncultivated child of nature, and shew their distinction rather in the mode than the reality of their debased condition.

The houses of great numbers of the labouring community in the manufacturing districts are filthy, unfurnished, and deprived of all the accessories to decency or comfort. What little furniture is found in them is of the rudest and most common sort, and very often in fragments—one or two rush-bottomed chairs, a deal table, a few stools, broken earthenware, such as dishes, tea-cups, &c. &c., one or more tin kettles and cans, a few knives and forks; no fender; a bedstead or not, as the case may happen to be; blankets and sheets in the strict meaning of the words unknown—their place often being made up of sacking, a heap of flocks, or a bundle of straw, supplying the want of a proper bedstead and feather bed; and these cooped in a single room, which serves as a place for all domestic and household occupations.*

In those divisions of the manufacturing towns occupied by the lower classes of inhabitants, whether engaged in mill-labour alone, or in mill-labour conjointly with hand-loom weaving, the houses are of the most flimsy and imperfect construction. Tenanted by the week, by an improvident and changeable set of beings, the owners seldom lay out any money upon them, and seem indeed only anxious that they should be tenantable at all long enough to reimburse them for the first outlay. Hence, in a very few years, they become ruinous to a degree. One of the circumstances in which they are especially defective, is that of drainage and water-closets. Whole

---

* We are here speaking from an extended series of personal inquiries; the tables which follow abundantly verify our description.

ranges of these houses are either totally undrained, or only very partially soughed. The whole of the washings and filth from these consequently are thrown into the front or back street, which being often unpaved and cut up into deep ruts, allows them to collect into stinking and stagnant pools, while fifty, or more even than that number, having only a single convenience common to them all, it is in a very short time completely choked up with excrementitious matter. No alternative is left to the inhabitants but adding this to the already defiled street, and thus leading to a violation of all those decencies which shed a protection over family morals.

The following Table, arranged by the Classification Committee of the Special Board of Health appointed during the late irruption of cholera into Manchester, affords the most decisive evidence upon this point:—

District	Number of houses inspected.	Houses requiring whitewashing.	Houses out of repair.	Houses wanting proper soughing.	Houses damp.	Houses ill ventilated.	Houses wanting privies.
1	850	399	128	112	177	70	326
2	2489	898	282	145	497	109	755
3	213	145	104	41	61	52	96
4	650	279	106	105	134	69	250
5	413	176	82	70	101	11	66
6	12	3	5	5	..	..	5
7	343	76	59	57	86	21	79
8	132	35	30	39	48	22	20
9	128	34	32	24	39	19	25
10	370	195	53	123	54	2	232
11	..	..	..	..	..	..	..
12	113	33	23	27	24	16	52
13	757	218	44	108	146	54	177
14	481	74	13	83	68	7	138
*Totals	6951	2565	961	939	1435	452	2221

* "These numerical results fail to exhibit a perfect picture of the ills which are suffered by the poor. The replies to the ques-

The next Table, the result of inquiries made by
the Special Board of Health, in 1832, shows the state
of the streets in Manchester, and shows how intimately
localities and characters are connected :—

Districts.	Streets inspected.	Streets unpaved.	Streets in part paved.	Streets ill ventilated.	Streets containing heaps of refuse, stagnant pools, ordure, &c.
1	114	63	13	7	64
2	180	93	7	23	92
3	49	2	2	12	28
4	66	37	10	12	52
5	30	2	5	5	12
6	2	1	0	1	2
7	53	13	5	12	17
8	16	2	1	2	7
9	48	0	0	9	20
10	29	19	0	10	23
11	0	0	0	0	0
12	12	0	1	1	4
13	55	3	9	10	23
14	33	13	0	8	8
*Totals	687	248	53	112	352

tions contained in the inspector's table refer only to cases of the
most positive kind, and the numerical results would therefore have
been exceedingly increased, had they embraced those in which the
evils existed in an inferior degree. Some idea of the want of
cleanliness prevalent in their habitations may be obtained from
the report in the number of houses requiring whitewashing; but
this column fails to indicate their gross neglect of order and absolute filth. Much less can we obtain satisfactory statistical results
concerning the want of furniture, especially of bedding, and of
food, clothing, and fuel."

* " An accurate inspection of this table, will render the extent of
the evil affecting the poor more apparent. Those districts which
are almost exclusively inhabited by the labouring population, are,
Nos. 1, 2, 3, 4, and 10 ; Nos. 13, 14, and 7, also contain, besides
the dwellings of the operatives, those of shopkeepers and tradesmen, and are traversed by many of the principal thoroughfares.

It very frequently happens that one tenement is held by several families, one room, or at most two, being generally looked upon as affording sufficient convenience for all the household purposes of four or five individuals. The demoralizing effects of this utter absence of social and domestic privacy must be seen before they can be thoroughly understood, or their extent appreciated. By laying bare all the wants and actions of the sexes, it strips them of regard for decency and modesty.

The brutalizing agency of this mode of life is very strongly displayed in the language employed by the manufacturing population, young and old alike.* Coarse and obscene expressions are in common and familiar use; and these things may be imputed, in a very considerable degree, to the promiscuous way in which families herd together,—a way that prevents all privacy, and which, by bringing into open day things which delicacy commands should be shrouded from observation, destroys all notions of sexual decency and domestic chastity.†

No. 11 was not inspected; and Nos. 5, 6, 8, and 9, are the central districts containing the chief streets, the most respectable shops, the dwellings of the more wealthy inhabitants, and the warehouses of the merchants and manufacturers. Subtracting, therefore, from the various totals those items in the reports which concern these divisions only, we discover in those districts which contain a large portion of poor, viz. 1, 2, 3, 4, 7, 10, 13, 14, that among 579 streets inspected, 243 were unpaved, 46 partly paved, 93 ill-ventilated, and 307 contained heaps of refuse, deep ruts, stagnant pools, ordure, &c.; and in the districts almost exclusively inhabited by the poor, viz. 1, 2, 3, 4, and 10, out of 438 streets inspected, 214 were unpaved, 32 partly paved, 63 ill-ventilated, and 259 contained heaps of refuse, ruts, stagnant pools, ordure," &c.

* *Vide* Mr. Cowell's Report in Factory Commission.

† " In addition to overt acts of vice, there is a coarseness and grossness of feeling, and an habitual indecency of conversation,

Many ranges of houses are built back to back, fronting one way into a narrow court, across which the inmates of the opposite houses may shake hands without stepping out of their own doors ; and the other way, into a back street, unpaved and unsewered. Most of these houses have cellars beneath them, occupied—if it is possible to find a lower class—by a still lower class than those living above them.

From some recent inquiries on the subject, it would appear, that upwards of 20,000 individuals live in cellars in Manchester alone. These are generally Irish families — handloom weavers, bricklayers' labourers, &c. &c. whose children are beggars or match-sellers in conjunction with their mothers. The crowds of beings that emerge from these dwellings every morning, are truly astonishing, and present very little variety as to respectability of appearance : all are ragged, all are filthy, all are squalid. They separate to pursue their various callings, either shutting up their dens till night, or leaving a child as sole occupant. A great portion of these wander about the town and its suburbs, begging or stealing, as the case may be ; others hawk little matters, such as pins, matches, oranges, &c. bringing back with them any fragment of meat or bread they have been able to procure. These cells are the

which we would fain hope and believe are not the prevailing characteristics of our country. The effect of this upon the minds of the young will be readily conceived ; and is it likely that any instruction or education, or Sunday schools, or sermons, can counteract the baneful influence, the insinuating virus, the putrefaction, the contagion of this moral depravity which reigns around them—

Nil dictu visuque fædum hoc lumina tangat
Intra quæ puer est ?"—JUVENAL.

—*Enquiry*, &c. p. 25.

very picture of loathsomeness : placed upon the soil, and partly flagged, without drains, subjected to being occasionally overflowed, seldom cleaned, each return of their inmates bringing with it a farther accession of filth, they speedily become disgusting receptacles of every species of vermin which can infest the human body.

The domestic habits of these improvident creatures are vile in the extreme—carrying their want of household decency one step further than those which have just been described. The Irish cottier has brought with him his disgusting domestic companion, the pig ; for whenever he can scrape together a sufficient sum for the purchase of one of these animals, it becomes an inmate of his cellar.*

It is here too that he displays his recklessness in another of his characteristic propensities—whiskey-drinking; an opportunity for the indulgence of which is furnished by the illicit distillers in his vicinity for a mere trifle. The disgraceful riots which are calling perpetually for the interference of the police, are mainly attributable to this cause, and a return from the lock-ups would abundantly show how terrible are the outrages inflicted upon each other during these drunken

* " In all respects the habitations of the Irish are most destitute. A whole family is often accommodated on a single bed, and sometimes a heap of filthy straw, and a covering of old sacking hides them in one undistinguished heap, debased alike by penury, want of economy, and dissolute habits. Frequently the inspectors found two or more families crowded into one small house, containing only two apartments, one in which they slept, and another in which they ate ; and often more than one family lived in a damp cellar, containing only one room, in whose pestilential atmosphere from twelve to sixteen persons were crowded. To these fertile sources of disease were sometimes added, the keeping of pigs and other animals in the house, with other nuisances of the most revolting character."—*Moral and Physical Condition of the Working Classes*, &c. p. 32.

brawls. When their passions are roused by intoxication, most severe and often bloody conflicts ensue between them, to the disturbance and degradation of the more peaceable inhabitants. Thus it appears that the inferior order of Irishmen have brought with them all their vices into the manufacturing districts, and aid powerfully by their example—independently of lowering the value of the labour of the English operative*—the demoralization which marks his general character.

Another fertile source of licentiousness in domestic manners, exists in the number of lodging-houses, which are very abundant in all the manufacturing districts. In towns they are thickly scattered through those divisions occupied by the poor. By a survey made in Manchester in 1832, there were found very near 300 of these houses. When it is remembered that these are but the temporary asylums of want and depravity, their number, great as it is, affords no criterion for ascertaining how many persons become their inmates during the year. In another point of view they are extremely injurious: the breaking up of the families, the consequence of mill labour, drives many of those who should be sheltered under a very different roof, to take up their abode in these haunts of crime; where, if not already debased by other causes, they are speedily reduced to the very lowest ebb of moral depravity. Their influence in this respect resembles very closely that brought about by a residence in prison; for the parties which are the habitual occupants of the one, are in their turn found living in the other.

* *Vide* Appendix—Table of Irish and English Settlements in Manchester. This Table shews to what an extent the immigration of impoverished Irish has been carried in the manufacturing districts.

The extraordinary sights presented by these lodging-houses during the night, are deplorable in the extreme, and must fill the heart of any man, open to the feelings of humanity, with pain and unutterable disgust. Five, six, seven beds—according to the capacity of the rooms—are arranged on the floor—there being in the generality of cases no bedsteads, or any substitutes for them; these are covered with clothing of the most scanty and filthy description. They are occupied by young men and young women ; men, wives, and their children—all lying in a noisome atmosphere, swarming with vermin, and often intoxicated. They serve as so many foci for crime—so many hot-beds for bringing into existence vices which might have lain dormant, if not roused into activity by their unnatural stimulus.

Maternal affection is one of those beautiful and beneficent instincts which so strongly mark the goodness and surpassing wisdom of the great Author of nature. In all ages, in all countries, in all stages of civilization—in war, in pestilence, shipwreck, or famine—whether roaming through the jungle or over the prairie—whether traversing the expanse of the continent or dwelling in the far off and isolated island—woman has ever been found with the hallowed character of a mother, and exhibiting, for the sake of her offspring, an abandonment of self—a pouring forth of her most holy affections, which has been the brightest and purest portion of her history.

Love of helpless infancy—attention to its wants, its sufferings, and its unintelligible happiness, seem to form the very well-spring of a woman's heart—fertilizing, softening, and enriching all her grosser passions and appetites. It is an instinct in the strictest acceptation of the word. A woman, if removed from all intercourse with all knowledge of her sex and its attributes, from the very hour of her birth, would, should she herself become a mother in the wilderness, lavish as much tenderness upon her babe, cherish it as fondly, hang over it with as fervent affection, attend to its wants, sacrifice her personal comfort, with as much ardour, as much devotedness, as the most refined, fastidious, and intellectual mother, placed in the very centre of civilized society.

Instincts are those dispositions for a certain train of actions, which have been impressed, more or less distinctly, upon the minds or nature of all living beings, whether endowed with reason or not;—and which, if allowed to take their own course, freed from the control of extraneous causes, are unerring guides for the attainment of particular ends. Education, change of locality and habits, will warp and derange their operations, but never entirely extinguish them. Maternal feelings and actions are rarely overcome in animals by domestication; and it would be supposed that woman, who, in addition to these instincts—which are fully as powerful within her, possesses reason and a capability of cultivating a host of affections, would exhibit, in her social condition, maternal love in its strongest, most durable, and most amiable form.

The system of factory labour* has, however, gone far towards annihilating this great and beautiful principle in woman's moral organization. The substitution of female labour for that of the adult male, has driven her to the mills, in which she is confined the whole day: this has torn asunder those links of affection which, under almost all other circumstances, have bound a

* *Vide* Moral and Physical Condition of the Working Classes, &c. p. 69.

mother to her offspring; and in doing so it has deprived woman of that moral characteristic, which is the
most influential in rendering her a loveable and loving
being.

Compelled to rise early—no opportunity given for
visiting home, during the day, but at the hurried meal-
times — her social affections warped, her frame little
calculated to furnish her child with support, she becomes
inaccessible to its appeals to her tenderness—leaves it
to the care of a hireling, or young person, often a mere
infant—suffers it to be filthy and half-starved; and, as
faculties develop, takes no interest in keeping it from the
contagion of vice and grossness.*

A system which thus depraves and perverts a mother's
love, or which demands those times and occasions a
mother ought to devote to her infant—which, from various
concurring causes, so far influences her domestic habits
as to interfere with the development of her social affections, and which, from its continued action upon her, at
length destroys or buries them beneath a load of grossness and sensuality—must be wrong.

If a mother's love be thus injured—a love springing
as it does from the very groundwork of her moral nature,

* " In consequence of the mothers being employed from home,
their children are entrusted, in a vast majority of cases, to the
care of others, often to elderly females, who have no infant families
of their own; and most of whom having in their youth had their
children nursed by others, have never formed those habits of
attachment and assiduous attention to their offspring, which could
alone afford a probability of a proper care of the children committed to their charge. These women often take care of several infants at the same time—their habits are generally indolent and
gossipping, and the children are restless and irritable from being
deprived of a supply of their proper food."—*Inquiry into the Manufacturing Population*, p. 17.

no wonder can be excited that the relations of husband and wife are perverted. The chastity of marriage is often disregarded, and an habitual indifference to sexual rights is generated, which adds one other item to assist in the destruction of domestic habits.

No amenity of manners, therefore, no gentleness of behaviour, mark the home of a factory labourer in a crowded population; often no regard is shown for conjugal obligations, no bashful reserve, no cultivation of those finer sensibilities, which give to married life its principal charms, when composed of its proper elements.

If the domestic manners of the parents are thus depraved, their example must of necessity influence their children. Brother and sister lose that connexion which ought naturally and properly to exist between them: disregard for each other's welfare, a separation of interests and feelings, a forgetfulness of what is due, one to another, destroy those bonds which should link together the hearts of individuals springing from the same source, endeared as they ought to be by the memory of their younger years—years which, unfortunately for them, have been passed in total disregard for home duties, uncared for likewise by their natural guardians, and separated at an early age.

Neither is the conduct of parent to child, and of child to parent, a whit more engaging, but is as remote as possible from the just observance of filial and parental duties. Insubordination on the part of the child, cruelty and oppression on that of the parent, quarrelling, fighting, a total alienation of affection, and, finally, a separation from home at an age when parental control and proper domestic discipline are essential to the future wellbeing of the child.

The instances of proper feelings between parents and

children are uncommon : those offices which should be mutually rendered are neglected, and a disregard for the well or evil doing of either party is exhibited.

A household thus constituted, in which all the decencies and moral observances of domestic life are constantly violated, reduces its inmates to a condition little elevated above that of the savage. Recklessness, improvidence, and unnecessary poverty, starvation, drunkenness, parental cruelty and carelessness, filial disobedience, neglect of conjugal rights, absence of maternal love, destruction of brotherly and sisterly affection, are too often its constituents, and the results of such a combination are moral degradation, ruin of domestic enjoyments, and social misery.

Dr. Ure, (in his *Philosophy of Manufactures*, p. 342, after quoting the opinion of Mr. Tufnel, one of the factory commissioners, to the effect that there is not a better or more certain mode of benefiting a country village than by establishing a cotton factory in it,) says—" It has been justly remarked, by one of the first manufacturers in the kingdom, that in large towns, and particularly with so mixed and fluctuating a population as that contained within the precincts of Manchester, with its various occupations, its hastily and imperfectly constructed streets, and crowded dwellings, and its many incentives to vice, it is no easy task to determine the effect of each particular kind of employment. The pure unmixed effect of factory labour will be best and most easily found in the country, where it affords regular employment during a series of years to the same families ; yet, even in Manchester, evidence enough to satisfy the candid inquirer may be obtained by inspecting the factories and dwellings of the working classes. It may be shown that the children of *orderly* parents, of both

sexes, are taught at home and in schools; and that
though there are too many heads of families *who wholly
neglect or set a bad example* to their children, still in
Manchester and in all other large towns, the attendance
at the Sunday schools of such as are employed in
factories, shows that that class of operatives furnishes
its full proportion of scholars."

This is unquestionably true; still it would be equally
unjust to take, as the sole ground for examination,
the establishment of the Messrs. Strutt, in the valley
of the Derwent, or any other country mill, conducted
by men of enlarged benevolence and active philanthropy. Nothing indeed can be more cheering to the
eye or gladdening to the heart than the admirable organization of a few out-town manufactories; and if an
opinion were to be formed from these, we should at once
assent to that of Dr. Ure; namely, that factory labour
is the best which can be found for the operative. The
instances adduced are rather beautiful examples of what
may be done, than illustrations of what is done. Why
is it that, as at Belper, Quarry-bank, Ramsbottom,
and other places, order, sobriety and morality characterize the labourers? Because they form, as it were,
one great family, bound together by common ties, and
dependent on one common master. "The population,"
says Mr. Tufnel, " surrounding a country mill, to the
number of one or two thousand, are sometimes entirely
dependent upon its master for work and subsistence;"
he is their landlord and their master; in short, they are
completely under his control and supervision; and if he
be a man with the honourable pride of seeing around
him a healthy and moral people, he has it in his power
to make them so. The whole of the system emanates
from and is dependent on him, and so complete is the

control he exercises, that any family which displays troublesome propensities is at once dismissed. The regularity required by factory processes renders any deviation from sobriety or social order a very sufficient reason for dismissal : thus Mr. Marshall, of Leeds, says, " that in their establishment they do not employ any operatives who are guilty of intoxication ;" and, in other country mills, where the proprietors have surrounded themselves by a distinct set of fixed labourers, the most happy results follow.

All country manufacturers, however, are not men who thus show that factory labour may be so conducted as to obviate its first grand evil—an evil which only partially exists in the best conducted country mills, as the workers, by intimate and daily association become greatly amalgamated ; in towns, however, the strict surveillance exercised in rural districts is impossible ; thus, says Dr. Ure— " In towns the tie that binds together employers and employed, is of course less strong ;" and, a few lines further on, acknowledges that even in the country many instances are to be found where the moral feelings and habits of the young are exposed to injurious influences. Another writer, whose observations refer chiefly to town manufacturers, and whose position and intelligence give his evidence a higher character than that due to the observations of a mere casual visitor, says : " Little advance can be made towards improving the morals of the manufacturing population, till a strict and scrupulous attention is paid by the masters to the character of those they employ. This is done in a few isolated cases, and with excellent effect ; but these instances are very rare. The great body of master-manufacturers pay no attention to the morals of their workmen, nor reprobate bad conduct, except as far as it

interferes with their daily labour. A large numbe of
their female hands are notoriously of immoral character, and a considerable portion of their men drunkards,
more or less confirmed." *   This is the plain and undeniable truth.

" Like master, like man," is a proverb no less applicable to public works than to private families. The mill-
owner, who has a nice sense of purity in heart and life, a
just comprehension of his own interest, and a conscientious concern for the well-being of his dependents, will
adopt every practicable measure to raise the standard of
their behaviour.   If, on the other hand, he is lax in his
own principles, and careless of their conduct, except as to
their punctuality at their task, he will experience the
consequences of this unconcern in slovenliness of work,
and in personal disrespect.   Let us figure to ourselves
a proprietor of extensive factories, a man of old experience, an unwearied worshipper of Mammon, and, of
course, a stranger to the self-denying graces of the
gospel.   Such a man knows himself to be entitled to
nothing but eye-service, and will therefore exercise the
most irksome vigilance, but in vain, to prevent his being
overreached by his operatives ; the whole of whom, by
natural instinct, as it were, conspire against such a
master.   Whatever pains he may take, he can never
command superior workmanship, he will find the character of his goods to be second-rate in the market, and
he will of course get a second-rate price and set of customers : his whole business is blasted, as it were, by an
evil eye.   Aware of his unpopularity with his work-
people, he strives to regain their favour, by conniving at

---

* Inquiry into the State of the Manufacturing Population, &c.
p. 35.

their vices; and views their intemperance on Saturday night and Sunday with indifference, provided it does not interfere with their labour on Monday morning.

Such policy may have been compatible with profit in times of narrow competition; but now it seldom fails, as I could prove by examples, to counteract prosperity, at least, if not to impair the fortunes' realized under better auspices. It is, therefore, excessively the interest of every mill-owner to organize his moral machinery, on equally sound principles with his mechanical; for, otherwise, he will never command the steady hands, watchful eyes, and prompt cooperation, essential to excellence of product. Improvident work-people are apt to be reckless, and dissolute ones to be diseased; thus both are ill qualified to discharge the delicate labours of automatic industry, which is susceptible of many grades of imperfection, without becoming so obviously defective as to render the work liable to a fine. There is, in fact, no case to which the gospel truth, ' Godliness is great gain,' is more applicable than to the administration of an extensive factory."*

These are sound observations; and after the description we have given of the domestic morals of labouring manufacturers, let us apply the above remarks to the past conditions of many extensive mill-proprietors.

THE EARLY MASTER MANUFACTURERS.

It may be laid down as a maxim, that whenever numerous bodies of men — whatsoever their rank, and whatsoever the cause which has led to their congregation—are brought together, a deterioration, more or

* Philosophy of Manufactures, p. 416.

less marked, in the moral condition of some portions
of the community, is the inevitable result.   Large
cities and populous districts have, in all ages, been
the foci from whence have emanated, if not great, at
least numerous crimes.

One principal effect of the steam engine has been,
to crowd workmen together, collecting them from parts
in which they had hitherto formed portions of a scattered
population.*

Example appears to be one of the most powerful
agents in the production of the common actions of life.
The various grades of society, from the most elevated
to the most debased, are led equally away by it.

Many of the first successful manufacturers, both in
town and country, were men who had their origin in the
rank of mere operatives, or who sprung from the extinct
class of yeomen.   It has been already explained that
this class had been driven, by the pressure of circumstances,† to the adoption of spinning, at the period when
trade was undergoing that series of changes which ended
in the introduction of steam.

The celerity with which some of these individuals accumulated wealth in the early times of machine spinning
and weaving, are proofs—if any such were wanting—
that they were men of quick views, and great energy of
character, possessing no small share of sagacity, and
by these means were able to avail themselves to the
utmost of the golden advantages which were presented
to their grasp, at a time when they supplied the whole
universe with the products of manufacture.

But they were men of very limited general informa-

* " Manufacturers naturally condense a vast population within
a narrow circuit," &c. &c.—*Philosophy of Manufactures*, p. 407.

† *Vide* Chap. I. *passim.*

tion—men who saw and knew little of any thing beyond the demand for their twist or cloth, and the speediest and best modes for their production.* They were, how-ever, from their acquired station, men who exercised very considerable influence upon the multitudes of work-men who became dependent upon them.

The acquisition of wealth, unfortunately for the in-terests of all parties, was not, in the first instance, attended by a corresponding improvement in their moral and social character ; on the contrary, all who had an opportunity of watching its effects, can only deplore and condemn the evil purposes to which, for many years, some portions of it were applied.

The extreme rapidity with which the returns were made for a considerable period—and this too with an immense profit—might well dazzle them. The animal enjoyments,—the sensual indulgences, which were wit-nessed at the orgies of these parties, totally unchecked by any intercourse with polished society, should have had the veil of oblivion drawn over them, were it not that, to some degree, they tend to explain the depravity which in a few years spread, like a moral plague, over the factory artisans.

The sprinkling of men of more refined habits amongst the early successful cotton manufacturers, was extremely scanty. Very few who brought large capital into the trade, were fortunate, or even made satisfactory progress. Neither will this fact be considered singular, when it is

* Arkwright, who may be styled the founder of our present manufactures, was a country *barber*. He acquired an immense fortune. Those who have followed in his steps, and of no higher origin, are, by the mere force of wealth, placing themselves in the path of our aristocracy. The House of Commons includes several of them already.

remembered with whom the battle had to be fought. They had to oppose men who had a practical acquaintance with machinery, and who laboured themselves, assiduously and diligently; whereas the previous pursuits and education of the capitalist, had unfitted him, in some respects, for that rapidity of action and quickness of calculation, which were essentially necessary, if he must keep pace with the daily improvements projected and carried on around him.

Master manufacturers then, at the commencement of this important epoch,* were in many instances men sprung from the ranks of the labourers, or from a grade just removed above these—uneducated, of coarse habits, sensual in their enjoyments, partaking of the rude revelry of their dependants—overwhelmed by success, but yet, paradoxical as it may sound, industrious men, and active and far-sighted tradesmen.

Wealth brought with it some of its usual accessories. Cottages were exchanged for mansions erected purposely for them, larger, more commodious, and furnished in a style of shew and expense, if not of taste, sufficiently indicative of the state of the owner's purse and prospects; and to these were transferred the manners which had unhappily disgraced their late more humble residences.

Destitute of every thing intellectual, and condemning every thing savouring of refinement, whether in manner or thought, they were in some measure driven to the indulgence of their animal sensations. This was

---

* Stockport, Hyde, Duckenfield, Stayley Bridge, &c.—places exclusively manufacturing—may be pointed out as illustrating the above. Many of the wealthy masters, in early life, worked as common labourers, either as hatters, shoemakers, carters, weavers, or at some other trade.

generally sought for in the use of ardent spirits, which roused them for a time into furious excitement, and rendered them unconscious of all that was due to decency or propriety. Thus wallowing in intemperance, little wonder can be excited that other passions were stimulated into active operation ; and from their situation, unbounded facilities were offered for their display.

The almost entire extinction of sexual decency, which has been one of the darkest stains upon the character of the mill artisans, the laxity in all the moral obligations which ought to exist between the sexes, and the consequent loss of this most important influence in the formation of social manners, may be traced, to some extent, to this period of their history.

Condemning, as every man must, the conduct of these parties, it may be remarked, that the mischief lay in no small degree with the particular juncture in which they were brought so conspicuously forward. Their want of education—the animal life they had previously led—the sudden accession of wealth—the contempt in some cases generated for refinement, by the discovery they soon made, that wealth, although burdened with blunt and coarse manners, was still an all-powerful agent for procuring worldly respect—the vanity which leads men to ascribe results to causes personal to themselves, keeping up their original vulgarity, in which they took a strange pride—the facilities for lascivious indulgence afforded them by the number of females brought under their immediate control—the herding together of workmen, the result of the factory system, more especially multitudes of boys and girls from ten to sixteen years of age, freed from domestic discipline—the separation of man and wife during the hours of labour—the dependence

H

which naturally grew up on the part of the labourers—
all these are matters which will serve to explain at
least, the immorality which marked the bearing of
many, though by no means the whole of the early
mechanical manufacturers.

There were amongst them, indeed, some who possessed a very elevated tone of moral thinking—men
whose sagacity clearly foresaw many of the evils which
threatened, and which have since fallen upon the operatives from these causes ; but the impulse was given—
the barriers of domestic virtue were broken down—and
nothing but a strenuous effort on the part of *all* the
masters could have checked and destroyed the evil
which was marching about them with giant strides, and
with almost irresistible force.

As these men became better established in their
several successes, and as they rose in importance by the
extension of their trade, and as, by its continuance and
diffusion, other parties, of better education and more
refined manners, joined the manufacturing phalanx, a
better order of things gradually developed itself, and
worked great and beneficial changes in the characters of
the masters.

One of the most permanently injurious consequences
resulting from the mode of life led by these individuals,
and one which has been severely felt and deplored by
them, was its influence upon their families. The demand
for hands necessarily led to the employment of all the
male relatives of the master manufacturer, at a very early
age. His own sons were invested with considerable
authority when mere children—taken from school to
superintend certain portions of the mills, and liberally
supplied with money. The same remark holds good
with reference to others, his relations. Boys, at an

age when they should have been sedulously kept apart from opportunities of indulging their nascent sexual propensities, were thrust into a very hot-bed of lust, and exposed to vicious example, in addition to other causes, irresistibly tending to make them a prey to licentiousness. The consequences of these criminal and unadvised proceedings were, that long after the masters had freed themselves from the vices incident to their first advancement, they had the shame and mortification of seeing their errors propagated through a series of ramifications, every remove seeming to become more and more depraved in its character.*

Numbers of these infatuated youths reaped their reward early, and were cut off on the very threshold of manhood, by a career of unbridled indulgence ; marriage was repudiated amongst them, and was indeed utterly at variance with the license reigning over all their sexual appetites.

Nothing can more clearly show the demoralizing effects of this pernicious intercourse than the fact, that a girl, who was known to have lived in a state of concubinage, found no difficulty in marrying subsequently amongst her equals. So debased became their tone of thinking, and so utterly were they lost to all sense of decency and shame, that not only was no difficulty found by these girls in procuring husbands, but this was even managed during the very time their intimacy was going on with their seducer, and which, not unfrequently,

* " The fact then undoubtedly is, that the licentiousness which prevails among the dense population of manufacturing towns, is carried to a degree which it is appalling to contemplate, which baffles all statistical inquiries, and which can be learned from the testimony of personal observers."--*Inquiry into the State of the Manufacturing Population*, p. 25.

was continued up to the very day of their marriage, and even subsequently.

This laxity,* or rather this entire absence of all regard for moral obligations relating to sex, extending, as it did, beyond the threshold of marriage, sapped the

* " On the subject of the general licentiousness and illicit intercourse which prevails in manufacturing districts, we cannot, for obvious reasons, dwell long, nor as minutely as the extreme importance of the subject would justify. In the few words we shall devote to this branch of our investigation, we shall be careful to keep within the limits of the most scrupulous accuracy, and to affirm nothing which we do not possess the materials for proving. First, then, we shall remark that nothing but personal observation, on the testimony of eye-witnesses, can be relied on for satisfactory information. The returns of illegitimate children (in the few cases where they can be procured) are worse than useless ; for it will be obvious, on a few moments' consideration, that in such cases they can afford us no possible criterion of the desired result. On this subject some writers on political economy betray the same ignorance as in their assertion of the extensive use of animal food among the manufacturing labourers. Both instances furnish an illustration of what appears to be a common source of error with them ; viz. a disposition to draw inferences from isolated facts, instead of resting their doctrines upon the basis of extensive and accurate observation. They conclude that because the proportion of illegitimate births appears to be greater among the agricultural than the manufacturing population, the females of the former are the more immoral of the two. We draw, without doubt or hesitation, exactly the opposite conclusion, and every one intimately acquainted with the south of Lancashire will bear us out in this opinion. This deduction is also materially confirmed by the practice which, it is painful to state, is far from uncommon among the abandoned females of these districts, of destroying, prematurely, the fruit and the evidence of their guilt."—*Inquiry into the State of the Manufacturing Population*, p. 24.

" The bonds of domestic sympathy are too generally relaxed, and as a consequence, the filial and paternal duties are uncultivated."—*Moral and Physical Condition of the Working Classes, &c.* p. 64.

foundations and overthrew the structure of the social virtues. Father, mother, son, and daughter, were mere words, leading to none of those delightful associations which are the fount from whence spring the best and most hallowed of man's pleasures and emotions; and the loss of these deprived the homes of the mill artisan of almost every thing which can give home value.

It must be understood that in pointing out a state of things and a mode of life happily greatly amended, the first manufacturers of this epoch must bear the blame of presenting an example, to which the peculiar circumstances of the times gave great and immediate force. Had a high sense of moral obligations taught them to introduce strict discipline into their mills, by separating the sexes as far as possible, and by keeping a watchful eye upon their own passions, a very different aspect would now be undoubtedly presented by this population. The impulse being given, the barrier of private decency being broken down, man's natural propensities, aided in their operation by collateral causes, will long prevent a filling up of the breach ; and till this is done, till the social virtues, till the morals of home are established among them, no theories of political economy, no bare intellectual education, no extension of political rights, ever can or ever will make them a happy, respectable, or contented race of men.

Of late years—we record the fact with great satisfaction—the master manufacturers have become aware that order, regularity, and punctuality, are important items in the character of their hands, and we are perfectly willing to believe that this has arisen from conscientious and pure motives. If it should not be so, it has arisen from the rapid improvement in the processes of manufacture, and in the organization and internal economy of their mills ; and from these has sprung the necessity for an orderly and steady set of work-people. As this organization proceeds, this necessity will be still farther felt ; and, eventually, some of the mischiefs attendant on the factory system will work their own cure.

Dr. Ure, the late Factory Commissioners, and others, who have theorised on the condition of the masters and operatives, contend, that as the internal economy of the mills goes on to perfection, order and morality must reign within their walls.   They overlook the fact, however, that before this consummation of what they style the " palladium " of British industry is reached, the operatives actually engaged will be reduced to a fragment, and that that fragment will consist almost entirely of women and girls.   Whether idleness is not likely to generate farther depravity in the male part of the community is not remarked upon, but reasoning and observation lead to an inference fatal to the opinion of those who advocate the moral and industrial advantages of the factory system ; the commercial economy of the system is another and distinct question.

CHAPTER IV.

_____

INFLUENCE OF TEMPERATURE AND MANNERS UPON PHY-
SICAL DEVELOPMENT, &c. AND UPON MORALS.

Puberty and sexual Appetence—Causes influencing their development—Vicious Example--Peculiarity of sexual Passions--Im-
portance of propriety of Manners--Want of Attention on the
Part of the Mill-Owners and Overlookers--A Want of proper
mental Growth--Error of Mothers—Influence of Temperature
on physical and sexual Development—Influence of Manners
upon physical and sexual Development — Late Acknowledgment of Puberty in Great Britain—Its Influence upon physical
Condition, &c. and upon Society--Importance of proper sexual
Restraint—Value of Refinement of Manners—Necessary Measures on the Part of the Masters--Present sexual Character in
manufacturing Districts.

_____

THE bringing together numbers of the young of both
sexes in factories, has been a prolific source of moral delinquency. The stimulus of a heated atmosphere,* the
contact of opposite sexes, the example of license upon
the animal passions—all have conspired to produce a
very early development of sexual appetencies. Indeed,
in this respect, the female population engaged in mill
labour, approximates very closely to that found in
tropical climates; puberty, or at least sexual propensities, being attained almost coeval with girlhood.

* The average temperature of the atmosphere in mills is about
70° to 75° Fahrenheit; formerly it was much higher.

The influence of these maturing causes is more strikingly seen in the female than in the male, in consequence of its effects being of a more prominent and observable character.

The advantages resulting from the simple observances of common propriety, may be judged of by the evils which attend upon their absence. Gross language, and allowance of word and deed pertaining to sexual gratification, are pregnant proofs of what the reality is when the outward form is so debased. The peculiar qualities of these passions — one of the most striking of these being the readiness with which they are roused by a word, a look, or a gesture, and the undying hold they take on the imagination, when once permitted to revel at large—render the want of some sufficient visible check very obvious.

Unfortunately little regard has been paid to these matters by the majority of mill-owners. A certain number of hands are required to superintend the labours of their untiring engine, with its complement of looms, &c. &c. for a certain number of hours, and for a certain amount of wages : so long as these are attained he looks no farther. He considers the human beings who crowd his mill, from five o'clock in the morning to seven o'clock in the evening, but as so many accessories to his machinery, destined to produce a certain and well-known quantity of work, at the lowest possible outlay of capital. To him their passions, habits, or crimes, are as little interesting as if they bore no relation to the errors of a system, of which he was a member and supporter.*

* " If the master acknowledges no common bond as existing between him and his labourers; if he does not even know their names or faces; if, avowedly or practically, which is the same

The early age at which sexual development calls into play a crowd of irrepressible sensations—which, when properly tempered and directed, form the basis of future character—and the unfavourable circumstances under which this forced development occurs, are, in a great measure, destructive to the well-being of those who may well be called its victims.

The mind does not keep equal pace with the body, though in some respects its faculties are precocious. Its better qualities are destroyed by the preponderance of animal sensations : it is a period when, even under the most favourable auspices, it is vacillating and uncertain in its determinations—now dreaming of sensual indulgence, and now devoting itself to the better purposes of which it is capable—hurried away by external associations—forming itself on the model of whatever is near it, and taking its impress, an impress which will never be entirely worn off, from the hands of those who may accidentally have the fashioning of it.

" Udum et molle lutum est, nunc properandus et acri,
    Fingendus sine fine rotâ."

The evil unfortunately does not end with the party first yielding to temptation : were it an isolated case, it might do so ; but here, extending as it does throughout a whole people, it descends from parent to child as an hereditary curse.

thing, he disclaims all regard to their conduct except as manufacturers ; if, in fine, he keeps wholly aloof from them—and under present circumstances it is not easy to see how he can act otherwise; then it is clear that some of the best feelings of our nature can never be called into exercise in the breast of the operative."—*Robertson on the Health of Manufacturers*, p. 23.

" Their employers know it would be unsafe to inquire into these matters."—*Inquiry into the State of the Manufacturing Population, &c.* p. 26.

The mother who has never felt her own moral and social rank injured by her sexual indulgences—who looks around her, and sees that all are like herself—who has experienced no difficulty in settling herself as a wife—who even, if, after her marriage, she has continued her former practices, has derived positive and substantial benefits in consequence, by improving the condition of her husband, and adding to the comforts of her family—forgets, if she ever felt, that she was sinning.

Her family inherit the same lax feelings; her sons and daughters are both subjected to the same causes which prematurely evolved her own propensities; are themselves in the same state of precociousness; have the same failings, and become fathers and mothers in their turn.

The additions which are incessantly made to the population of the manufacturing towns, and which additions are made up chiefly of increments from the surrounding agricultural districts, are very rapidly assimilated, as to moral perversity, with those amongst whom they become sojourners.

It is true that those who have already attained maturity cannot undergo the same physical changes which have determined the moral condition of the parties whose early youth has been spent in the enervating atmosphere of a large mill; but their union with those who have suffered these changes soon obliterates any difference which might originally have existed between them: or if it should fail in doing this, as far as regards the senior members of these immigrations, it never fails to do so with the juniors. In the end, therefore, although each addition modifies, to a limited extent, the universality of the evils complained of,—these, constant as they are, produce no permanent impression upon the leading traits of the whole community. The rapidity with which generation succeeds generation, and the continuance of the same energetic and efficient causes, operating upon the moral framework of society, must ever prevent any decided improvement—providing this improvement is left to the natural course of events, unaided and unsustained by remedial measures of a more decided character and more cogent operation.

The influence of temperature upon physical development has been tolerably investigated, or at least fully acknowledged, by those who have paid attention to external causes operating upon the human race. Travellers in all tropical countries have rendered the early age at which sexual intercourse takes place sufficiently familiar ; and this has been generally taken as a sort of acknowledgment of an equally early puberty. That it is influenced to some extent by climate cannot be doubted ; but it may be seriously questioned whether as an accelerating agent it has not been greatly overrated.*

* If temperature were the sole cause in producing early sexual development, it might reasonably be concluded that the inhabitants of the extreme north would exhibit a very protracted celibacy. That this is not the case is abundantly proved by northern voyagers and travellers—witness Hearne, Franklin, Parry, Lyon, Crantz, Richardson, &c. &c. Parry declares that in no country is prostitution carried to a greater extent than among the Esquimaux—that no people are more libidinous and dissolute. Mention is more than once made of girls of ten years of age being taken as wives. Mr. Richardson remarks, " that the women marry very young." Examples are given of wives of fourteen, sixteen, and eighteen years of age.—*Vide* Parry's First and Second Voyages ; Franklin's First and Second Journey ; Hearne, &c. &c.— Humboldt, in speaking of the tribes of northern Asia, says, " that girls of ten years are found mothers." The evidence of Clarke and other writers who have visited the northern countries all agree in the same facts.

If the influence of temperature has been exaggerated upon these points, there is one question which has been neglected in taking into account the causes which govern sexual maturity; and that is, the customs, habits, and modes of life which prevail in the countries in which observations have been made. These are unquestionably far more important agents than mere temperature, both in calling into being sexual desire, and accelerating, in consequence, the period of puberty. It is quite needless to enter into any argument to prove—that whatever excites the generative organs will have a tendency to develop their specific functions. The same remark is applicable not only to these organs, but to any and to every organ composing the human body. An attentive examination of the writings of various travellers and observers * would demonstrate the accuracy of this opinion very sufficiently, and would show that sexual indulgence precedes and leads to what is here considered premature physical perfection. This is dependent not so much upon any constitutional peculiarity, as upon manners, which encourage and keep up libidinous feelings, and examples brought to bear upon passions so excitable and active as are those having reference to sexual enjoyments.

It has long been noticed, that in warm countries, and in nations still barbarous, or only in a state of partial civilisation, very early marriages take place, and that

* *Vide* Russel's " Natural History of Aleppo;" Marsden's " Sumatra;" Winterbottom's " Natural History of Sierra Leone;" Ellis's " Polynesian Researches;" Buchanan's " Journey through Mysore," &c.; Crawford's " Indian Archipelago;" Long's " Jamaica;" Collins's " New South Wales;" Forster's " Voyage Round the World;" Cook's " Second Voyage;" Raffles's " History of Java," &c.; Volney, Madden, and a host of others.

women become mothers at a time which appears singularly premature to northern ideas; at a time, indeed,
when girls are looked upon as mere children, alike
unknowing of and incapable of being roused to sexual
appetence. The moral and religious institutions which
have prevailed in Great Britain have discountenanced
the intercourse of the sexes, till, comparatively speaking,
a late period of life. Jurists and legislators have also
lent the weight of their authority to the protraction of
adult age till such time as it was supposed both body
and mind would be equally matured.* These arrangements are, however, merely conventional; but they have
nevertheless produced very decided effects upon the
physical nature of the population, by acting as so many
powerful checks upon the display and early development
of puberty. The germs of its maturity were nevertheless in being; and, were these checks removed, it
is unquestionable that a great and striking change
would take place in the social arrangements at present
existing.†

---

* The English law makes it felony to have intercourse with
a child under ten years of age; and a misdemeanor if above that
age and under twelve.

† The experience of medical men engaged in manufacturing
towns affords evidence of this, for in these situations the restraints
of law and decency are unacknowledged. A case is related in
Mr. Robertson's paper in the "North of England Medical and
Surgical Journal," as having occurred to a respectable surgeon,
where a girl working in a cotton factory had become pregnant
during her eleventh year, and that in all respects she was a full-
grown woman, and that the menses had appeared prior to this.
Two similar cases have occurred to the author, and very many
others to his professional friends. It is far from uncommon to
find mothers at fifteen years of age, a period perhaps full as
early as that in tropical countries.

One of the most important advantages which has attended the past and present delay in acknowledging and countenancing the occurrence of puberty till so late a period, has been, that time and opportunity are given for the growth of those feelings of reserve and delicacy which both sexes have been necessarily driven to adopt for their mutual protection. It is this protection, dependent upon, and having its origin in, the causes just mentioned, that eventually becomes the armour shielding the chastity of sex : it is this, too, which forms the grand distinguishing mark between a nation far advanced in civilisation and refinement, and one commencing its career, or still wallowing in the coarseness of savage existence : it is this which gives its charm to the associations of common life, shutting out and completely excluding the grosser topics, which are subversive to so many of the social virtues—for virtues they are, even though matters of form.

By thus ridding the communion of all grossness, the best guarantee is given for its moral propriety. The character of the sexes is raised in the estimation of each other. It clothes them with a covering of purity, which must be first removed before man's animal nature can be fully displayed ; and this is generally prevented by the high tone of public and private morality. Or if, in spite of these, it is rashly cast aside, the wanderer is condemned to the persecution of a host of troubles and vexations, which in the one sex ends by its expulsion from its natural rank in the social confederacy.

In speaking thus strenuously on the observances of the forms of society, it may perhaps be imagined that too much stress is laid upon them, and that the natural instincts of mankind, its moral tendencies, its religious

feelings, are too little consulted ; in fact, that the com-
position of the essence is overlooked in its fragrance and
beauty.

The form here, however, constitutes whatever there is
of reality.   Man cannot be taught to forget that he is
a man, or that the breathing and blushing being before
him is a woman ; that she is endowed like himself with
an ardent temperament—a desire for gratification ; that
she has within and around her a world of delights which
he is framed for and destined to enjoy ; and that she has
passions which, if roused into activity, would overwhelm
all sense of shame or propriety.   Neither can he forget
that he has a fire within his own breast, which, if
freed from the asbestos coating of moral decency, would
overthrow all obstacles standing between him and the
object of his desire ; nor that he has the capability of
stirring into vigorous life his own and woman's propensities.   These he cannot be taught to forget—the voice
of nature is potential.   But he may be taught that his
own welfare, and more especially that of the creature
before him, are intimately connected with the suppression and concealment of their separate desires and capabilities.   His sense of justice as to what is due to
himself, to her, and to the still wider circle in which he
moves amongst his fellows, may be called into action,
and thus become his own safeguard, and the safeguard
of the woman, against the machinations of their respective
passions ; and hence it is that the forms of society are
worthy the greatest attention and the most sedulous
cultivation.

Considerable sexual laxity has been brought about
in the manufacturing population, more especially in the
large towns.   It is the triumph of sense over morals—
a great revolution in the period of physical development

—a consequent premature indulgence of sexual appetite, unchecked by any sufficient impediment, and producing important effects upon all that relates to the morals and well-being of those subjected to their influence.

The change in the moral and physical attributes of this population has been operated by temperature partly, but more especially by the force of example and manners already existing.   Both are no doubt powerful agents, but there can be no difficulty in saying which must bear the principal onus of imputation. Cooperation has manifestly aided the effect of each separate influence, and has been the reason of its unexampled and rapid spread, and its permanence must of course depend upon the continuance or abstraction of the same causes.

As yet no sufficient moral or religious check or impediment is in force to prevent the displays, necessarily resulting from this change ; nor are there any modifying and correcting agencies powerful enough to lessen its mischievous tendencies.

Had it been the wish of the early manufacturers to have made their workmen an orderly, moral, and domestic race, their own example would, in the first place, have been of the utmost importance. Failing in this, the next most important point would have been to have entrusted the overlooking department to individuals of good character, of untainted morals, and of humane and considerate dispositions.   Then the separating, as far as possible, the sexes, during the hours of labour, and carefully suppressing any display of grossness and immorality, so long as they were confined to the mills. Great improvements have taken place, and are taking place in these respects.   Next, dismissing or disgracing any party guilty of improper practices : and finally, rejecting steadily and as an inviolable rule, all and every applicant for work who did not bring some testimony that he was a sober and moral person.

These regulations have, however, been neglected or overlooked, and a power which the masters might have exercised easily in the first instance, it would now be difficult, if not impossible to assume. The numerous causes of dissension and suspicion which have arisen between them and the labourers are so many impediments in the way of beneficial and salutary inspection; till these are removed, little expectation can be had of any striking amelioration proceeding from their interference. There are, however, certain changes in progress, that will, ere long, most probably enable them to do this easily and efficiently, if, in the mean time, the dangerous elements composing the manufacturing population do burst out into active operation, and destroy the whole system of which they form the foundation.

As it is, the baleful influence of the circumstances already detailed are in full and undisguised action; licentiousness and depravity* shewing themselves at a very early age, and to an extent painful to contemplate. The exhibitions of the utter absence of sexual delicacy common in manufacturing towns, are notorious to the most superficial observer. The robe of Arthur's mistress would be tried in vain on the great majority of the females.†

---

* " The depravity of large numbers in Manchester exceeds aught I ever before saw."—*Report of the Ministry to the Poor*, p. 17.

† So intolerable a nuisance is the unblushing effrontery of the lower class of the junior mill-operatives, that in Manchester, Stockport, and other places similarly circumstanced, respectable females never pass along the streets during the period of their going to and returning from work.

It is not denied that there are many girls who, from a coincidence of favourable causes, or from their possessing a higher and more just sense of what is due to themselves, escape some of the many evils which beset them, and grow up decent and moral women, fitted to make good wives and good mothers. These are nevertheless exceptions; not so rare as to be extremely remarkable, but still standing out in strong relief from the mass to which they are attached.

The causes which are so injurious to the female are operating, in a similar degree, and with similar force, upon the male, and produce precisely similar effects, both upon his moral and physical organization.

" There is," says Dr. Kay, " a licentiousness capable of corrupting the whole body of society, like an insidious disease, which eludes observation, yet is fatal in its effects :" and hence it must be that the Factory Commissioners failed in the discovery of the sexual depravity so notoriously existing amongst mill artisans. The unnatural substitution of the labour of the child for that of the parent, has led to the evil of early marriages, fostered by premature development. Pregnancy generally precedes marriage ; as it is a well-known fact, and one familiarly spoken of the operatives, that a woman who is not fruitful is unfit for a wife, because the men look forwards to the labour of their children as their resource against dismissal from the mills.

CHAPTER V.

SOCIAL CONDITION—DOMESTIC HABITS, &c. &c.

Social Confederacy—Mode of life pursued by the Factory Labourer—Hour of commencing Work—Breakfast—Dinner—
Tea, or Baggin—Their Constituents, &c.—Diet of the Manufacturing Population—Use of Tobacco—State of Market—Saturday's Market—Description of the Morning and Evening—
Effects of want of solidity in Diet—Dram-drinking—Increase
of Gin Vaults and Beer Houses—Description of a Gin Vault—
Visit of the Male Labourer to the Gin Vault—Visit of his Wife
and Child—Girls and Young Women, their Visit to the Beer
House—Conduct of Wives — Pawnbrokers' shops — The Use
made of these by the Operative—Illicit Distilleries—Their
Extent—Their localities described—Irish Population—Country
Mills.

THERE is nothing which so truly marks the character
of a community, in a moral point of view, as domestic
manners,—nothing which affords so correct a criterion
by which a judgment may be formed of its happiness
and comfort. Politically speaking, the common people
may be a dead letter, whilst their homes exhibit private
independence and social enjoyment. Politically speaking, a people may possess many immunities, many
rights, may even exercise a very marked control over
the actions of their rulers, whilst their homes exhibit
social disorganization and moral worthlessness.

The social condition of the present generation is full
of anomalies. Possessing, as the great bulk of the
population does, many advantages never known or

dreamt of by their forefathers; education rapidly progressing; its wants liberally relieved; its sicknesses carefully tended; religion afforded it, nay, even brought to its doors, and applied to its senses; a practicability of earning something towards a livelihood; continual accessions of political privileges; it is, nevertheless, filled with immorality, irreligion, improvidence, political discontent, refusal to earn any thing, ingratitude, ignorance, and vice, in every conceivable form in which these can develop themselves.

The mode of life which the system of labour pursued in manufactories forces upon the operative, is one singularly unfavourable to domesticity. Rising at or before day-break, between four and five o'clock the year round, he swallows a hasty meal, or hurries to the mill without taking any food whatever. At eight o'clock half an hour, and in some instances forty minutes, are allowed for breakfast. In many cases, the engine continues at work during meal-time, obliging the labourer to eat and still overlook his work. This, however, is not universal. This meal is brought to the mill, and generally consists of weak tea, of course nearly cold, with a little bread; in other instances, of milk-and-meal porridge. Tea, however, may be called the universal breakfast, flavoured of late years too often with gin or other stimulants. Where the hands live in immediate proximity to the mill, they visit home; but this rarely happens, as they are collected from all parts, some far, some near, but the majority too remote to leave the mill for that purpose.

At twelve o'clock the engine stops, and an hour is given for dinner. The hands leave the mill, and seek their homes, where this meal is usually taken. It consists of potatoes boiled, very often eaten alone; sometimes with a little bacon, and sometimes with a portion of animal food. This latter is, however, only found at the tables of the more provident and reputable work-men. If, as it often happens, the majority of the labourers reside at some distance, a great portion of the allotted time is necessarily taken up by the walk, or rather run, backwards and forwards. No time is allowed for the observances of ceremony. The meal has been imperfectly cooked, by some one left for that purpose, not unusually a mere child, or superannuated man or woman. The entire family surround the table, if they possess one, each striving which can most rapidly devour the fare before them, which is sufficient, by its quantity, to satisfy the cravings of hunger, but possesses little nutritive quality. It is not half masticated, is hastily swallowed in crude morsels, and thrust into the stomach in a state unfavourable to the progress of those subse-quent changes which it ought to undergo. As soon as this is effected, the family is again scattered. No rest has been taken; and even the exercise, such as it is, is useless, from its excess, and even harmful, being taken at a time when repose is necessary for the digestive operations.

Again they are engaged from one o'clock till eight or nine, with the exception of twenty minutes, this being allowed for tea, or baggin-time, as it is called. This imperfect meal is almost universally taken in the mill: it consists of tea and wheaten bread, with very few exceptions.

It must be remembered, that father, mother, son, and daughter, are alike engaged; no one capable of working is spared to make home comfortable and desirable. No clean and tidy wife appears to welcome her hus-band—no smiling and affectionate mother to receive her children—no home, cheerful and inviting, to make

it regarded. On the contrary, it is badly furnished—
dirty and squalid in its appearance. Another meal
sometimes of a better quality, is now taken, and they
either seek repose, or leave home in the pursuit of
pleasure or amusements.*

The staple diet of the town-mill artisans is potatoes
and wheaten bread, washed down by tea or coffee.†
Milk is but little used. Meal is consumed to some
extent, either baked into cakes or boiled up with
water, making a porridge at once nutritious, easy of
digestion, and readily cooked. Animal food forms a
very small part of their diet, and that which is eaten
is often of an inferior quality. In the class of fine
spinners and others, whose wages are very liberal,
flesh meat is frequently added to their meals. Fish
is bought to some extent, though by no means very
largely. Herrings are eaten not unusually; and though
giving a relish to their otherways tasteless food, are not
very well fitted for their use. The process of salting,
which hardens the animal fibre, renders it difficult of
digestion; it dissolves slowly, and their stomachs do not

---

* " The artisan seldom possesses sufficient moral dignity, or
intellectual or organic strength, to resist the seductions of appetite.
His wife and children, subjected to the same process, have little
power to cheer his remaining moments of leisure."—*Moral and
Physical Condition of the Working Classes*, p. 25.

† The increased consumption of tea and coffee, as compared to
the increase in population, shows the change in the habits which
has been going on so rapidly during the present century. The
quantity of sugar consumed in 1814 was 1,997,000 lbs.; in 1832,
3,655,000 lbs., an increase of 83 per cent.; increase in population,
24 per cent.; tea, in 1814, 19,224,000 lbs.; 1832, 31,548,000 lbs.,
increase 65 per cent.; coffee, in 1814, 6,324,000 lbs.; 1832,
22,952,000 lbs., increase 183 per cent, against an addition of population amounting to 24 per cent.

possess the most active or energetic character. Eggs, too, form some portion of the operative's diet. The staple, however, is tea and bread. Little trouble is required in preparing them for use ; and this circumstance, joined to the want of proper domestic arrangements, favours their extensive use amongst a class so improvident and care- less as the mill artisans.

Tobacco is very largely consumed by the male and female labourers indiscriminately ; hundreds of men and women may be daily seen inhaling the fumes of this plant, by means of short and blackened pipes.* Smoking, too, is an almost universal accompaniment to drinking—a pernicious habit, as will be shortly seen, prevailing to a frightful extent in this portion of the population.

The difference exhibited both by the buyers and sellers, of animal and vegetable food on the Saturday, which is the general provision market-day and the pay-day of the labourers in the morning and evening, very strikingly illustrates the different grades into which the community of a manufacturing town or district is divided.

Speaking generally, the markets are well supplied, both as regards quality and quantity. Animal food, consisting of beef, mutton, veal, and pork, is plentiful, and of the best sorts—certainly not surpassed by any market in the kingdom. Vegetables are equally abundant, and of an equally good quality. Lancashire has indeed long been famous for the excellence of its potatoes, a native rarely meeting with any fit to be compared with them for

* The consumption of tobacco has increased from 1814 to 1832, from 15,000,000 lbs. to 20,000,000 lbs. that is, about 31 per cent. against an increase in population of 24 per cent. It is much less used now than formerly by the upper and middle classes.

growth and flavour. Cheese, flour, butter, &c. &c. are
also in like manner good and abundant; in short, there
is nothing eatable but what may be found at a moderate
price, and in any quantity.

In the morning the markets are crowded with well-
dressed, respectable persons, making their purchases
for the ensuing week—order, civility, decency being
preserved as far as these things can be on such occasions.
The best animal food, whether it be flesh, fish, or fowl,
is of course first carried away to the larders and cellars
of the middle and upper classes, and the same with the
vegetables. The day wears on, and about noon a change
is observable in the appearance of the markets. The
morning's trading had pretty well cleared them, a tolerably accurate balance being preserved between the supply
of prime and first-rate articles, and the probable demand.
At this time they are beginning to fill again—the
butcher's stalls are replenished — the vegetables start
into being — the sides of the streets in the principal
market thoroughfares become lined with baskets or
petty stalls, the property of sellers of every variety of
minor article likely to tempt the cupidity or taste of
vulgarity.

It might be supposed that a supply of similar quality
to that of the morning was now to be found,—but it is
widely different. Coarse, badly fed, too long kept, and
not unfrequently diseased animal food, stands in the
room of the excellent article of the morning. The
vegetables have undergone an equal deterioration, consisting of the refuse of the morning's supply. These
are retailed out, not by the respectable dealer or
grower, but by a congregation of small buyers who have
selected their stocks, not from their excellence, but
from their cheapness; and the same inferiority holds

throughout. And what a scene is Saturday night's market—what a hubbub of discordant sounds—what jangling, swearing, drunkenness, noisy vociferation, confusion worse confounded, riot, and debauchery! Thus passes Saturday till near midnight—a scene of turmoil, strife, and roguery.

If the perfection of social and domestic life consisted in limiting and stinting the supplies of man's natural wants, as to food,—or if this perfection consisted less in the limiting these supplies, than in an indifference as to their quality,—a very great portion of the lowest classes in the great manufacturing towns are rapidly approaching, or rather have already nearly approached perfection. If true wisdom, as to eating, consists in simply satisfying the cravings of appetite, without reference to the nature of the food or place of doing this, then do these people exhibit a high order of wisdom. There is, however, an intimate relation between moral and domestic virtues and modes of living.

The Irish hand-loom weaver, who rarely tastes any food but potatoes, has reduced his scale of living to its utmost simplicity, and he holds the lowest rank in the very low classes even in these situations. Recklessness and improvidence may be ever detected by coarse, inferior, and badly cooked diet. Poverty, even in its very extremity, if still retaining any trace of self-respect, any tincture of a wish or hope for better things, will have its meals, even though they may be hardly worthy the name, with a regard to common decency and decorum. The savage, who feeds promiscuously upon whatever comes before him, from his own species to ants and caterpillars, affords, by this very omnivorousness, the most decisive proofs of his want of civilisation, and domestic forethought and economy. So does the work-

man, in a different order of society, who consumes the
refuse merely of those around him, without regard to its
quality,—he proclaims, if possible, in still more decided
language, the extent of his moral and social debase-
ment.

The mere supply of the wants of nature, with respect
to food, absorbs but a very small amount of the wages
earned by the majority of the manufacturing labourers,
confined, as the supply is, to the coarsest and most
simple viands. Men may be found who have not yielded
to the indifference and destructive habits of the mass,
who are living in comfort and decency upon the average
amount of wages earned by the whole population—a
sufficient proof, if proof were wanting, that the mischief
lies full as much with the labourers themselves, as in
the system of labour, bad as that is, acknowledged
to be.

The extinction of decent pride in their household
establishments, which at present characterizes the mass
of the manufacturing town population, presents them in
a very unfavourable point of view. There are none of
the minor comforts of existence—nothing but a hut of
squalor and filth, alike repulsive to sight and smell, and
injurious to health—having few of the requisites of
home. It is stripped of every thing which might render
it pleasant or delightful, and has, in consequence, no hold
upon the affections.* The labourer leaves it without
regret—he anticipates no joy on his return—he finds
there nothing but want—and all these are in a great

---

* " Domestic economy is neglected, domestic comforts are too
frequently unknown. Home has little other relation to him than
that of shelter—few pleasures are there," &c. &c.—*Moral and
Physical Condition of the Working Classes,* &c. p. 25.

measure the results, not of the pressure of actual want, but of his own bad and improvident habits.

The operative having no home, therefore, which can cheer the brief period allowed him from labour—too often destitute of moral principle, unguided and uninfluenced by good example—flies for relief to the gin-vault or the beer house, dissipating in these haunts of crime and depravity, resources which, if properly applied, would furnish his house decently, supply his table with wholesome and nutritious food, and provide him with ample means to make him a respectable member of society.*

The plainness and want of solidity and proper stimulus in the food of the labourer, is attended by some other evils, bearing strongly upon his domestic habits.

His labour is continued so interruptedly, that whether it is morning, or noon, or night, he leaves the mill or workshop, and devours his watery meal with feelings of mental depression, exhaustion or wearisomeness, and he eagerly swallows a stimulus in the shape of spirits or beer, to supply, by its temporary exciting influence, the want of proper food on the one hand, and of due relaxation on the other.

* " If I were to form a judgment of the whole town from the small number of families which I have visited, I would divide the working class into three parts : two of these parts have the means of making a comfortable living, their wages being sufficient to provide them with plenty of food and clothing, and every thing needful to make a family comfortable, if well laid out ; but I am sorry to say that a large number of these are as destitute of clothes, bedding, and furniture, and occasionally of provisions, as the poorest families in the town. They drink more money than would amply provide them with every substantial necessary for their families."—*Report of the Ministry to the Poor—Manchester,* 1834, p. 17.

The increase which has of late years taken place in the number of gin vaults, and the more than equal increase in the number of low beer houses, since the passing of the bill termed the Beer Bill,—though its more correct designation would have been a " Bill for the Demoralization of the Working Classes,"—is sufficiently indicative of the prevalence of dram-drinking and tavern-haunting.*

In Manchester alone there are very near, if not quite, one thousand inns, beer houses, and gin vaults. Of these more than nine-tenths are kept open exclusively for the supply of the labouring population,† placed in situations calculated for their convenience, decked out with every thing that can allure them, crowded into back streets and alleys, or flaunting with the most gaudy and expensive decorations in the great working thoroughfares. They are open at the earliest hour, when the shivering artisan is proceeding to his work, holding out to him a temptation utterly irresistible ; and remain open during a considerable portion of the night, ministering their poisons to thousands who flock to them, in place of seeking excitement and pleasurable stimulus in fire-side comforts and enjoyments.

* Mr. Braidley, the respectable and intelligent boroughreeve of Manchester during 1832-3, observed the number of persons entering a gin shop, in five minutes, during eight successive Saturday nights, and at different periods, from seven o'clock till ten. The average result was 112 men and 163 women, or 275 in forty minutes, which is equal to 412 per hour.—*Moral and Social Condition of the Working Classes*, p. 58.

† Manchester is divided into districts for municipal convenience. Of these, Nos. 1, 2, 3, 4, belong exclusively to the labouring population ; including with these, Nos. 5 and 6, there are, in these localities, 270 taverns, 216 gin shops, and 188 beer houses ; total, 674, which minister almost entirely to the wants of the poor.—*Ibid.*

Nor is it the adult male labourer who alone visits these receptacles for every thing that is wicked and degraded. Alas! no. The mother with her wailing child, the girl in company with her sweetheart, the mother with her daughter, the father with his son, the grey-haired grandsire with his half-clad grandchild, all come here, herding promiscuously with prostitutes and pickpockets, the very scum and refuse of society,—all jumbled together in an heterogeneous mass of evil, to the ruin of every thing chaste and delicate in woman, and the utter annihilation of all honourable or honest feeling in man.*

It is a strange sight to watch one of these dens of wickedness throughout an evening: it is a strange, a melancholy, yet, to the meditative man, an interesting sight. There approaches a half-clad man, a hand-loom weaver, or an improvident spinner, shivering even beneath the summer breeze which is singing around him. He comes with faltering step, downcast eye, and air of general exhaustion and dejection. He reaches his accustomed gin vault, disappears for half an hour or less, and now comes forth a new creature: were it not for his filthy dress, he would hardly be recognised, for his step is elastic, his eye is brilliant and open, his air animated and joyous. He inhales the breeze as a refreshing draught, and he deems himself happy. His enjoyment is, however, shortlived, and purchased at an immense sacrifice; for the

" —— Price is death!
It is a costly feast."

* The dram shops, Tom and Jerry shops, and public houses; swarm the Lord's day over (except an hour or two during service-time) and overflow at night by the addition of gamblers, and

Now comes a woman, perhaps his wife, bearing a sickly and cadaverous-looking infant, wailing and moaning as if in pain, or wanting nutriment. She is indeed offering it the breast, but it is flaccid and cold as marble. She has no endearments for her child, it is held as a burden—passively and carelessly. She is thin, pale, and badly dressed—is without bonnet, and her cap is soiled and ragged; her bosom is exposed, her gown is filthy, her shoes only half on her feet, and her whole aspect forlorn and forbidding. She too disappears for a time within the gin shop, remains longer than her husband, but returns equally changed. The child is now crowing in her arms, clapping its tiny hands, and is filled with infantine mirth, whilst its mother views it with fondness, joins in its vociferations, tosses it in her arms, and kisses it like a mother. She passes on cheerily, her whole gait is altered, her cheeks are flushed, and she thinks herself happy, for her maternal feelings are aroused, and her inebriated child seems to her own disordered senses the very paragon of beauty and delight.

The pair have now reached home; night is far advanced, and the fumes of their intoxication are worn off or become converted into sullenness. The child is in a stupor, and the husband and wife meet without a single kindly greeting. There is no food, no fire: bickerings arise, mutual recrimination, blows, curses— till both at last sink into the stupified sleep of drunkenness, worn out by toil, excessive stimulus, and evil passions.

Here come several girls and young women, tolerably

multitudes of females, lost to all sense of shame, and totally destitute of every virtue that makes woman lovely and respectable."— *Report of the Ministry to the Poor—Manchester,* 1834, p. 15.

dressed ; some with harsh, husky voices, shewing the premature development of puberty, others full and perfectly formed women. All, save one, have the same pallid hue of countenance, the same coarseness of expression, the same contour of figure. One amongst them is however beautiful, and beautiful as an innocent girl alone can be,—the very purity of her heart and her soul gleaming in her face. Her figure is plump and round, and her cheeks, though somewhat pale, are yet firm in their outline. It is evident that she is scarcely at home in the presence of her companions, nor one of them in feeling, though it would seem that she is condemned to the same labour. Yes! it is so. She is not many weeks returned from a distant town, in which she had been apprenticed to a respectable trade. Adverse circumstances have, however, driven her home, and she has no resource but to become a weaver, and this she has been for upwards of a week. She hesitates to enter the beer shop—she withdraws timidly, but at length is lost within its door, amidst the laughter and jeers of her companions. They remain long : and now approach a number of young men with soiled dress, open necks, and of obscene speech. They too enter the beer house. Laughter long and loud resounds from it ; time wears on, but the drunken revel continues unabated, now shewing itself in bursts of obstreperous merriment, now by vollies of imprecations—now by the rude dance—and now by the ribald song. But where is that delicate and beautiful girl ? Can she be one sharing such scenes ? Can she, whose eyes and ears evidently revolted from the bold gestures and speeches of her companions, be remaining to share such coarse orgies ? Eleven o'clock, and the party reappear. Cursing, swearing, hiccuping, indecent displays, mark their exit ; and *there is* the fair

girl, whose " unsmirched brow" so lately gave token of
her purity. But now she is metamorphosed into a
bacchanal, with distended and glowing cheeks, stag-
gering step, disordered apparel—utterly lost, to herself; and when the morning bell rings her to her
appointed labour, she will be one of the herd, and will
speedily lose all trace of her purity and feminine
beauty.

If there is one period of the day when these displays
excite more unmingled disgust than another, it is during
the hours of labour, when those wives and mothers of the
absent artisans, who are either unable to work, or cannot procure it, are left at home. No domestic cares
occupy them, except in a few rare cases. Their hearths
are unswept, their persons and houses uncleaned, their
rooms untidied. On the contrary, they are seen in
groups of two or three, lounging about the gin or beer
shops, wasting any trifle of money they may have re-
served, or procuring a supply by pawning some
portion of their wretched apparel, or equally wretched
furniture.

Pawnbrokers' shops have an affinity in their demoralizing agency to the gin and beer houses, and are
almost as numerous, occupying the same localities, and
giving unhappy facilities to the poor man to protract his
Saturday night's or Sunday's debauch throughout the early
part of the week. Article after article is pledged for small
sums, to be redeemed the next pay-day, and homesteads
which, on the Saturday mornings, are destitute of every
necessary utensil, are found, in the evening, possessing
some of these. They have been fetched from pledge, a
loss has been sustained upon them, and in ninety-nine
cases out of one hundred they are again missing before
the middle of the ensuing week. The same with regard

to dress—coat or trousers, cloak, dress, or under dress, shoes, stockings, &c. &c. all have a constant round. Sacrifice after sacrifice takes place, till at length the articles are either left unredeemed, or are become so far worn and tattered as to be no longer a valid security to the pawnbroker, even for the very small sum he advances upon them, be it twopence, fourpence, sixpence, eightpence, or one shilling.

This disregard for personal comfort and household decency in the mass of town manufacturers, strongly demonstrates the miserably low ebb to which their domestic relations are reduced, and proclaims, in a voice which it is impossible to misunderstand, how deplorable, how pitiable is the condition, which thus deprives itself, like the untutored and uncultivated savage, of every thing humanizing, for the sake of a momentary excitement ; which leaves matters in an infinitely worse state than before, and precipitates the unhappy being who thus blindly indulges a depraved taste only the more rapidly upon his inevitable ruin.* Truly did Mr. Hunter remark

---

* Neither has this passion lessened since the day of the acute Hunter. At the treaty of Chicago, in 1821, the commissioners ordered that no spirits should be issued to the Indians. A deputation of the chiefs was sent to remonstrate against this precautionary measure; and at its head was Topnibe, chief of the Potawatomic tribe, a man upwards of eighty years of age. Every argument was used to convince them that the measure was indispensable ; that they were exposed to daily murders ; and that, while in a state of intoxication, they were unable to attend to the business for which they were convened. All this was useless, and the discussion only terminated by the peremptory refusal of the commissioners to accede to their request. " Father," said the hoary-headed chief, when he was urged to remain sober, and make a good bargain for his people ; " father, we care not for money, nor the lands, nor the goods ; we want the whiskey. Give us the whiskey."

that of all the products of civilisation, the North American savage was anxious alone for brandy and gunpowder ;
and with equal truth it may be said, that the nearer a
people approach to the destitution of savage life, the
more eagerly do they seek to participate the enjoyments
of intoxication. Distilled spirits afford a cheap and
effectual oblivion of cares and wants, and however much
the indulgence may increase the sum of human sufferings, it is not surprising that they who have no other
pleasure within their reach should madly snatch at this
solitary comfort.

Independently of these open and recognised means,
which are within the reach of the labourer and his
family, there are others of most extensive operation for
demoralizing him, through the agency of drunkenness
and its attendant vices. The lowest class of the population, in the manufacturing towns, is, to a very considerable extent, made up of Irish, who inhabit the cellars,
and those portions of the towns which, to the casual
observer, would appear totally uninhabitable. In these
places, however, is congregated a very numerous body
of people, who have introduced with them the same
spirit of recklessness and improvidence, with the same
systematic evasion of, or violent resistance to, law and
order, which have so long disgraced their native country,
and gone far towards ruining its resources. Here, and
by these individuals, illicit distillation is carried on to a
great extent. It has been calculated, upon not very
perfect data, that there are not less than one hundred
stills in constant operation in Manchester alone,* producing genuine potheen of the highest strength.

* During the year 1832, thirty persons were committed to the
New Bailey, Manchester, for having either been detected in dis-
tilling or hawking illicit spirits. Nearly the whole of these were

From many seizures which have been made, it appears that the average size of the tubs may be about thirty gallons, and if each distillery should produce no greater quantity than this, the whole amount would be very considerable ; and this is drunk, be it remembered, almost exclusively by the lowest classes. Reckoning thirty gallons as the weekly produce, it would give annually 156,000 gallons, which pays no duty, and the manufacture of which is carried on under circumstances in the highest degree unfavourable to the welfare of a peaceable population. This estimate is, however, most probably underrated ; the difficulty of detection is extreme, occupying, as the distilleries do, sites apparently the most improbable, and unfitted for the purpose. These generally are dark cellars, having no outlet except a trap-door, opening into some obscure court, half filled with filth, or excavations dug in the sand-stone rock, beneath tenements occupied by persons either knowing nothing of their subterranean neighbours, or being in league with them. The requisite apparatus is so simple and so little expensive, that detection is no hinderance, and a seizure valueless. The fine inflicted, £30, is of no moment to the successful speculator ; and if it should so happen that he is unable to pay it, the short imprisonment which is the alternative only hardens him in crime, and turns him out upon society a more determined and experienced scoundrel.

Amongst the higher classes of factory operatives, such as fine-spinners and dressers, where a very ample amount of wages is earned, the houses, and the manners of their inhabitants, are often found of a very superior

Irish ; one half had been known to have carried on the trade before, and one-third had been previously convicted, and suffered imprisonment.

kind. ' The spinners, indeed, form a fast-improving body of men ; they are the most influential part of the hands in the factories, and they are fully aware of it. Their interests are in general strictly guarded by combinations ; and of late years, since the rapid advance in automatic labour, they have been compelled to throw aside habits which at one time rendered them a most disorderly and licentious class.

The domestic habits of the manufacturing population in out-town districts are of a better order than those found amongst town-operatives ; their houses are built by the mill-proprietor, and in immediate contiguity with the mill.   Every thing connected with their mode of life is immediately under bis eye ; they form a colony, as it were, detached to a very considerable extent from foreign associations.   Their entire interests are concentrated in and about the mill ; and it is to parties thus circumstanced that Dr. Ure's observation applies, namely, " that all the conveniences, and not a few of what our forefathers would have reckoned the luxuries of life, are attainable by the factory population, and are very generally to be found in their dwellings."* Striking out the word generally, and substituting in particular cases, where the masters take pains to superintend and furnish with every convenience the houses of the labourers, this is true.

The establishment of Mr. Ashton, of Hyde, where Dr. Ure found houses " more richly furnished than any common work-people's dwellings I had ever seen before. In one I saw a couple of sofas, with good chairs, an eight-day clock in a handsome mahogany case, several pictures in oil on the wall side. In another house I observed a neat wheel barometer with its attached

* Philosophy of Manufactures, p. 372.

thermometer, suspended against a snow-white wall. In a third there was a piano, with a little girl learning to play upon it;" New Lanark mills on the Falls of Clyde, where little strong liquor of any kind is taken by the operatives, water being the usual drink at dinner; where many of the females wear silk dresses on Sundays; and Deanston, near Stirling;—instances deduced from these establishments are not to be taken as examples of the social condition of the bulk of the manufacturing population. A few weeks' residence in Hyde, and a knowledge of the painful steps by which the principal proprietors have elevated themselves into social estimation, would satisfy Dr. Ure that he has painted an outside picture of the moral and social condition of the manufacturers, and that in his enlarged *mechanical* views he has overlooked the human agent except in so far as it forms a subordinate part in his great drama of steam and machinery.

A detailed history, indeed, of the rise and progress of manufactures in Hyde, Duckenfield, and Staley Bridge, would form a valuable Appendix to the " Philosophy of Manufactures," as it would exhibit all the good and the evil of the factory system, from the time when the principal manufacturers were hatters, shoemakers, and carters, and the neighbourhood thinly inhabited, to the present, when the same hatters, shoemakers, and carters, are become wealthy and intelligent men, and the district peopled by sixty thousand inhabitants.

The domestic habits of the operatives will improve as their moral condition is amended. There are to be found many detached sections, distributed in favourable localities, and governed by moral and religious masters, which clearly show that it is not factory labour, considered in itself, which produces the social evils which have followed upon its steps. The separation of families, which is generally complete in towns and populous manufacturing districts, is the primary evil ; and this, though it cannot be altogether done away with, may be to some very considerable extent remedied.

For the rest, a system of moral and religious education will do much ; and it should be made a rule that mothers should in all cases be confined to domestic duties, and should on no account be permitted to become mill-workers. It was a fine and correct expression of Madame Campan to Napoleon, when he asked what more was required for the education of the children of France—" Mothers, sire, mothers ;" so we would say that mothers are wanted for the mill artisans of Great Britain.

CHAPTER VI.

INFANT LABOÚR—FEMALE LABOUR.

Infant Labour—Small and Simple Machinery—Mill Labour by
Children from Five to Twelve Years of Age—Apprentice Sys-
tem—Size and Locality of the first Spinning Mills—Excess of
Labour—Dr. Percival's Inquiries in 1796—Sir Robert Peel's
Evidence—Free Labour—Introduction of Steam Power—En-
largement of Machines—Great improvement of Mills—Propor-
tion of young Children employed in Factories—Increase of Adult
Labour—Effects of improved Machinery upon Adult Labour—
Cause of Women and Children being preferred by Masters—
Equalization of Infant and Adult Labour—Material organization
of Childhood described—Progress of Ossification—State in the
Embryo, in the Fœtus, in the new-born Child, described—
Periods of completion of different points according to function
—Progress of Ossification subsequent to Birth—Physical conditions, &c.—Childhood—Importance of proper Nutrition—Ne-
cessity for Exercise, &c. &c.—Condition of the Factory Child—
Effects of Disturbing healthy Nutrition—Earthy deposit in Bone
—Rickets, Scrofula, is hereditary, in what sense—State of Factory Child prior to commencing Labour—Necessity of this being
properly understood—Error of Abolitionists—Healthy Children
fit for Labour at eight or nine years of age—State of a Child from
the country—Its change when placed in a large Town—Difference of capability for bearing labour in a Town and Country
Child at nine years of age—Their Conditions compared—Factory
Labour, consequences to Children described—Deformity, how
produced—Inhalation of Dust, Effluvia of Oil, &c.—Odours, influence of upon Health—Temperature—First impression upon
Children—Ventilation—Deoxigenation of respired Air—Continuance of Mill Labour—Consequences—Examination of Children—Opinion of Dr. Baillie—Influence of Deformity on the

Female—Mischiefs of present Social Condition—Difficulty of
alteration—Want of restriction, &c. &c.—Factories Regulation
Act—Female Labour, its extent.

"THE discoveries of Arkwright, Watt, Crompton,
and other great benefactors of mankind," remarks an
intelligent and extensive manufacturer, in his evidence
before a Committee of the House of Commons, on the
employment of Children in Manufactories, " produced
a complete revolution in the spinning manufactures of
cotton, of wool, and of flax, which might now be more
properly termed mechanical productions : by the application of the power of waterfalls, and of ingenious
mechanism, adults were superseded by children, whose
wages were lower, and who soon acquired a great dexterity : the production of the manufacturers was enormously increased, because the extraordinary cheapness
produced a consumption in proportion to the great aug-
mentation of the wealth and revenue of the nation.
The very moderate exertion of the children, and the
great expense of the mechanism, introduced the custom
of working twelve hours per day in the mills.   Under
these circumstances it became the duty and the advantage of every proprietor to render his mill as healthy as
possible, by cleanliness, ventilation, spaciousness, and
temperature, and to interest himself generally for those
employed by him.   As the children grew to be adults,
notwithstanding their acquired expertness, they became
too big for the machinery, and their labour too expensive.   In consequence of the introduction of the revolving steam engine, factories were established in manufacturing towns ; the establishments in manufacturing towns
were more calculated for adults, and machines of greater
size and complication were constructed for the more

difficult and finer kinds of spinning. If this arrangement had not taken place, and the business continued
to extend, a numerous population of children would
have been formed, and employed in remote situations,
without an adequate demand for their labour when
adults; the employment of adults by such suitable
establishments in manufacturing towns, therefore, ob-
viated this evil. It has likewise produced that excellence in the operations which could never have been
obtained or rewarded, except in the great and open
market of talents in large towns. The labour of adults
is infinitely more regular in machinery than in manual
employment, *but can never be controlled and reduced to
the uniformity of attendance of children.* On the other
side, they are capable of greater exertion, and possess
far greater skill. The system of employing adults
restores society to its proper direction, which had been
changed by sudden discoveries, and probably neither
a younger nor a greater number of children will be
required to be trained in the mills upon the new scale,
than that proportion which is necessary to supply the
demand for adults in many other labouring classes of
society."

The simplicity of the first machines adapted for spinning, and their small size, fitted them for being tended
by children. The localities in which the mills were at
first erected for the convenience of water power,
were often remote from towns or villages, from which
alone an adequate supply of hands could be obtained:
hence, in the early period of mill labour, apprentices,
from six to twelve years of age, were almost the only
workers. These apprentices were chiefly taken from
the workhouses of large towns, such as London, Bir-
mingham, &c. and from foundling hospitals, and trans-

mitted in droves* to the different mills, where, in many instances, it is to be feared they suffered very severely.• Villages, however, sprung up in the vicinity of the mills, and the parents of children very naturally took advantage of their labour, and hence, free labourers became superadded, and, in time, displaced the apprentice system to a considerable degree.

The construction of the first mills was, of course, fitted only for small machines ; they were consequently small, and the rooms in them were low, and of very contracted dimensions, and very little precaution was used, either as to ventilation or temperature. The time of labour was extended to twelve hours, with very little interval ; the immense profits which accrued from their produce pushing aside all ulterior considerations. Nor was this all : unsatisfied with the day labour, the night was almost uniformly spent by one portion of the hands in the mill ; the owners or occupiers thus securing twenty-three hours out of the twenty-four for making their machinery valuable.†

There cannot be a question but that child-labour, urged to this extent, and under these circumstances, was prejudicial in every way, and gross immorality was one result. In 1796, the evil of it had aroused the attention of various philanthropic individuals, amongst whom the name of Dr. Percival stands conspicuously forward ; and he, in conjunction with others, stirred themselves to produce some alteration and amendment.

On the establishment of the Manchester Board of Health, the following statement was made by him, on

---

* Mr. Arkwright's first mills were almost entirely filled with very young children. The house of Peel and Co. employed at one time a thousand of these children.

† The practice of night work is nearly abolished at the present day.

the 15th of January, 1796 :—" The Board have had their attention particularly directed to the large cotton factories established in the neighbourhood and town of Manchester, and they feel it a duty incumbent on them to lay before the public the result of their inquiries : 1. It appears that the children and others, who work in the large cotton factories, are peculiarly disposed to be affected by the contagion of fever; and that when such infection is received, it is rapidly propagated, not only amongst those who are crowded together in the same apartments, but in the families and neighbourhoods to which they belong. 2. The large factories are generally injurious to those employed in them, even when no particular diseases prevail, from the close confinement which is enjoined, and from the debilitating effects of hot or impure air, and from the want of the active exercises which nature points out as essential in childhood and youth, to invigorate the system, and to fit our species for the employments and the duties of manhood. 3. The untimely labour of the night, and the protracted labour of the day, with respect to children, not only tends to diminish future expectations, as to the general sum of life and industry, by impairing the strength, and destroying the vital stamina of the rising generation ; but it too often gives encouragement to idleness, extravagance, and profligacy in the parents, who, contrary to the law of nature, subsist by the oppression of their children. 4. It appears that the children employed in factories are generally debarred from all opportunities of education, and from moral and religious instruction."

According to the evidence of Sir Robert Peel, who was himself very extensively engaged in manufactures at this period, contagious and epidemic diseases were very common in the people, or rather children, employed in these badly constructed mills, and under the influence of such continuous labour. He remarks, that they were uniformly of stinted growth, and that although in his own case they were fed and lodged under his roof and at his own expense, they still looked to be in ill-health.

That gross mismanagement existed in numberless instances there can be no doubt; and that these unprotected creatures, thus thrown entirely into the power of the manufacturer, were over-worked, often badly fed, and worse treated. No wonder can be felt that these glaring mischiefs attracted observation, and, finally, led to the passing of the Apprentice Bill,* a bill intended to regulate these matters. It may be questioned whether the bill of itself did much good, but from the discussions it excited, and the vast superiority displayed by some mills over others, when general inquiries were made, very beneficial consequences were the result, and some attention began to be paid both to the better ordering of the mills, and to the welfare of the children.

The machines for spinning were, day after day, becoming more bulky, and requiring greater skill and exertion for producing fine numbers, so that adults gradually found their way to them. The application of steam as a moving power, which became general from 1801 to 1804, produced a great change in all respects. It did away with the necessity for so much water power, and hence mills were more commonly built in towns or populous districts, favourable as to coal, &c., and where a population was at hand for their occupation. The uniformity, the increased rapidity of motion, and the greater size of the machines, called in some departments for active labour, and grown-up men and women were

* The Apprentice Bill was passed 1802.

now largely engaged in spinning ;—but still children formed the majority of hands, many processes being better calculated for them than for adults. But they were not put to work quite so young, few before ten years of age—an age, in fact, which the masters found to be as soon as they could be properly useful.

The hours of labour have not undergone any very material alteration since the universal application of steam, and since the doing away with night labour as a general custom. Notwithstanding this the condition of the children has undergone great amelioration. This has arisen not from increased wages, but from the improvement in the construction of the mills. Subsequent to 1806, when the steam-loom was first brought into operation, many of the first mills were either much enlarged, or in very numerous examples abandoned by the more wealthy manufacturers, and in their stead large buildings were erected, fitted to receive, in addition to the spinning processes, a quantity of looms.

Nor was this increase in size the only advantage. The rooms were much more lofty, generally of large proportions, had numerous windows, so arranged as to afford excellent ventilation, whilst improved modes of warming them did away with many of the inconveniences which had hitherto attended upon this necessary portion of their interior economy. This consisted in carrying through the room pipes conveying steam, or heated air, which enabled the overlooker to regulate the temperature according to the necessity of the season. Various improvements took place in the cleaning the cotton, so as to free the mill from a great part of the flue or fine cottony down, which in the old mills, spinning coarse numbers had been nearly suffocating. Cleanliness began to be cultivated, and this was materially aided by the

use of cast-iron floors. These were much more easily
cleaned than wood, which had absorbed the oil drop-
pings, and soon became offensive and exceedingly difficult to get off; added to which was the gradual
substitution of iron in the frame-work of machinery :
this by its diminished bulk materially increased the
empty space in the rooms, the wooden frames having
been large and massy, and always getting filled with dirt.

The number of young persons employed in factories
since the breaking up of the apprentice system, and since
the divisions of labourers have fairly settled themselves,
has not till of late years varied very largely, when estimated as to the proportion they bear to the remainder
of the hands. In 1816, a return from forty-one mills in
Scotland gave a total of ten thousand persons engaged
in them. Of this number,

Under ten years of age.	From ten to eighteen years of age.	Above eighteen years of age.
191 Males. 224 Females.	1179 Males. 2810 Females.	5596.
415	3989	
Total under 18 . . . 4,404.		

A similar return from forty-eight mills in Manchester
gave a total of 12,940 hands.

Under 10, 793; 10 to 18, 5460; above 18, 6687.

This approximates very nearly to the Table first
given.

A return from thirty-six mills in Stockport, in 1833,
gave a total of 11,444.

Under 10, 326; 10 to 18, 4017; above 18, 7101.*

* *Vide* Table in Appendix for details, as to number of hands
employed, with their age, sex, &c.

The diversity in the foregoing Tables arises from several causes. Wherever spinning is more especially prosecuted, there the number of hands under eighteen years of age will appear proportionately increased; and wherever weaving is the staple manufacture, there the number of hands upwards of eighteen will be in greater ratio. There can be no question indeed, but that since steam-weaving became general, the number of adults engaged in the mills has been progressively advancing, inasmuch that very young children are not competent to take charge of a steam-loom. The individuals employed at them are chiefly girls and young women, from sixteen to twenty-two or twenty-three years of age; indeed, the weavers in many mills are exclusively females, and it is not likely that any very material alteration in this respect will occur. In spinning, children are as valuable workers in many of its processes as adults, in some degree more so.

Yet a change is rapidly taking place in the condition of the operatives, and a disposition is developing itself to have recourse to the labour of women and children in preference to adults. The causes which have led to this are, the great improvements which are taking place in machinery, and its application to an infinite variety of minute operations, requiring the nicest management, the requisite power being given by steam. Nearly the whole of the hands employed in the silk factories are females, as well as in the Scotch flax, cotton, and woollen mills.

The labourer is indeed become a subsidiary to this power. Already he is condemned, hour after hour, day after day, to watch and minister to its operations,—to become himself as much a part of its mechanism as its cranks and cog-wheels,—already to feel that he is but

a portion of a mighty machine, every improved application of which, every addition to its Briareus-like arms,
rapidly lessen his importance, and tend to drive him
from a participation with it, as the most expensive and
unmanageable part of its materials.

The contest, however, between human and steam
power, as applied to manufactures, is not yet so far
advanced as to annihilate its value to its possessor. In
another portion of this work it is satisfactorily shown
that the labourer, though losing rapidly his independent
character, is paid for his labour a sum amply sufficient,
when properly applied, to supply all his natural wants,
and to provide him with comforts and opportunities for
making provision for sickness or old age, without becoming a burden upon the fixed capital of the nation.
This observation, it must be understood, refers to those
artisans who work aided by mechanism and steam. The
hand-loom weavers are, on the contrary, crushed by their
mighty opponent to the dust, and keep up a warfare with
it upon the most unequal and untenable grounds.

The necessity for human power thus gradually yielding before another and more subservient one, has had,
in the first place, the effect of rendering adult labour of
no greater value than that of the infant or girl ; the
workmen are reduced to mere watchers, and suppliers of
the wants of machinery, requiring in the great majority
of its operations no physical or intellectual exertion ; and
the adult male has begun to give way, and his place
been supplied by those who in the usual order of things
were dependent upon him for their support.

It may be asked why, if adult labour was still efficacious, though its physical and intellectual energies
were not demanded, it was thrown aside, and women
and children brought to perform its functions ; thus

reversing the law generally acknowledged, that man, as a husband and a father, should furnish his wife and family with support till such periods as his offspring were themselves arrived at an age when the development of their physical powers fitted them for earning a separate and independent support, or at least assisting their parent, and lessening in some degree his burdens. Why take from their homes and proper occupation women and children, and employ them to the exclusion of their husbands and fathers,* and subject them to labour which, in the instance of the children, their physical organization was unable to bear, and in that of the women must of necessity lead to the neglect of all the domestic offices—household economy—and conjugal and maternal duties ; why throw the active labourer into idleness and dependence, and thus lower immensely his moral importance ? and why thus, laying the axe to the root of the social confederacy, pave the way for breaking up the bonds which hold society together, and which are the basis of national and domestic happiness and virtue ?

The previous sketch of the progress of the manufactures in reference to machinery and its influence upon labour, and the conditions and localities in which the mills were first established, will explain the employment of children in the spinning department to the exclusion of adults ; the introduction of the steam loom, the subsequent excellence and simplification of the machinery, and lastly, a history of the combinations, will be sufficient to unravel the question, and to explain why masters, taking advantage of steam power, and finding that the child or woman was a more obedient servant

* This substitution is felt very acutely by the operatives themselves—they denounce it as an unchristian and most cruel policy.

to himself, and an equally efficient servant to his machinery, were disposed to displace the male adult labourer, and throw him for support upon his family, or send him, as it might happen, a pauper or depraved being to prey upon the community at large.

It may be supposed that the masters, in thus wishing to rid themselves of a turbulent set of workmen, were influenced by other causes—that women and children could be made to work at a cheaper rate, and thus add to his profits.   This has had considerable weight doubtless.   The mode of payment now universally adopted by the trade, which is payment for work done, piece work as it is called,—the spinner for the number of pounds of yarn he produces, the weaver for the number of cuts or yards turned off from his loom,—places the active girl upon a par with the most robust adult.* It is true there are some of the processes which do require the exertions of strength and skill, and in these, of course, men are still employed ; but these processes are few, and even now machinery is making them still fewer, as the manufacturer has to pay very high wages, and is therefore striving to do away with the adult and expensive labourer.

It has happened, then, that in consequence of the great improvements in the adaptation of machinery to

* " In the cotton factories of Lancashire," says Dr. Ure, " the wages of the males, during the period when there is the greatest number employed, from eleven to sixteen, are on the average 4s. 10¾d. per week; but in the next period of five years, from sixteen to twenty-one, the average rises to 10s. 2½d. a-week, and of course the manufacturer will have as few at that price as he can. In the next period of five years, from twenty-one to twenty-six, the average weekly wages are 17s. 2½d.   Here is a still stronger motive to discontinue employing males as far as it can practically be done."

complicated and delicate processes, and the steam-engine, affording a moving power capable of exercising any requisite degree of force,—that, in consequence of machines, thus impelled, requiring merely feeders or watchers, and these watchers or feeders, being not, of necessity, strong in body or intellect,—that adult male labour having been found difficult to manage, and not more productive,—its place has, in a great measure, been supplied by children and women ; and hence the outcry which has been raised with regard to infant labour, in its moral and physical bearings. .The moral considerations have been partly discussed in another portion of this work. The important question of infant labour as to health and physical development, two points intimately connected with the future welfare, well-being, and happiness of the mill artisans, now remains to be examined.

The material organization of childhood is decidedly unfavourable to labour. The functions of nutrition, which are those peculiarly active, leave little either of nervous or muscular energy beyond what is required for their due supply. The whole body is in a state of rapid alteration, full of vascular excitement, and requiring long periods of repose. The constitution at large is very excitable, abounding in vitality, and prone to irregular action. The osseous system is incomplete, its structure, as yet, being in a very great proportion cartilaginous, and hence beautifully adapted for accommodating itself to the growth and extension of the body. It is, however, soft, yielding, bends beneath pressure, and is easily made to assume curvatures and alterations in direction, incompatible, more or less, with the natural arrangements, which are, in all instances, full of harmony and architectural and mechanical

beauties.   The long bones, those of the arms and legs,
do not´become completely ossified till the body has
attained its full growth.   The flat bones, those of the
head, pelvis, &c. become hard sooner, serving, as they
do, for the walls of cavities, or supports for delicate
and important viscera, essential to life.

It will be useful to trace the progress of bone from
its mucous state in the fœtus to its complete perfection
in after-life, as it bears very considerably upon the
fitness or unfitness of young children for labour, and
will sufficiently demonstrate that external agencies
may have a very important influence upon its due
development.

The first stage in which the anatomist can detect
bone, or rather the rudimentary parts, which a re subsequently to become the depositories for bony matter, is
at a very early period, at a time when the whole embryo
is a mere mass of transparent matter, which is so soft
and unresisting that it yields beneath the finger like a
firm pulp. At this time, however, the forms of the bones
are discernible, holding their proper respective positions
in the frame of the fœtus.   This is the condition in
which they will be found in the very early periods of
pregnancy.   Gradually they become firmer, more cartilaginous, and about the end of the first month of utero-
gestation, specks of bony deposit appear in the centre of
the long bones, and in one or two or more places in the
flat bones.   From these specks, as from centres, radiate
osseous fibres towards the extremities of the various
separate portions, into which the long bones and the flat
bones, forming the cavities, are divided.   In the long
bones these osseous striæ, or streaks, are longitudinal,
running towards their extremities; in the flat bones,
they take a star-like course, diverging towards their

edges; and in the short bones, such as the bones of the hand and foot, they proceed from the interior to the surface.

Previous to the deposit of bone, the cartilaginous parts were nearly without' colour, merely indeed tinged with a yellowish hue; but now a red dot is perceived in the point where the bone is forming, and blood-vessels gradually show themselves. This red spot is synchronous with the earliest bony formation; not that the cartilaginous parts were before destitute of circulating fluids, but that its circulation consisted of colourless matter.

This bony formation steadily progresses till the period of birth, and has generally touched, in one or more points, the extreme length of the long bones, and the edges of the flat and small bones. But the whole is very far from being complete. The heads or extremities of the long bones offer distinct points of ossification; in the flat bones, those of the head and pelvis, and shoulder blades, several distinct points are also often found, each forming a small centre for the divergence of similar striæ to those of the primary ones. The bones of the head, which in later life become one continuous case or surface, are at this period divided into several plates, that gradually stretch out their ossific rays, and indent into the edges of those next them, forming serræ, or teeth, which dovetail one into another, and finally make a very firm and immovable union, the bone breaking before these give way, as the edges are thickened purposely to strengthen and fortify this point of junction.

The Divine Architect, whose omniscience has contrived a mechanical apparatus like the human body, has also, in the mode of its growth, and the periods

appointed for the completion of particular parts, clearly
indicated the order in which their functions should be
called into active employment. Respiration being
immediately essential to the new-born creature, the
points of bones to which the muscles are attached,
chiefly concerned in that office, are the very first to
show signs of ossification. So early as the end of the
first month of gestation, the collar-bones and ribs are
hardening, and at birth are sufficiently firm to afford
unyielding fulcra for them to act upon. The spinal
column shows early marks of ossification, as it is, in a
considerable degree, interested in the same function;
while the extremities of the flat bones are still incomplete, and the process of hardening in the small bones
of the hands and feet is hardly commenced.

At this period (the time of birth) the osseous system
is a great series of detached portions of bone, incapable
of supporting the soft parts without yielding beneath
their weight—the connecting medium between them
(cartilage) is flexible, the only portions which have
assumed a very decided formation being those connected
with respiration.

Month after month, as the infant acquires muscular
vigour, the bones solidify in ratio as the peculiar organs
are called into play. Point after point hardens, and is
connected with the shafts of the long bones, or firm
ridges spring up along the surface of the flat bones,
giving origin or insertion to the moving powers which
are destined to enable the child to perform the actions
of locomotion, lifting weights, &c. &c.

It is not till complete growth has been attained, which
is from the seventeenth to the twentieth year, that all
the bones are completely ossified, and till this period
they are more or less liable to give way under continued

pressure. They have, however, assumed a very considerable firmness of structure long prior to this, and little danger need be apprehended of evil consequences from any common labour or exertion which the purposes of life require.

The system of bones—the skeleton—is the basis or frame-work on which all the soft parts are, as it were, hung. It sustains their weight, affords points of support for muscular action, and by the beauty and order of its articulations, is capable of assuming a variety of directions, while its symmetrical proportion is most perfect, and admirably adapted for the packing and convenient arrangement of the numberless components of which a man's body is made up.

During the growth of the child, then, its bones are to some extent soft and yielding, — a circumstance familiar to many mothers, in whose infants the bony structure has not, from some fault in its peculiar nutrition, gone on apace with muscular development : this, by inducing the child to support its weight upon its feet, causes its legs to give way beneath the body, and bow out,—a very common case in strumous families.

It has been said that the child's system was one full of excitement, of rapid changes in structure, and that its sensibilities were acute. The world brings to the infant, for many years, a constant succession of new sensations; and its activity, its variableness, its jocund laugh, its quiet repose, are all evidences that, like the young of other animals, its life was intended by the Creator for unrestricted bodily enjoyment, for to it motion itself ever seems a high gratification.

No one familiar with the wants and habits of a child is ignorant how irksome confinement is to it—how utterly unfit it is for settled occupations—how listless and heartless it speedily becomes when shut out from its instinctive mode of life—how soon it droops and pines, and loses the vigour and freshness of the wild flower.

Whatever causes tend to derange digestion must of necessity interfere with nutrition ; for, in fact, the terms may be considered as almost synonymous. The growth of every part depends intimately upon this first process being well performed. Whatever interferes with this deranges the whole circle of the animal economy, and, if continued, will lay the foundation for a series of irregular actions, which may either run into scrofula, if such taint already exists, or may bring about, independently of such taint, the same or some analogous affection. Whatever vitiates this series of operations,—and it is liable to be vitiated by many causes,—puts the whole animal machine out of equilibrium ; and irregular formations, strumous swellings of the cancellated heads of the long bones, as at the knees, ancles, elbows, and wrists, or a similar train of evils in the glandular structure, evidenced by swellings in the neck, terminating in sores difficult to heal, or of the mesenteric or other glands of the abdomen, or of derangements in the mucous surfaces of the mouth, eyes, breathing apparatus, bowels, &c. &c.—all these are results, more or less marked, of any continued derangement in that most important function of childhood—nutrition.

Light, air, recreation, freedom from toil, proper clothing, wholesome food, attention to the bowels, &c., are all essential to this function being well performed. Children placed even under the most favourable conditions, if deprived of their necessary amount of unrestricted physical enjoyment, show very plainly their want of it. In fashionable boarding-schools, and in private families, where tuition is commenced early, and where little proper exercise is taken, but where every attention is paid to food, &c., the pallid face and spiritless demeanour of the children very soon show that nothing can compensate for the abstraction of their necessary stimuli.

The factory child,* from the very earliest period of its existence, is, in large towns, subjected to all the necessary causes for the production of the physical evils, resulting from derangement of the digestive organs. Its food is coarse, and the times of feeding irregular; it is exposed to cold, ill clad, allowed to be filthy. It inhales the impure atmosphere of a badly ventilated and uncleanly house, and the equally impure one of an unpaved and unsoughed street; is allowed to get wet, goes barefoot, no attention is paid to its dietetic comforts, and consequently vast numbers die very young, and the remainder who live exhibit symptoms that they have suffered from neglect and exposure. They have pale and flaccid features, a stunted growth, very often tumid bellies, tender eyes, and other marks that the *primæ viæ* have been permitted to go wrong. The effect of all the other causes is aided by the abominable practice, so general amongst this class, of cramming children with quack and patent medicines, to quiet their irritability, increased as it is by their digestive derangement, or the equally pernicious one of giving them gin for the same purpose.†

* Vast numbers of these children are hired out at the rate of 1s. 6d. per week.

† "In consequence of the absence of the mothers, these children are entrusted, in a vast majority of cases, to the care of others, often of elderly females. These women often undertake the care of several infants at the same time; the children are

Whatever tends to disturb that function, the products
of which furnish the materials for the building up of the
body, or which alters and depraves those materials,
must necessarily impede and retard the completion of
the healthy structure of the system.   In childhood,
much has to be done in these respects; muscles have
to be strengthened and brought into use; the bony
fabric solidified; growth carried on, by the deposition
of new matter in every portion of the body; preparation made for sexual development: all these keep the
feeders in incessant action.   The vessels which are to
be the first stage in preparing the new matter, and
carrying it to its final depositories, are all connected
with the alimentary canal : these convey the chyle they

restless and irritable from being deprived of a supply of their
natural food (as when the mothers suckle them, they can only perform that duty in the intervals of labour), and the almost universal
practice amongst them is to still the cries of the infant by admi-
nistering opiates, which are sold for the purpose under several
well-known and popular forms.   The quantity of opium which
from habit some children become capable of taking is almost
incredible, and the effects are correspondingly destructive.   Even
when the children have a healthy appearance at birth, they almost
uniformly become in a few months puny and sickly in their aspect,
and many fall victims to bronchitis, hydrocephalus, and other
diseases, produced by want of care, and the pernicious habits we
have detailed.   We may mention, also, that spirits, particularly
gin, are given frequently when the infants appear to suffer from
pain in the bowels, which from injurious diet is very common
among them."—*Inquiry, &c.* p. 17.
   " The child is ill-fed, dirty, ill-clothed—exposed to cold and
neglect, and in consequence more than one half of the offspring of
the poor die before they have completed their fifth year.   The
strongest survive, but the same causes which destroy the weakest
impair the vigour of the more robust, and hence the children of
our manufacturing population are proverbially pale and sallow,
though not generally emaciated, nor subjects of disease."—*Moral
and Physical Condition of the Working Classes, &c.* p. 70.

have elminated from the food. If, however, this chyle
is imperfectly formed, which must inevitably be the
case when digestion is impaired by the causes already
mentioned, it cannot fulfil perfectly its destined offices
in the system—growth is retarded, and particular struc-
tures unfinished.

The formation of bone, the necessary earthy deposit
upon which its hardness depends, is one singularly
under the influence of the digestive operations. Ricketty children are ever wrong in this respect: the food
they take furnishes but little nutriment: their bowels
are disturbed; assimilation goes on imperfectly; all
the processes connected with absorption and deposition
are irregular, and do not preserve that reciprocity of
action, that balance of quantity, which is necessary for
proper growth.

Without going more diffusely into the pathology of
the two diseases, scrofula and rickets, which are in
their origin clearly traceable to disturbed digestion, it
may be sufficient to state, that both, when they have
been fairly established, seem to be transmissible from
parent to child,—to become hereditary. By the term
hereditary, however, when applied to diseases, whether
mental or physical, it must be understood only in a
general sense, as meaning, that a parent endows his
offspring with certain peculiarities of constitution, certain
tendencies to take on diseased actions; not that he
transmits the disease in its distinct form, but that he
gives a liability to have it called into action by causes
which would not develop a similar disease in a child
descended from parents perfectly free from any such
taint. With scrofula this is decidedly the case, scrofulous parents very frequently having offspring with all
the traces of its peculiar diathesis, light eyes, fair

skin, &c. &c. With rickets this transmission is less observable, probably because its incipient stages are not
so strongly marked.

The factory child then, from its birth, is placed under
circumstances certain to deprave its nutritive functions,
and to produce effects injurious to the healthy stamina of
its physical organization. Its soft parts become flabby,
relaxed, open to disease ; its osseous system becomes
firm very slowly and irregularly, yields to superincum-
bent weight, producing deformity more or less marked,
and more or less prejudicial, as affecting parts more or
less connected with important outlets or cavities.

But farther than this, the child which is descended
from parents who have themselves been subjected to
like causes of physical debility, must have an organization weakly from its very origin ; must have inherited,
to some extent, their debilitated constitution, and in
consequence be much less able to resist the influence of
the unfavourable conditions to which it is exposed
subsequent to birth.

This condition, it must be constantly borne in mind,
has nothing to do with labour—as yet the child has
undergone none : it has been allowed to run wild, half-
clad and half-starved. It is of the utmost consequence
to a correct understanding of the question of infant
employment, that this preliminary state should be properly considered and correctly appreciated. It would,
indeed, be a monstrous perversion of every thing like
justice, both to the masters and to the system of factory-
labour, to burden the one with the moral responsibility
of this prior condition, or the other with all the results
for which it paves the way ; a state, be it remembered,
little likely to be ameliorated or improved if the child
were permitted to remain in idleness at home, since it

would be still exposed to the same causes of physical and moral depravity. If, indeed, it could be shown that abstinence from the mill would, to some very considerable extent, give it an opportunity for regaining during youth what it had lost during infancy, a powerful argument would be afforded for government interfering with what the abolitionists of this species of labour do not hesitate to term infanticide, and compare it to the Hindoo Gangetic superstitions, and the Chinese systematic child-murder. A perversion of words is, however, no argument; it may be ingenious, and serve party purposes, but it leaves the question at issue precisely in the same state in which it found it.

There can be no question that a child of nine or ten years of age, if it has been placed under circumstances to permit the healthy development of its· organs, is capable of performing light work. If a child gets over its fifth year, even when it has shown symptoms of slight scrofulous or rachitic affections, it generally pushes forward, and does well, providing that it is properly nurtured, and is well fed and well clothed.

A child from an agricultural district, eight or nine years old, blooming with rosy health, full of vitality, is transported to a crowded town ; its parents are compelled to leave it whilst they prosecute their work at the manufactories ; it is exposed to miasmatic evaporations, shut up in a narrow street, its home is damp and cold, its food poor and badly cooked : in a few months, from the force of these circumstances, the Hebe-looking child has become pallid ; its muscular system loses its tone ; but it seldom goes down below this, its bony fabric having attained already so much firmness and completeness of ossification as to prevent it from yielding to any very great degree. In consequence,

however, of the lessened efficiency of its digestive
apparatus, it is much more liable to chronic diseases,
glandular enlargement, irregular developments, at the
expense of the whole ˌsystem. This train of circumstances is independent of labour : it is brought about
simply by its change of locality, the altered habits of its
parents, and its damp and unwholesome home.

The difference between the child born and subjected
to these mischievous agencies, and the one born under
more favourable auspices, in the influence of which it
has lived till seven years of age, and then brought under
the same train of mischiefs, as to living, &c., when
they are examined at nine years of age, is less striking than would have been previously supposed, from
a comparison of data. Externally they, present but
few points of dissimilarity in physical structure; but a
more attentive inspection will very readily enable the
inquirer to ascertain that, in their several capabilities of
bearing labour, or continued exertion, they are widely
disproportioned, the preponderance of ability leaning
vastly to the child whose prior healthy development had
enabled its organs to make a decided progress.

In this instance its nutrition, for several years, had
been unimpaired ; its long bones had become in a great
measure ossified ; the whole increments of its system'
had been eliminated from a healthy source, through a
series of vessels equally healthy and capable of performing their functions, and a degree of growth established,
which no subsequent derangement could materially
injure or deface. Not so the child whose destiny has
fixed it here from birth : not only is its muscular system
flaccid, supplied with thin watery blood ; its mucous
surfaces unhealthy ; its glandular system deranged ; but
the groundwork upon which these are built, the frame-

upon which they are arranged, is incomplete in comparison. The bony fabric has had no opportunity for becoming properly solidified—contains as yet too large a proportion of cartilaginous matter ; so that the child whose early years have been passed in healthy localities, and had home-tendance, is far more advantageously framed for work, and much less liable to the yielding of its osseous supports, than the child differently circumstanced.

Factory labour is a species of work in some respects not unfitted for children. Being cooped up in a heated atmosphere, debarred the necessary exercise of one set or system of muscles chiefly called into activity, it cannot be wondered at that its effects are, to some extent, injurious to the physical growth of a child. Where the bony system is still imperfect, the vertical position it is compelled to retain influences its direction ; the spinal column bends beneath the weight of the head, bulges out laterally, or is dragged forward by the weight of the parts composing the chest ; the pelvis yields beneath the opposing pressure downwards, and the resistance given by the thigh-bones : its capacity is lessened, sometimes more and sometimes less ; the legs curve, and the whole body loses height, in consequence of this general yielding and bending of its parts.*

* " Had five hundred children, from five to eight years of age ; work thirteen hours, one hour and a half for meals. I very soon discovered that these children, though well fed, and well clothed, and well lodged, and very great care taken of them when out of the mills, their growth and their mind were very materially injured by being employed at these ages within the cotton-mills for eleven and a half hours per day. It is true that these children, in consequence of being well fed, well clothed, and well lodged, looked fresh to a superficial observer, healthy in their countenances, yet their limbs were very generally deformed, and their growth was stunted."—*Evidence before Committee.*

These effects are necessarily produced only in instances where ossification has been retarded, and it has
been shown how the conditions of the child born and
bred up in large towns tend to this state. With regard
to the general health of the child, there is nothing in the
labour to which it is subjected which is likely to injure
it ; and it may be questioned whether, *cæteris paribus,*
it has not full as good a chance of its health being unimpaired in the mill, as if it were left at home, neglected
as it inevitably must be.

The inhalation of dust, &c., the effluvia from oil,
steam, &c. with which the atmosphere of the rooms is
infected, are in no other way injurious than by showing that ventilation is imperfect: of themselves they
have no ill effects upon health, provided the consumption of the oxygen of the respired air be replaced
by sufficient portions of fresh air.   Odours, however
disgusting—nuisances though they be—and though
upon those unaccustomed to their foetor,* they produce
squeamishness, and a temporary indisposition for taking
food, experience has proved are by no means delete-
rious.   On the contrary, there are certain gases, which
would appear to be even conducive to human health,

* To prove that odours are not of themselves injurious to
health, it may be remarked, that the oyster fishing affords as
striking an example as can perhaps be found bearing upon the
subject :—"It is a curious fact that these numerous couttôs (or
heaps), each containing an enormous mass of oysters, all putrefy
together on a narrow extent of soil, and emit the most detestable
odours ; yet the health of the precarious and crowded population
gathered there is in no ways affected. During two consecutive
years," says M. de Noè, " that I did duty at the fishery, I never
saw a soldier of my regiment sick : Europeans and Sepoys all
equally enjoyed good health."—*Memoires relatifs à l'Expedition
Anglaise de l'Inde en Egypte.*

though sufficiently disgusting. Soap-boilers, chandlers, stable-men, dealers in oil, curriers, tanners, are generally healthy men, and to some extent have appeared to enjoy an immunity from contagious diseases. Neither is the dust in the carding-rooms of cotton-mills so great as to produce any marked effect upon health. The temperature in which the infant portion of factory labourers work is not so high as to be actively pernicious, except in the first instance; nor does it extend beyond a certain point.

When a child is first introduced into the mill, the warmth often produces slight fever; this, however, does not go so far as to prevent the sufferer working, neither is it at all contagious, being simply the effect of temperature, and preceded by considerable perspiration whilst at work. This of course produces some degree of debility and a paleness of skin, rarely recovered from; but the health does not continue to suffer from this cause—use soon reconciles the constitution to it. The mischief is, that in the climate of England it is difficult, during certain seasons, to keep up an increased temperature without prejudicially interfering with ventilation; for when great numbers of individuals are congregated together, that portion of the atmosphere which is essential to life is rapidly removed, and a gas evolved fatal to animal existence.

The proportion with which a room may be impregnated with this, may have no very visible immediate effects, yet it lowers the powers of life, and depresses the action of the heart; and thus adds to the physical declension under which the child of the factory labourer already suffers. Great numbers of mills have however been examined, in which these disadvantages are in a great measure done away with, by a system of ventilation and

M

cleanliness, adopted as far as is compatible with the nature
of the operations carried on in them ; and where the
amount of mischief resulting from the inhalation of
floating particles, or of deoxygenated air, is so small, as
to be worthy of little notice.*

Nothing appearing then in the condition of the labour,
considered *per se*, to which children are subjected, of an
actively† injurious character, as far as physical health is
concerned, the evils, if any, have their origin in causes
foreign to it,—and these are, first, its continuance, and
secondly, the prevention of all recreation and exercise
necessary for sustaining or repairing their already shat-
tered constitutions : and to these must be added the
moral effects of example, of independent earning and
appropriation of wages, the evils of which have already
been detailed.

· The continuance of labour for so many hours is the
one great physical agent for keeping up and increasing
the inconveniences resulting from depraved nutrition.
The whole burden, however, must not therefore be
thrown upon factory labour ; one half the mischief is done

---

* Nothing can more strongly mark the puerility which so often
disgraces the opinions of scientific men, than the stress which has
been laid upon the importance of a certain number of cubic feet
of space being devoted to each individual in mills. The space
(generally about 1200 feet) is more than enough, if ventilation is
well performed, and is ridiculously small if this is imperfect.

† " It must be admitted that factory children do not present the
same blooming, robust appearance as is witnessed among children
who labour in the open air ; but I question if they are not more,
exempt from acute diseases, and do not on an average suffer less
sickness than those who are regarded as having more healthy
employments. The average age at which the children of this district (Preston) enter the factories is ten years and two months."—
Report of Inspectors of Factories for 1834, *to the Home Secretary,*
pp. 52, 53.

long before the child is engaged in it, and even were the period in which it is engaged deferred, the home and habits, of which it is the victim, are not those materially to assist in its regeneration.

To avoid misconstruction, it is highly necesssary that the state of the child, preparatory to its being brought into the mill, should be correctly understood. To call out a number of children, and examine into their moral and bodily conditions, and to charge the whole of whatever is found bad in both or in either upon the mill directly (however truly it may be charged with it remotely), would be manifestly unjust. " Suum cuique tribuito," should be strictly observed; the evils are sufficient without adding any thing beyond what fairly and properly belong to the actual conditions of the mills.

Of late years a vast improvement has taken place in the internal economy of factories. In the first stages of the system, when mills and machines were small, ventilation imperfect, and night work common, serious injuries were inflicted upon the infantile workers.

It is beyond all question then, for it is abundantly *proved by physiological and pathological considerations,* that factory labour, continued for twelve or fourteen hours, is liable to produce certain distortions of the bony system in children, if there be previous want of healthy growth ; that it prevents proper and natural exercise; and that, in conjunction with a continuance of imperfect nurture, and want of domestic comforts, it keeps up an unhealthy condition of the digestive organs, making the body peculiarly prone to take on a variety of chronic diseases ; and that it checks growth, the necessary supplies being impaired.*

* The opinion of Dr. Baillie, one of the most enlightened and judicious physicians who have adorned the annals of British medi-

An inspection and admeasurement of 2000 children,
taken indiscriminately from several large establishments
ten years ago, strikingly verified the accuracy of the foregoing results deduced from reasoning upon the known
functions and operations of the body in a state of
health and disease. The children were stunted, pale,
flesh soft 'and flabby ; many with limbs bent, in most
the arch of the foot flattened ; several pigeon chested,
and with curvatures in the spinal column ; one hundred and forty had tender eyes, in a great majority the
bowels were said to be irregular, diarrhœa often existing, and ninety shewed decided marks of having sur-
vived severe rachitic affections.

In the early period of factory spinning distortion was
very common, from the lowness of the old water-
frames.

The employment of children in manufactories ought
not to be looked upon as an evil till the present moral
and domestic habits of the population are completely
reorganized. So long as home education is not found
for them, they are to some extent better situated when

cine, is coincident with the actual conditions as described above,
and is the more valuable, as having been entirely drawn from the
general operations of the animal economy.

" I cannot," he says, " say much from experience, but I can
say what appears to me likely to arise out of so much labour, from
general principles of the animal economy. I should say, in the
first place, that the growth of those children would be stunted—
that they would not arrive so rapidly at their full growth—that
they would not have the same degree of general strength—that it
is probable their digestion would not be so vigorous as in children
who are more in the open air, and less confined to labour—and
that they would probably be more liable to glandular swellings
than children who are bred differently."—*Evidence before Committee.*

engaged in light labour, and the labour generally is light which falls to their share.* The duration of mill labour, from the natural state of the body during growth, and where there is a previous want of healthy development, is too long.

There can be no question but that very considerable practical difficulties lie in the way of any extensive change as to the hours of labour,—difficulties on the part of the masters and the men equally. It is doubtful if any legislative interference can be effective; on the other hand, it is a question whether it may not materially injure the future prospects of the labourers, and accelerate a fate already too rapidly approaching them : still some modifications might be made to satisfy the claims of nature and humanity, contradistinguishing these from fanaticism and bigoted ignorance.

It can admit of little dispute, that by diminishing the length of time which the factory child now spends in the mill, some advantages would be gained by it physically; or, that the same advantages might be to some extent derived from periods of relaxations during the day. As it is, the perpetual necessity for attention prevents any thing like bodily repose, so that, although no labour, in the common meaning of the word, is undergone, fatigue necessarily results.

* " The labour is these mills is not perpetual labour—it is attention. The employment is not at all laborious—it is more a matter of attention than of labour."—*Evidence before Committee.*

" In those manufactories in which the time of work is not very long, where the children are not taken in at a very early age, and where the proprietors are men of enlarged minds, and possess some degree of benevolence, to induce them to look after the welfare of those from whom they derive their support and their wealth, the children are perhaps better off than in many other situations."— *Evidence before Committee.*

If any regulations tending to do away with some of
the evils attendant upon child labour were introduced,
and generally acted upon, it may be safely asserted, that
the man who would abolish it in large towns does not
understand the position in which children are there
placed : or, if he does, he suffers himself to be led away
by false notions of philanthropy, and is no friend to the
best interests of his species.   The interior economy of
mills has been so much improved as to remove most of
the obnoxious agents, which fell with such dreadful
severity upon the parish apprentices, who first became
their victims ; and there is nothing whatever in a well-
regulated mill directly injurious to life, save only the
length of time spent there, and its consequences.   The
real evil lies in the habits of the people themselves ;
 habits, it is very true, generated by the system of factory
labour: and one half the mischiefs suffered by the children
are inflicted upon them prior to their commencing work.

The influence of infant labour upon the mental faculties is a subject of less importance than is generally
imagined.   The children employed in mills exhibit the
peculiar intellectual traits which distinguish the town
child from that of a rural district. 'They are acute and
of quick intelligence—a circumstance arising from the
greater variety of objects brought under their notice
early in life, and to their being left to their own resources.   It is not, indeed, improbable that the exclusive attention which is required to one particular
employment, may, in some degree, limit and confine
the general capacity for acquiring diversified knowledge.
This is, however, by no means proved to be the case ;
neither if it were would it signify much, as this is a
species of knowledge which would not add to their
individual happiness.

Much has been said as to the cruelty and injuries supposed to be inflicted upon children in mills. There is, however, but little ground for the extravagant accusations which have been made on these heads. Children are punished by their employers in the factories for carelessness, and other faults, and now and then a hasty-tempered spinner may carry the punishment into actual violence. The masters are in very few cases to blame, the fault lying principally with the operative. A humane master of course attends to any flagrant act of oppression, and this is the best shield for the child. The general reports of the Factory Commissioners are tolerably satisfactory on this subject. Cases were indeed found of harsh treatment and over-working, in the old and small mills, and in the flax, woollen, and silk factories, but they are not *now* of very common occurrence ; neither are injuries so frequent as formerly, and as machinery improves, they will become less and less common.

The outcry raised regarding Infant Labour was one main cause of the Factories Regulation Act of 1833. This Act applies to all cotton, wool, flax, tow, hemp, and silk mills in which machinery is moved by steam or water power. Its enactments are as follows :—

No child can be employed at all before it is nine years old.

No child younger than eleven must work more than forty-eight hours in one week, or more than nine hours in any one day.

After the 1st of March, 1835, the same restriction applies to children under twelve, and after the 1st of March, 1836, to children under thirteen.

To prevent these restrictions being evaded, no child

must, on any pretence, remain more than nine hours a-day in any working apartment of the mill.

Persons under eighteen years of age must not work more than sixty-nine hours in a week, or twelve hours in a day ; nor at all between half-past eight o'clock at night and half-past five in the morning.

Children under nine may be employed in silk mills.

One hour and a half allowed for meals, exclusive of working hours.

Two whole holidays, and eight half-holidays, to be allowed to young persons annually.

Children prohibited working more than forty-eight hours per week must attend school· two hours every day. The master is not allowed to employ any child who has not a certificate of such school attendance from the teacher.

School to be chosen by parent, guardian, or in default of these, by the factory inspectors, who are appointed with very wide and loose powers to see the above enactments carried into effect.

Of this Bill it may be truly said that it is an absurdity, being founded upon the most singular ignorance of the interior economy of mills. This economy consists of a series of operations in which the child performs an essen--tial part. There is a mutual dependence of the entire labourers one upon the other ; and if the children who are employed principally by the spinner are dismissed, his work ceases, and the mill is at a stand still. The absurdity of the measure lies in the gradations, if we may so term it, which it appoints. Supposing that perjury and evasion fail in rendering the act nugatory, in what position do the masters stand ? That they must reduce their working hours to the lowest ·limit, eight hours per day, for the whole of their establishment; or that they must have relays of young hands to enable them to work full time ; or that they must dismiss all young persons under thirteen years of age. Every one of these alternatives would be attended with considerable loss and annoyance to the master, but would press far more heavily upon the labourers.

The following remarks of Dr. Ure on this point are perfectly just:—" The twenty-first clause of the Factories Regulation Bill is an act of despotism towards the trade, and of mock philanthropy towards the work-people who depend on trade for support. It requires every factory child, twelve years of age, to produce every Monday morning a certificate of having attended school for two hours at least in six days of the preceding week, on pain of dismissal from the mill in which he earns his livelihood. Against this absurd law strong remonstrances have been made by the real friends of the poor. Few mills, in fact, are situated near schools which are open at hours convenient for these busy children, namely, early in the morning and late in the evening, and therefore to make the requirements practicable, one or more factories should have a school or schools subservient to them, open at suitable times of the day. The school clauses exhibit an ingenious sample of legislative wisdom, for they have had the diametrically opposite effect of their avowed purpose. Instead of protecting and improving the condition of the children, the supposed victims of the mill-owners' avarice, they have deprived them of the means of subsistence, causing them to be turned adrift to sympathize with the listless progeny of the farm-labourer.

" The mill proprietor, after finding that this factory act, like its predecessors, was the fruitful parent of deceit and perjury to the young operatives and their guardians, and a law-trap to himself, has had no alternative but to dismiss from his works all children under twelve years of age—an event fraught with wide-spread privation. The children so discharged from their light and profitable labour, instead of receiving the education promised by Parliament, get none at all : they are thrown out of the warm spinning rooms upon the cold world, to exist by beggary or plunder—in idleness and vice."

This is the truth : but we would pause a moment to ask the writer how far the statement is in accordance with his previous account of the moral and saving habits of the parents of these children ? because, surely, if such were the fact, these parents would guard against their children sinking down into thieves and beggars. That they become such we know—a notable illustration of our description of the moral and social habits of the mill artisans.

" After the first of March, 1836, all children, even up to thirteen, will be in danger of being dismissed from factory employment, by a prospective ordinance, which, under the mask of philanthropy, will aggravate still more the hardships of the poor, and extremely embarrass, if not entirely stop, the conscientious manufacturer in his useful toil. This law will no doubt be evaded in many ways by the indignant artisans, whose families it tends to starve; and it will thus prove operative only for evil, by perverting their moral principles. A proprietor of a large factory in Manchester lately told me, that, on the first of March this (1835) year, having discharged thirty-five children as being under proper age, he was surprised to find that, within a week or two, the whole of them had resumed their work, under the sanction of legal surgical certificates, which the managing partner of the concern had no leisure to investigate, and could not reject."*

In other words, the operatives perjured themselves, and the master connived at it. It did not require the experience to be derived from this Bill to demonstrate *the low state of morals amongst these people; Hobhouse's Act had already shown, in the most vivid colours, what might be expected.* " In fact," says Dr. Ure, " the perjury of the witnesses placed an effectual barrier against conviction, and compelled the masters in Manchester to abandon all attempts to enforce by law the provisions of Hobhouse's Act with regard to the age of the children and hours of work."

Does this plain confession argue a moral population? We readily grant the stern necessity of the case, for it amounts to neither more nor less than this; that, by the change from the natural order of industry, the labour of the child supersedes that of its father, who, thus thrown into idleness and poverty, is ready to forswear himself, and lead his child to tell a deliberate lie that he may not starve. Is this a moral or satisfactory condition of the hundreds of thousands engaged in mill labour?

Dr. Ure's view of the restrictive clauses of the Factories Regulation Bill is, however, exceedingly narrow, and overlooks some of the most important considerations connected with them. One of them, and not the least is, the influence these restrictions will have upon the progress of mechanical development; this will be discussed in a subsequent chapter, remarking here only, that it affords a singular proof of the extensibility of this development. Another is, their effect upon the population of the manufacturing districts, if the plan contemplated by the masters of having two sets of chil-

* Philosophy of Manufactures, p. 406.

dren, for a time, be carried into general operation. This would, in the first place, produce considerable immigration to manufacturing towns, and swell enormously the amount of unemployed male and adult labour; and in the second, increase the dangers already threatening from this cause very materially.

There is no employment to be found for adult males; on the contrary, they are becoming daily more and more a clog in the way of the masters, and the hand loom, with its necessary companion, utter poverty, is alone open to them. The attempts made by the Poor Law Commissioners to encourage the depressed agriculturists to emigrate into the manufacturing districts, is at once strange and unaccountable, and can only serve to derange the present trembling balance which connects the human labourer to many mill processes, and to lower the value of labour generally, at a crisis when such a process will be dangerous to the prospects of that vast branch of industry dependent upon manufactures.

The Factories Regulation Act, then, is absurd in its details, complicated in its machinery, and worse than useless for the purposes aimed at. It is not founded on the reports of the commissioners appointed expressly for procuring information on which government might proceed, having been passed, to crown the absurdity of the entire proceedings, seven months before the returns were completed.

The only measures which can be brought to bear beneficially upon the labour of infants, and upon the general welfare of the operatives, would be the establishment of a well-organized system of national education, having schools for very young children, and a prohibition to the employment of children under twelve years of age. This is early enough for regular labour to be undertaken; and if the child has beèn properly attended to, morally and physically, the subsequent attendance at a Sunday school will furnish all the information it requires.

At this age, the labour imposed upon it in a modern and well-regulated factory will be innocuous, although not favourable to a full development of its physical powers, nor to a condition of high and robust health. After this period, if it is to work in the mill at all, it must become an integral part of the machinery of that mill, and as such must be subjected to the general economy regulating the whole. No interference can avail it, and should never be attempted. It is the steam engine that should be legislated for, and not the child who is its passive minister.

Another point which connects itself very naturally with infant labour, is female labour. The causes which have led to the substitution of female for male workers have been already explained.

The extent to which this substitution has been already carried is extraordinary. Thus there are, in the—

	Male.	Female.
Cotton factories in Lancashire and Cheshire ..	100	to 103
Cotton factories in Scotland	100	to 209
Flax factories in Leeds	100	to 147
Flax factories in Dundee and East Coast of Scotland	100	to 280

On this Table, Dr. Ure remarks, in his Appendix, " that factory females have in general much lower wages than males, and they have been pitied on this account with perhaps an injudicious sympathy, since the low price of their labour here tends to make household duties their most profitable as well as agreeable occupation, and prevents them from being tempted by the mill to abandon the care of their offspring at home. Thus Providence effects its purposes with a wisdom and efficacy which should repress the short-sighted presumption of human devices."

It would be well if this statement expressed the actual condition of the factory women, and if the partial disappearance of the sex, noticed when they reach their twenty-fifth or twenty-sixth year, could be accounted for so satisfactorily. It is true that at this age many are married, but it is not true that they devote themselves to domestic duties. They quit the factories, not voluntarily, but because accouchemens and other causes unfit them for the unvarying attendance required by the system of factory labour. They are compelled to have recourse to fustian cutting, hand-loom weaving, or some other less unbroken labour, when no longer engaged in mills.

If, as Dr. Ure states, and he states the truth, that the dismissal of a child from the mill necessarily sends it out a beggar or a thief, when its wages were certainly not more than 2s. 6d. per week, what is to become of a family, in which the earning of a wife, the most important item of their means of support, is cut off? The excess of female over male factory labourers, shows clearly enough, that providing they were unmarried, as Dr. Ure hints, they could not marry factory men, and therefore could not enjoy the advantages so glowingly painted as attending on factory earnings; besides, the liberally paid male operatives form a very small proportion of the whole.

No; factory women generally marry some one who has been a factory labourer, but who has been driven from this branch of industry because he grew to be a man, and who has since either sunk down into a hand-weaver, or been compelled to seek some other and more precarious trade. Hence, for the first few years after marriage, for they marry early, in order that children may result, they do labour in the mills universally, and it is not till circumstances interfere with the regularity of their attendance that they quit them.

In cases where they marry young men whilst engaged in the mills, both husband and wife continue their occupation as long as it is possible ; but unless the husband be engaged in the higher departments of mill-labour, he is displaced to make room for his child, or for a junior hand, whose wages are about one-tenth those of the skilled adult labourer, or of the labour of those hands who, by strict union, have hitherto compelled the master to pay high prices—namely, the spinners, dressers, &c. &c.

Dr. Jarrold, an old medical practitioner in Manchester, says of women—" Brought up to factories, that they can have no domestic habits, and are consequently inattentive to cleanliness. That they make wretched wives." We have already said the same thing, and it is too notorious to admit of question.*

* "The children run wild in the streets, their parents being often engaged in labour."—*Moral and Physical Condition of the Working Classes*, p. 70.

CHAPTER VII.

PHYSICAL CONDITION.

" ' WITH, civilisation and barbarism, food and clothing appear intimately connected. We should beforehand be induced to imagine that the most excellent development of every animated species would be effected, where all its wants were supplied, its powers all duly called forth, and all injurious and unpleasant circumstances least prevalent, and *vice versâ*. But experience teaches us that no change can by any means be brought about in an individual, and transmitted to his offspring. The causes of change in a species must therefore operate, not by altering the parents, but by disposing them to produce an offspring more or less different from themselves.' Such is Mr. Hunter's view of the question, and it is certainly confirmed by every fact. Uncivilized nations, exposed to the inclemency of the weather, supported by precarious and frequently unwholesome food, and having none of the distinguishing energies of their nature called forth, are almost invariably dark coloured and ugly, while those who enjoy the blessings of civilisation, that is, good food and covering, with mental cultivation and enjoyment, acquire, in the same proportion, the Caucasian characteristics."

" ' The different effects of the different degrees of civilisation,' says Dr. Smith, ' are most conspicuous in those countries in which the laws have made the most complete and permanent divisions of rank. An immense difference exists between the nobility and peasantry of France, Spain, Italy, and Germany. It is still more conspicuous in eastern countries, where a wide difference exists between the highest and lowest ranks of society. The naires, or nobles, of Calicut, in the East Indies, have, with the usual ignorance and precipitancy of travellers, been pronounced a different race from the populace, because the former, elevated by their rank, and devoted only to martial studies and achievements, are distinguished by that manly beauty and elevated stature, so frequently found with the profession of arms, especially when united with nobility of descent : the latter, poor and laborious, and exposed to hardships, without the spirit or the hope to better their condition, are much more deformed and diminutive in their persons, and in their complexion much more black.' ' In France,' says Buffon, ' you may distinguish by their aspect, not only the nobility from the peasantry, but the superior orders of the nobility from the inferior, these

from citizens, and those from the peasants.' " The
field slaves in America,' says Dr. Smith, ' are badly
clothed, fed, and lodged, and live in small tents on the
plantations, remote from the example and society of
their superiors.   Living by themselves, they retain
many of the customs and manners of their ancestors.
The domestic servants, on the other hand, who are kept
near the person, or employed in the family of their
masters, are treated with great lenity : their work is
light, they are fed and clothed like their superiors, they
see their manners, adopt their habits, and insensibly
receive the same ideas of elegance and beauty.   The
field slave is in consequence slow in changing the aspect
and figure of Africa.   The domestic servants have
advanced far before him in acquiring the agreeable and
regular features of civilized society.   The former are
frequently ill shaped—they preserve, in a great degree,
the African lip, and nose, and hair—their genius is dull,
and their countenance sleepy and stupid : the latter are
straight and well proportioned, their hair extended
to three, four, and sometimes even to six or eight
inches ; the size and shape of their mouth handsome,
their features regular, their capacity good, and their
looks animated.'"

   " ' The South-Sea islanders, who appear to be all of
one family, vary according to the degree of their cultivation.   The people of Otaheite and the Society Islands
are the most civilized and the most beautiful.   The
same superiority,' says Captain King, ' which is observable in the eeces, or nobles, throughout the other
islands, is found also here.   Those whom we saw were
without exception well formed, whereas the lower sort,
besides their general inferiority, are subject to all the

variety of make and figure that is seen in the populace of other countries.' "*

Food and clothing, then, are intimately connected with civilisation, and civilisation is intimately connected with personal appearance. The half-starved and ill-clothed negro, snatched from maritime provinces, utterly barbarous in his habits, and exchanging only one sort of slavery for another, has long since stamped the notion of ugliness upon all the coloured races of men. Bruce, Denham, Clapperton, Lander, and other travellers in the interior of Africa, give assurances that there are numerous tribes, and portions of tribes, possessing, in an eminent degree, bodily excellence, and exhibiting in their persons but few traces of the negro lip or nose, his monkey calf, or pointed shin-bone. Neither can these assertions be doubted, when it is remembered that they are described as having made some progress in the arts of life, and are distinguished into classes or castes. The Dahoman and Ashantee Caboceers, according to Bowditch and Norris, are in many points widely dissimilar from the inferior natives,—their personal appearance improving as they recede from the houseless and precarious condition of the rude African tribes.

The pastoral Caffres of Southern Africa Mr. Barrow describes as a remarkably well-built and handsome race of men ; they have made some advances in civilisation, and present as perfect a picture of patriarchal existence as can well be imagined.† In all these respects they

* Elliotson—Blumenbach's Physiology.
† " From the fertility of their soil, the abundance of their rivulets, and the pleasant situation of their craals, may probably arise that settled and contented turn of mind which in time of peace so remarkably distinguishes the Caffre. To him a neat little dwelling, solidly constructed in the centre of a corn-field,

offer a striking contrast to the Bosjesman, or Bushmen, who appear at some not very remote period to have derived their origin from the same source. The combined evidence of Barrow, Lichstenstein, Vaillant, Campbell, and Burchell, prove that the Bushmen are as ugly a race as any under the sun; leading a wandering life; frequently half-starved; then indulging ravenously, and to a most enormous extent, in eating—rivalling even the Esquimaux as to quantity; almost naked; and hunted by the colonists and their dependents. Their bodily form is but an index of their barbarism. There is, however, no reason to doubt but that if their wandering and predatory habits should, in course of time, yield to a more settled mode of life, it would be followed by a great improvement in their physical conformation.

Thus, then, it seems evident that barbarous habits, occasional want of food, bad clothing, one and all, produce bodily inferiority. The records of all nations prove this, where an absolute division into castes is in force; by nations still termed savage, yet having amongst them a superior and inferior order, whether of governors, priests, or warriors; by slaves imported, presenting no apparent social or bodily disparity, yet, in a few years, or in one or two generations, undergoing very decided modifications, when favourably placed for that purpose; by tribes inhabiting similar districts, and obviously tracing their origin to similar sources—the one becoming cultivators and men of settled habits, and quickly losing their coarseness of bodily form; the

that was once cultivated by his ancestors, is sufficient to claim the agreeable appellation of his country. The Caffres must certainly be acknowledged a more civilized people—their industry is more perceptible, and their acquaintance with some of the necessary arts of life greatly superior."— *Le Vaillant.*

other leading a doubtful and precarious existence, depending for support upon the uncertain products of the chase or plunder, and retaining all their aboriginal ugliness and peculiarities.

If it were necessary to bring forward as proofs other quotations from the historians of mankind, to substantiate the position, that the mill artisans, in consequence of their mode of life, must exhibit great inferiority in figure and personal proportion, they might be readily found. Wherever men are condemned to toil—wherever wide distinction of caste separates them from their superiors—wherever their manners and domestic habits are coarse and improvident—their bodies uniformly become stunted, ill-shaped, wanting elegance of contour, and that development and arrangement of parts constituting beauty. The universality of this truth needs no confirmation or illustration to those who have read or inquired into the subject, or whose observation has been exercised upon a comparison of bodily forms, infinitely varied as they are, in common society.

The population engaged in mill-manufactures, since the application of the steam engine has so assimilated and simplified their condition, offers an admirable field for examining how far external causes, aided by morals, can modify the physical proportions of man, and. how far this modification is likely to influence the offspring of parents thus changed, providing the same causes continue to operate through several successive generations.

The personal appearance of the domestic manufacturer is still well remembered by those whose memories carry them back to the days of quoit and cricket-playing—wakes—May-day revels—Christmas firesides, and a host of other *memorabilia*, now ranked but as things that were! Some faint traces of these by-gone times are still discoverable in the remoter rural districts : they are, however, only the " disjecta membra" of a large division of the community.

He was a robust and well-made man, reaching the average altitude of his race; clean-limbed, and with an arched instep; ruddy complexioned: his general contour rounded from the deposition of adipose matter, and from muscular development, possessing considerable physical power, and delighting in athletic sports. Not called into active and permanent labour till his frame was to some extent set, and his bony system perfected, he ran no danger of any shrinking or yielding in these parts; neither were his animal passions pushed into premature activity by high atmospheric temperature, aided in its exciting operation by vicious example at home and abroad. His offspring were, like himself, a chubby and rosy-faced set of urchins—healthy from their birth upward; tended by affectionate mothers, whose domestic occupations never interfered with their maternal duties. Permitted to range at will in the free and balmy air of heaven, their young minds inhaled a love of nature with their daily and hourly growth, while their social affections were fostered and directed under the eye and admonition of their parents.

The same ruddy and healthy appearance marked the whole household of the domestic manufacturer, as, at the present day, characterise the rural population of other countries enjoying moderate prosperity; they were, in fact, a strictly rural people, partly indeed engaged in the various processes of manufacture, but partly also in cultivating the soil as small farmers, either in their own right, or as leaseholders or yearly tenants of farms, averaging in extent from four to eight acres.

Their manners were, no doubt, coarse and rude, but their habits were a thousand times more moral and civilized than those of their descendants. This was owing very materially to their intercourse with their superiors, and by their living in immediate contact with them. They derived, in consequence, essential advantages from their example, which kept up a spirit of private and public decorum, quite at variance with open and avowed vice and profligacy. Hence their persons exhibited no traces of debilitating excesses ; their nerves were well strung ; their step elastic, and their feeling of existence buoyant and joyous. Their days were passed in sport or labour, as their necessities demanded, and their nights in deep and profound sleep, the result of active physical exertion.

The deterioration in personal appearance which has been brought about in the manufacturing population,* during the last thirty years, a period not extending over one generation, is singularly impressive, and fills the mind with contemplations of a very painful character. If hardship—if low wages—if an impossibility of acquiring the means to secure the necessaries of life, or of clothing fit for protection against the influences of a variable climate ; if one or all of these causes had been in operation, their effects might have been anticipated. But nothing of this sort has been in operation. On the contrary, with the exception of one particular class (hand-loom weavers) wages have been and are good, and more than amply sufficient to supply all that is wanted even for liberal support.

Any man who has stood at twelve o'clock at the

* The fact of this deterioration having occurred is familiar to the most partial observer. The opinion of the operatives themselves (worthless as it is) may be seen in Mr. Cowell's Report.

single narrow doorway, which serves as the place of
exit for the hands employed in the great town mills,
must have been struck with their appearance. Their
complexion sallow and pallid,* with a peculiar flatness
of feature, caused by the want of a proper quantity of
adipose substance to cushion out the cheeks. Their
stature low ; the average height of four hundred men,
measured at different times, and different places, being
five feet six inches. Their limbs slender, and playing
badly and ungracefully. A frequent bowing of the legs.
Great numbers of girls and women walking awkwardly.
Many have flat feet, accompanied with a down-tread,
differing very widely from the elasticity of action in the
foot and ancle attendant upon perfect formation. Hair
thin and straight; many of the men having but little
beard, a sprawling and wide action of the legs, and an appearance, taken as a whole, giving the world but " little
assurance of a man," or if so, " most sadly cheated of
his fair proportions." Beauty of face and form are
both lost in angularity, while the flesh is soft and flabby
to the touch, yielding no " living rebound" beneath
the finger. The hurry of this juncture brings out very
strongly all their manifold imperfections.

" It is," says Dr. Ure, " perfectly true that the Manchester people have a pallid appearance, but this, for
two reasons, is certainly not attributable to factory
labour ; first, because those who do not work in factories are equally pallid and unhealthy-looking with
those that do ; and the Sick Society returns show that
the physical condition of the latter is not inferior.

---

* Dr. Hawkins was greatly struck by the pale and delicate
appearance of factory operatives ; that of the hand-loom weavers
is perhaps equally striking, poverty and starvation having weighed
heavily upon them.

Secondly, because the health of those engaged in country cotton-factories, which generally work more hours than town ones, are not injured even in appearance. Many a blooming, cheerful countenance may be seen in Mr. Ashton's mill at Hyde. The apprentices in Mr. Greg's mill at Quarry Bank, near Welinslow, are equally well-looking."*

There are several errors in this statement, one of which is that the non-factory labourers are as pale and unhealthy-looking as the factory labourers; on the contrary, the out-door artisans of Manchester and its vicinity are a fresh-looking, healthy set of men, when of sober habits. It is in vain to refer the reader to Mr. Ashton or Mr. Greg's mills as examples of the excellence of factory labour; or rather the reference shows, joined to the admission of the squalid appearance of the mill-workers in general, how strong an impression the contrast produced upon Dr. Ure's mind. In the chapter devoted to the Health of the Mill Artisans will be found some further observations on this subject.

The opinion of Mr. Thackrah, of Leeds, a man accustomed to compare and estimate the appearances of operatives, is worth the report of a hundred casual visitors. "I stood in Oxford Road, Manchester, and observed the stream of operatives, as they left the mills at twelve o'clock. The children were almost universally ill-looking, small, sickly, barefoot, and ill-clad. Many *appeared* to be no older than seven. The men generally from sixteen to twenty-four, and none aged, were almost as pallid and thin as the children. The women were the most respectable in appearance ; but I saw no fresh,

* Philosophy of Manufactures, p. 399.

fine-looking individuals amongst them. **** Here I
saw, or I thought I saw, a degenerate race—human
beings stunted, enfeebled, and depraved."*

Mr. Thackrah remarks that this was a "mournful
spectacle." It may be witnessed every day at twelve
o'clock, near any of the outlets of the large factories in
Manchester. The conclusions of the Factory Commissioners and Factory Inspectors are based upon what
mill-labour and mill-operatives may possibly become—
not upon what they are, nor upon what they have
been.

Lancashire has long been celebrated for the beauty of
its women ; " the Lancashire witches " being a standing toast in all private and public convivialities. In the
higher and middle classes of society there are certainly
to be found many exquisite specimens of female loveli-
ness—many exceedingly graceful and feminine beings.
But these must not be sought for amongst the preco-
ciously-developed girls herding in town factories. Here, on
the contrary, will be found an absence of grace and feminine manners—a peculiar roughness of voice—a peculiarity owing to various causes, a principal one of which
is, too early sexual excitement, producing a state of
vocal organs closely resembling that of the male. Here
is no delicacy of figure, no elegance of tournure, and no
retiring bashfulness ; but in their place an awkward and
ungainly figure—limbs often badly moulded from imperfect nutrition — a bony frame-work, in some points
widely divergent from the line of womanly beauty—a
beauty founded upon utility—and a general aspect of
coarseness and a vulgarity of expression quite opposed

* On the Effects of Arts, Trades, &c. on Health and Longevity,
p. 147.

to all ideas of excellences in the moral and physical attributes of the sex.

Sir David Barry, in the Second Factory Commission Report, has given some highly-coloured details, drawn from inspecting a number of girls in the New Lanark Mills. He says, " A most extraordinary degree of attention is devoted in the New Lanark Mills to the education of the children of the workers, candidates for admission to employment in the mills. They are taught reading, writing, with the elements of geography, music, dancing, natural history, &c. in fine spacious rooms. I witnessed considerable proficiency in some of these branches, and saw eight young persons, from ten to thirteen, dance a quadrille in the very best style, under their dancing master. Employment in the mill is looked forward to by their children with much ambition as the reward of diligence in their studies. It is quite clear that Mr. Walker, the managing resident partner, devotes the kindest attention to his people—he is beloved by them all." *

Children thus nurtured have nothing to fear from factory labour; but they are nurtured so only in a few detached mills, superintended by men like Mr. Walker, who is deservedly beloved by his people. In these instances Sir David found many perfectly formed women, at which he candidly expresses his surprise, not being able to believe but that the frame must have suffered. It will never suffer in instances like the above-mentioned. The only remarkable part of Sir David's observations is, where he says, " There is one thing I feel convinced of from observation, that young persons, especially females, who have begun mill-work, at from ten to twelve, independently of their

* Second Factory Commission Report, p. 53, A. 3.

becoming much more expert artists, preserve their
health better, and possess sounder feet and legs at
twenty-five than those who have commenced from thirteen to sixteen and upwards."* This is singular even
on physiological grounds, and quite opposed to existing
realities in the mass of labourers. Such details as are
here given by Sir David do not bear upon the general
factory system; they are bright spots in it, indeed, but
at present nothing more.

There is something in the female figure strongly indicative of its aptitude for the performance of certain
functions peculiar to her sex. Child-bearing is one of
these, and the nourishment she is subsequently destined
to afford her offspring, another. The gait of women who
labour under any alteration in the axis of thigh-bone is
singular—a sort of waddle, an alternate side-long progression. This alteration is brought about by any
change in the direction or bearing of its socket, which is
seated in the pelvis—or by changes operated upon the
thigh-bone itself—or by changes in the direction of the
action of certain great muscles which have their origin
on the spine, pelvis, or adjacent parts,—all of which are
liable to be influenced more or less by the circumstances in which she spends her infant years, and by
that derangement in the primæ viæ, and their effects,
which her occupation and habits expose her to.† This
gait may be detected in great numbers of factory girls
and women, and is exceedingly ungraceful—ungraceful

* Second Factory Commission Report, p. 4.

† Instances of positive deformity are not very common *now* in
mill workers. Formerly many were absolutely crippled. Mr.
Tufnel's admirable Report, as well as that of Mr. Cowell, contains
the evidence given before the Factory Commissioners on this head.
It is, as in other, quite contradictory.

in itself, and still more so in its impression upon the mind, by the evidence it gives of certain alterations in form peculiarly unsexual.

The condition of those organs from which the child is to derive its first aliment is not less strikingly illustrative of their habits. Very early in life, from ten to fourteen years, the breasts are often found large and firm, and highly sensitive, whilst at a later period — at a period indeed when they should show the greatest activity and vital energy—when in fact they have children to support from them, they are soft, flaccid, pendulous, and very unirritable — both states giving the most decisive proofs of perversion in the usual functional adaptation of parts. That the physical energies of the factory women are injured is proved by the fact, that miscarriages are exceedingly common amongst them. We have had many opportunities of noting this circumstance both in girls engaged in silk and cotton mills. Parturition is not particularly difficult, but they are liable to copious discharges. Young women not unfrequently re-enter the mill within ten days after confinement.

The moral influence of woman upon man's character and domestic happiness, is mainly attributable to her natural and instinctive habits. Her love, her tenderness, her affectionate solicitude for his comfort and enjoyment, her devotedness, her unwearying care, her maternal fondnesses, her conjugal attractions, exercise a most ennobling impression upon his nature, and do more towards making him a good husband, a good father, and a useful citizen, than all the dogmas of political economy. But the factory woman cannot have this beneficial agency upon man's character. Her instincts, from their earliest birth, have been thwarted and pushed aside

from their proper channels ; they have had no field in
which they could be cultivated, no home where their
aberrations might have been checked, no legitimate
object on which her love could be lavished; on the
reverse,—her passions have been prematurely developed, her physical organization stimulated into
precocious activity, her social affections injured, whilst
her occupation has destroyed her home sympathies and
maternal affections.

Under these circumstances, woman is reduced to precisely the same grade in the social rank which she holds
in half civilized countries. She is no longer the companion of man, in the proper meaning of the term ; but
is a mere instrument of labour, and a creature for satisfying his grosser appetites. It is true, her condition
differs in some respects from that of her sex in countries
which are called savage ; she is not the slave, though
she is no longer the companion of man; neither is she
the subordinate being whose interests are esteemed so
secondary as to be totally unregarded ;—but, as far as
concerns the better portion of her attributes, she is upon
the same degraded level.

Nothing would tend more to elevate the moral
condition of the mill artisans, than the restoration of
woman to her proper social rank ; nothing would
exercise greater influence upon the form and growth of
her offspring, than her devotion to those womanly occupations which would render her a denizen of home.
No great step can be made till she is snatched from
unremitting toil, and made what Nature meant she
should be—the centre of a system of social delights.
Domestic avocations are those which are her peculiar
lot.

The poor man who suffers his wife to work, separated

from him and from home, is a bad calculator. It destroys domestic economy, without which no earnings are sufficient to render him comfortable; it produces separate interests and separate sets of feelings—they lose their mutual dependence upon each other—their offspring is suffered to starve or perish*—to become, even as a child, the imitator of their bad example—to have its frame permanently injured—to acquire bodily conditions which it must, in its turn, transmit to its own children, for, by their being thus early implanted, they become part and parcel of its very nature.

Another circumstance, which shows very decidedly the extent of moral and social degradation in the female sex among this population is this—that upwards of two-thirds of all the children born to this class in Manchester are brought into the world by the aid of public charity; that decent and proper pride, which should lead women to prepare for an event so interesting to her as a mother, is abolished; and, like the Indian squaw, she pursues her labour almost till the hour of her delivery, to abandon her tender and delicate infant, after the interval of a few days, to other and hireling hands, again to pursue her usual routine of work.†

* Mr. Roberton, a very competent authority, a surgeon in Manchester, stated to Dr. Hawkins, that out of every one hundred children born in that town, fifty-four died under five years. This is about 20 per cent. above the average.—*Factory Commission Report.*

† " The number of married women delivered annually by the Manchester Lying-in Charity, on the average of the last two years, is upwards of four thousand three hundred. Now it is well known to those conversant with statistics, that the number of baptisms occurring annually in England is in the proportion of one baptism to thirty-four inhabitants nearly. This is about the average for the kingdom. But the births are somewhat more numerous than

The mean appearance already acquired by the
inferior order of manufacturers—even though one
generation has scarcely passed away since the processes
in which it is engaged have been so essentially changed,
by the application of steam—is not the less remarkable
for its own sake, than as it arouses examination into the
probable alterations their descendants must undergo,
placed, as they inevitably must be, as still more abject
and passive slaves beneath machinery.

Physiological inquiries will serve to develop these

the baptisms, because some children are still-born, and others die
before they are baptized, and some are christened who are not
entered into the public registers. When we have made allowances
for these incidental circumstances, the annual rate of births in
Manchester may be stated to be, at the very highest, as one to
twenty-eight of the existing number of inhabitants—perhaps one
to thirty would be nearer the truth.

" The application of this, with the view of showing what proportion of the inhabitants produce the number of births, attended
annually by the Lying-in Charity, is a sufficiently simple process.
Taking it for granted that the four thousand three hundred births
before-mentioned as the average annual number that may be anticipated regularly to occur (and I am sorry to say that there is no
prospect of the number decreasing),* it follows that since the production of one birth annually requires twenty-eight inhabitants,
the production of four thousand three hundred births will require
one hundred and twenty-four thousand four hundred inhabitants ;
in other words, if we take the population of Manchester at two
hundred and twenty-seven thousand, we have thus considerably
more than half of the whole, who are in so destitute a condition,
or, if you will, so degraded, as to have their offspring brought into
the world by the aid of a public charity."—*Roberton on the Health,*
&c. p. 22.

---

* Mr. Roberton's anticipations have proved correct enough,
the present number of women delivered by the charity being very
near 5000.

changes to some extent; facts of observation are likewise in abundance,* and both prove, that a body worn
down and debilitated, although the generative faculty
may be uninjured as to intensity in either sex, cannot
give the necessary pabulum for the production of a vigorous offspring, endowed with active vitality. Bodily
deformity, bodily defect, or ugliness, may not, nay, in
general, will not be transmitted; but an universal
weakness and want of tone in all the organs, a disposition little able to resist disease, sufficiently prove, that
although the child has not inherited the peculiar failings
of its parents, yet it has, as an heir-loom, their weakened constitution, attended with all its liabilities to
physical inferiority. That parents so circumstanced
may occasionally produce fine and robust offspring,
goes for nothing; the mass must be depraved and
deteriorated, and how far this may extend no human
sagacity can foretel.

Nature may, indeed, raise up some countervailing
influence; her powers of modification and adaptation are
extraordinary, and their extent unknown; but neither
the extent nor effect of this can be predicated. Judging
from those things upon which judgment should alone be
formed, namely, an accurate examination into the existing
state of things, and the causes which have led to that
state, and proceeding upon the belief that similar causes
must be attended with similar results, it may be asserted
—that a race, possessing little muscular strength, and
fitted as labourers *only* to act in subservience to a more

* The lines of Horace are founded upon nature and her work-
ings—

      " Fortes creantur, fortibus et bonis;
       Est in juvencis, est in equis patrum
       Virtus."

powerful agent, will be the product of the present mode of manufacture.* Steam, which has been the principal instrument in rendering human force and skilled.labour † valueless, will, in time, be the means of generating a set of helpers, peculiarly its children, and doomed to depend entirely upon it for support.

The want of sympathy and proper intercourse between the master manufacturer and those employed by him is one very. powerful cause which tends to keep down their moral habits and their physical condition. Living, as the majority of the operatives do, in the midst of large towns, and incessantly occupied, they see nothing around them but beings like themselves. There is no middle class to which they can look for countenance and example. The family of their employer they either detest, and studiously avoid imitating its manners, however humbly or remotely, or they see so little of it, and are treated so coldly and harshly by it, that they nurse their own grossness in direct and avowed opposition to it.

The force of external circumstances in modifying bodily form, is seen acting forcibly in another and more pleasing point of view in the manufacturing districts. Many of the masters have raised themselves from the very humblest rank of labourers—in many instances after a family had been born to them in humility. These individuals with their families, at this period, of course possessed all the traits distinguishing their

* The difference of weight between boys engaged in factories, and those not engaged in factories, was found by Mr. Cowell, after an extensive series of examinations, to be 3 lb. on the average.— *Report*, p. 87.

† *Vide* chapter on the Influence of Machinery on the Value of Human Labour.

grade, both moral and physical. Change of condition, better food, better clothing, better housing, constant cleanliness, mental cultivation, the force of example in the higher order of society in which they are now placed, have gradually converted them into respectable, and even handsome families. The first remove places them still more favourably, and, *ceteris paribus*, they become elegant and intelligent females, and well-formed and robust men. They now resemble but slightly, in their general aspect and deportment, the class from which they have risen.

It has been said by Mr. Thackrah, in the work already quoted, that, " on conversing with a mill-owner, he urged the bad habits of the Manchester poor, and the wretchedness of their habitations, as a greater cause of debility and ill health than confinement in factories; and from him, as well as from other sources of information, it appears that the labouring classes in that town are more dissipated, worse fed, housed, and clothed, than those of the Yorkshire towns. Still, however, I feel convinced that, independently of moral and domestic vices, the long confinement in mills, the want of rest, the shameful reduction of the intervals for meals, and especially the premature working of children, greatly reduce health and vigour, and account for the wretched appearance of the operative." Some observations on this subject have already been made in the chapter devoted to Infant Labour.

CHAPTER VIII.

HEALTH—RATE OF MORTALITY.

———

———

THE health and physical condition of the mill artisans are dependent in a great degree upon the perversion of their moral and social habits, and upon the early age at which factory labour commences.

The fallaciousness of the opinions deduced from the existing state of the population, held by men of considerable information is very strikingly shown by one circumstance. Mr. M'Culloch, and other writers of his school, from observing the improvement in the value of human life, and coupling this with its known rate of increase, have come to the conclusion that the health and comfort of the people at large must have materially improved. Joining this fact to a consideration of the change which has been going on in the occupation of the people, namely, their rapid conversion into manufacturers—a conversion so rapid and extensive, that whilst the entire population has increased from 1801 to 1831 rather more than 50 per cent., in the manufacturing towns and districts this increase has advanced 140 per cent.—they suppose that the increased longevity of the whole must indicate that manufactures are decidedly healthy, notwithstanding since steam became the moving power, they were of necessity confined to particular localities for the convenience of fuel, and crowded into towns and populous districts for a supply of hands.*

According to Mr. M'Culloch, the average rate of mortality in 1780 was 1 in 40; 1810, 1 in 53; 1820, 1 in 57 ; and, it may be added, in 1833, 1 in 60.

Mr. Finlayson's calculations enabled Sir G. Blane to draw up the following Table, which shews very distinctly the comparative mortality at two distant periods. These calculations, it must never be forgotten, are to be looked upon rather as approximations to reality than reality itself ; still they are highly valuable :—

* *Vide* Mr. Senior's Lecture on Wages.

Ages.	Mean duration of life.		The increase of vitality is in the inverse ratio of 100 to
	In 1693.	In 1789.	
5	41.05	51.20	125
10	38.93	48.28	124
20	31.91	41.33	130
30	27.57	36.09	131
40	22.67	29.70	131
50	17.31	22.57	130
60	12.29	15.52	126
70	7.44	10.39	140

The changes which have taken place in the different classes of the community are equally curious, as shewing the progress of manufactures from 1811 to 1821. These changes have been reckoned upon ten thousand of each class.

	Agriculture.	Manufactures.	Unproductive as professions, &c.
England .	Decrease 168	Increase 175	Decrease 7
Wales . .	do. 555	do. 63	Increase 422
Scotland .	do. 211	do. 34	do. 178

Taking the counties separately, the increments of agriculturists are 1437, for trade and manufactures 10,658, a proportion seven times greater than the first.

According to Mr. Marshall's analysis of the population in 1821 and 1831, it appears that in the manufacturing districts it had increased one-fourth, and in the agricultural only one-eleventh.

The rapidity of increase in the mill population, and its extraordinary growth, compared to that engaged in agriculture, is indicated by the fact that, in 1801, it was calculated as six to five, in 1821 as eight to five, and in 1830 as two to one.

This transition, for so it must be called, is still farther elucidated by the following Table, drawn up from the Report of the Committee of the House of· Commons, on manufacturers' employments, in July 1830, and from the census of 1831.   In a period of thirty years, the following increase per cent. ·appears in the manufacturing towns :

Places.	1801 to 1811.	1811 to 1821.	1821 to 1831.	1801 to 1831. } Total.
Manchester ..	22	40	47	151
Glasgow	30	46	38	161
Liverpool	26	31	44	138
Nottingham ..	19	18	25	75
Birmingham..	16	24	33	90
Great Britain .	14.2	15.7	15.5	52.5

The population of Lancashire, ·which is the great centre of the cotton trade, in 1700 was 166,200; in 1750, 297,400 ; in 1801, 672,731; in 1811, 828,309; in 1821, 1,052,859 ; in 1831, 1,335,800.

When the increase is compared with that of an agricultural country through the same periods, the disparity will be strikingly seen.   Norfolk, for example, in 1700, 210,000; in 1750, 215,000; in 1801, 273,371 ; in 1811, 291,999 ; in 1821, 344,368; in 1831, 390,000; an increase of one and three-fourths; whilst Lancashire in the same period has added to its population ninefold.

These details are amply sufficient to shew the rapid growth of the population, engaged in mill manufactures when compared with the general increase of the inhabitants of the kingdom at large, and with that division more immediately connected with agriculture. The numerical disproportion which is steadily progressing shews very clearly, when joined to the diminished rate of mortality evidenced by the general increase, that there can be nothing in the processes of manufacture necessarily destructive of human life. On the contrary, it may be asserted that the improvement in its average duration is intimately dependent upon the conversion of the bulk of the population from agriculturists to manufacturers.

Paradoxical as it may sound, it by no means follows that because the duration of life is extended the people are a more salubrious race than their forefathers, whose lives averaged hardly 1,35. It is indeed true, that many of the fatal diseases which formerly at certain times nearly depopulated whole provinces, are no longer in active and extensive operation : plague, sweating sickness, petechial fevers, small-pox, the scourges which, during their periodical visitations, destroyed hundreds of thousands, are themselves gone to the " tomb of the Capulets."

This salutary change has been brought about not by improvement in the art of medicine—though very great and very admirable discoveries have been made, and, above all, the treatment of disease has been much simplified and become more rational,—but has been in a great degree produced by the alteration which has been gradually going on in the habits of the people, and their modes of living. The rush-covered floor, generally unflagged, a receptacle for the filth of weeks —the animal diet, the ale drinking, the popular sports and seasonal celebrations, each in their way induced a state of health unfavourable to longevity. The narrow and crowded streets, the small and low rooms, with their contracted windows and thick walls, nearly dark and badly ventilated, the want of proper drainage, and half occupation, were all predisposing causes for the generation or propagation of mischievous contagions.

War, famine, want of medical aid amongst the poor, were other abundant sources of destruction.

Notwithstanding these drawbacks, the population of Great Britain enjoyed much better health than it does at the present period, and this too notwithstanding the diminished rate of mortality. Taken as individuals, they were more robust, fuller of organic activity, enjoyed in much higher degree the feelings of existence ; but, in consequence, their diseases were of a much more acute character, and infinitely more fatal in their tendency.

Health may be defined that condition of the body in which all its functions or operations go on without exciting uneasiness. Nature no doubt meant, that as far as mere existence is concerned—that is, that every thing connected with the taking of food, and its necessary changes, constituting nutrition, and every thing connected with sensation, the link which binds man to the material world around him,—should be a source of pleasurable feelings, or, at all events, that it should be unattended by pain ; were it otherwise, mankind would be stretched upon the rack of its own sensibilities. Whatever produces an opposite state of things must be looked upon as causative of disease, or that condition of body, in which some of its functions are so far deranged as to interfere with personal comfort, inducing uneasiness or pain, or proceeding farther, and deranging and disordering the action of parts, so as to interfere with the operations essential to life, and, in the end, producing its extinction.

The rate of mortality among savage tribes, and in states just emerging from barbarism, is universally high ; one in thirty, as far as data can be collected, being the average. The health of individuals composing these tribes or states is nevertheless, according to all travellers, exceedingly vigorous, and their frame generally robust, indicated by the great fatigue they are capable of enduring, the severe wounds from which they rapidly recover, the rarity of chronic diseases amongst them, and the few decrepid and premature old men who burden their huts or wigwams. Infanticide and voluntary abortion, neglect in the early periods of life, the little estimation in which female children are held, and the want of remedial means of even doubtful efficacy, destroy vast numbers shortly after birth.

A great deal is often said as to the hardihood of the Indian mother, and the vigorous nature of her offspring, evidenced by her easy delivery, generally unassisted and uncared for, and from the circumstance of her slinging her infant on her back, and almost immediately joining the march, or pursuing her household or field labour; but if a list of children who perish from want of proper attention could be obtained, it would present a frightful picture of infantile mortality.*

The habits of women in civilized countries are repugnant to the simple forms of savage life; and in most cases, the infant is tenderly nurtured, and, in consequence, vast numbers are reared, which, under a different regime, must have inevitably perished; and this is one very important item in the account of the comparative mortality in the two conditions. Again, the adult male population in savage nations is seldom at peace—war being the maximum of their animal existence and happiness. This is especially destructive, by cutting off in their prime the very flower of the men,

* *Vide* James's Expedition to the Rocky Mountains; Humboldt's Travels; Cruze's New Zealand; Dobrizhoffer; Collin's New South Wales; Franklin's First and Second Journeys; Parry's Voyages; Vaillant, Bruce, &c. &c.

and laying the remainder of the tribe open to exter-
minating aggression. It is, indeed, rare to find an adult
labouring under sickness, nine-tenths being carried off
either by war or accidents in the chase, or falling victims
to acute inflammatory disease. Famine is another
powerful agent in the destruction of tribes, whose existence depends chiefly upon the produce of hunting or
fishing, or upon the imperfect cultivation of a very
limited portion of ground; and this again exposes them
to contagious or epidemic diseases, which often sweep
away a whole people. The rate of health is, however,
high, and their bodily vigour well known to all inquirers,
frequently, indeed, presenting splendid examples of
almost animal perfection.

The condition of man in a state of civilisation differs
of course very widely in some of these particulars. He
is better lodged, better clothed, and exposed to fewer
and less important variations. In the agricultural districts, where labour is moderate and food abundant and
nutritious, the labourer has, in many points, a bodily
constitution closely resembling that of the savage. He
possesses great physical development, high health,
uninfluenced by intellectual irritability, and is, consequently, open to the attack of acute diseases, which
soon destroy him when brought under their influence.

Fevers, inflammations in important viscera, resulting
from deranged circulation in a system of blood-vessels,
gorged with nutritive fluids, are rapidly fatal, without
the most prompt and energetic measures for their relief,
and which he is usually unfavourably placed for obtaining. An examination of the lists of patients of a
country practitioner, in a district exclusively agricultural,
will verify the correctness of these observations; the
majority of deaths resulting from inflammation of the

chest, head, and abdominal or pelvic viscera, or the consequence of accidental violence, and exhibiting very few chronic diseases, except the anomalous ones amongst females.

Thus the state of health is high in agricultural districts, and amongst savage and semi-barbarous tribes. It is, indeed, very common to hear individuals, so circumstanced, declare that they have never known a day's sickness, or been plagued with ache or pain, when a rapid disease seizes them, and their vigorous health and great vascular activity become the agents of their destruction.

In comparing this state of things with the correspondent ones in manufacturing towns and districts, a very striking contrast is observed. In the former case, it may be truly said that life is physical enjoyment, and disease hasty death; in the latter, that life is one long disease, and death the result of physical exhaustion.

The population crowded into the large manufacturing towns, which have sprung into being almost with the rapidity of Aladdin's palace, and where their growth has preceded all efficient police regulations, is exposed to many causes tending very powerfully to depress its vital activity. Unpaved and unsewered streets, ricketty houses, huddled into heaps, undrained, unprovided with needful conveniences, badly ventilated, and crowded with inmates; the habits of the population itself, its improvidence, its neglect of domestic comforts, its indulgence in dram-drinking, its general immorality, its thin and innutritious diet; and these, joined to the peculiarity of their labour, continued unremittingly for twelve or fourteen hours, cooped up in a heated atmosphere, and debarred from the cheering influences of the green face of nature, and of fresh air ; and, finally, deprived of all recreation in ,open and salubrious situations—all these are agents for lowering the tone of the system, and produce a series of diseases widely dissimilar from that which has been explained as proving so destructive to a population placed under opposite conditions.

In these towns disease generally assumes a' chronic type ; its progress is slow, and often interferes but little with the proper functional actions which are essential to life. Neither, in many instances, does it, of necessity, shorten its duration ; but rather, by keeping the standard of vital energy somewhat below par, it abstracts the system from the impression of more fatal affections, which kill by disturbing the circulation. To illustrate this, the following Table, including 5833 patients, who came under the care of one medical gentleman attached to the Manchester Infirmary, has been drawn, specifying the nature of the diseases in as simple a manner as possible. These cases occurred in the four years from 1826 to 1830.

Inflammation of the Brain, &c.	6	Common Catarrhal Fever (Colds)	550
Inflammation of the Tonsils, &c.	41	Measles	8
Inflammation of the Bronchiæ, &c.	31	Scarlet Fever	24
		Small Pox	19
Pleurisy, &c. &c.	80	Chicken Pox	2
Affections of the Liver, &c.	32	Erysipelas	26
		Purpura	4
Inflammation of the Bowels, &c.	26	Nettle Rash, &c.	47
		Simple Cough	640
Inflammation of Bladder, &c.	17	Hooping Cough	21
		Asthma and Difficult Breathing	297
Rheumatism	569	Loss of Voice, &c.	8
Intermittent Fevers	47	Consumption	228
Remittent Fevers	11	Secondary Syphilis	48
Common continued Fever	861	Bronchocele	5

Dentition	5	Apoplexy	1
Abortus	1	Paralysis	50
Scrofula, common . . .	18	Epilepsy	25
Hæmorrhages	62	Hysteria	20
Dyspepsia, &c.	203	Chorea	27
Jaundice	19	Convulsion (Children) .	3
Cholera	45	Palpitation	12
Diarrhœa	191	Anginæ Pectoris . . .	1
Dysentery	323	Nervous Pains	26
Constipation	755	Diabetes	4
Colic	72	Ischuria	8
Verminatio	44	Dropsies	110
Hemorrhoids	15	Amenorrhœa, &c. . . .	47
Hypochondriasis . . .	28	Leucorrhœa, &c. . . .	14
Headaches	51	Poison	1

This singular Table very clearly and satisfactorily shows the prevailing character of diseases amongst the operative population, medically considered. The great majority of these are compatible with a very extended life; few are fatal of themselves, and still fewer with the aid which is liberally afforded them. The acute diseases are limited in number when compared to the whole; and this is the more worthy of notice, since they are precisely those which are the most likely to come under the observation of the medical officers attached to this admirable institution. It will be remarked that the cases of dyspepsia, constipation, and other affections dependent on derangement of the digestive apparatus, are more than one-third of the entire cases. This most distinctly indicates the vast amount of these peculiar derangements; for great as their number is in this one Table, they must have been extreme cases to bring them under notice. Another peculiarity distinguishing the list is, that one-fifth of the number is made up of coughs, &c., while scrofula and consumption, in its varied forms, are exceedingly limited.

The number of patients annually receiving advice and medical assistance at the various munificent charitable institutions in the metropolis of the manufacturing world,* will afford another valuable document to estimate the rate of health enjoyed by the community ; all, however, that are relieved here are not of the class of operative manufacturers. The number of individuals resorting to these charities cannot be less than 30,000 per annum,† an immense proportion out of a population of 240,000. There are, in addition to these, 133 surgeons, 26 physicians, 76 druggists and apothecaries, making a total of 235, all and each of whom procure a livelihood by ministering to the ailments of the different classes of society. Besides these there are a host of quacks, at all times a flourishing order, sellers of patent medicine to a great amount annually ; those too who adhere to domestic medicine, and lastly, and by no means a small item, the numbers who resort to many physicians and younger surgeons for gratuitous advice, perhaps not less than 2,000 in the year. To this must be also added the female patients of the Lying-in Hospital, amounting, at the present period, to 5,000 more, who are supplied with medicine for diseases incident to gestation, accouchement, and subsequent recovery ; also their infants till arrived at a certain age. Taking all these together, it may be inferred, very safely, that 3-4ths of the entire population require medical aid annually ; a vast proportion certainly, and in all probability greater than what exists in other large towns

* Manchester.

† In 1831, patients admitted at the Royal Infirmary, 21,196; House of Recovery, 472 ; Ardwick and Ancoat's Dispensary, 3,163 ; Workhouse, 2,100; Children's Dispensary, 1,500; Lock and Eye Institutions, 1500 ? Chorlton and Hulme Dispensaries, 1,000 ?

more favourably placed in some respects than Manchester.*

It might be supposed, in looking at this formidable list of disease, with the number of charities, and the array of medical men devoted to its alleviation, that death would sweep away a great proportion of a people possessed of so little physical energy; that, consequently, manufactures, with their necessary crowding together of men in towns and mills, would be singularly injurious to the average duration of human life. To some extent, doubtless, this is so, but a little examination will show the fallacy of judging of this from the state of health enjoyed or suffered by communities.

The very imperfect registries of births and deaths—so generally complained of in Great Britain—exist in full force in the manufacturing districts. It is, indeed, utterly impossible to form any estimate even approaching to accuracy as to the rate of mortality in any given amount of population. The increase depends, very materially, upon immigration from surrounding neighbourhoods, to

* If a judgment may be formed of the number of sick from the number of medical men, Manchester is very unfavourably placed in this respect; though the criterion is far from being a fair one. Taking the population of London at 1,200,000, in 1821—

There were Physicians . . . . 174 or 1 to 7,000
Surgeons . . . . . 1,000 or 1 to 1,200
General Practitioners 2,000 or 1 to 600
Druggists, &c. . . . 300 or 1 to 4,000

Paris at 800,000, in 1821—
Surgeons . . . . 128 or 1 to 6,000
Physicians . . . . 600 or 1 to 1,300
General Practitioners 180 or 1 to 4,450

London Total 3,474, or 1 Medical Man to every 345 inhab.
Paris . . . 1,310, or 1 . . . . 900 ——
Manchester . 235, or 1 . . . . 121-3 inha-
[bitants, in 1831.

which again many of those who die are removed for
interment.   Great numbers of interments take place in
the towns from the out-townships, so that the registries
which do exist exhibit burials only, without any particular
specification which can be depended upon.

The registries of baptisms, as data for births in a particular town or locality, are no guide whatever, looked
at generally; a very great proportion of the baptisms
at the established churches, where alone any tolerable
register is kept, being from out districts.   The chief
difficulty, however, lies in the circumstance of the majority of the inhabitants engaged in manufactures being
dissenters; and from the fact, which is much to be
regretted, that amongst them, as a body, it is out of the
question to collect satisfactory statistical details.

Again, immense numbers of the children born to
parents in the lowest grades of society are never baptized at all, and if these perish, they are buried in the
free burial grounds without the slightest attention to
registration.   The population, too, is an exceedingly
fluctuating one, differing widely from that in agricultural
districts, and presenting insuperable obstacles to the
collection of accurate details.   When all these things are
taken into consideration, it must be quite obvious that
with so many sources of error in the way of partial
examination, it will be safer to adhere to the general
rate of mortality for the whole kingdom, which can be
ascertained with considerable accuracy, and establish
deductions taken from that.

It has been universally asserted that the mortality,
in counties largely engaged in manufactures, was much
higher than in agricultural counties.   The following
Table shows the generally received opinion upon this
subject:—

Manufacturing Counties.	Deaths to population.	Agricultural Counties.	Deaths to population.	Wales.	Deaths to population.
Middlesex .	47	Sussex . .	72	Anglesey. .	83
Chester . .	55	Monmouth .	70	Brecon . .	67
Lancashire .	55	Gloucester .	64	Cardigan. .	70
Yorkshire .	60	Suffolk . .	67	Pembroke .	83
Stafford . .	56	Wilts . . .	66	Carnarvon .	69
Warwickshire	52	Hereford. .	63	Glamorgan .	69
Average . .	53		67		73

This Table, which has been selected in consequence of having been drawn up for a very opposite purpose, and which gives the extremes, might at once seem decisive as to the question of mortality. When fairly explained, its disproportionate results will be materially changed.

In the agricultural counties, as it has been before remarked, the population is a fixed one, and, generally speaking, one attached to the Church, and exceedingly scrupulous in every thing relating to deaths and baptisms. The following Table will verify this:—

Manufacturing Counties.	Established Churches.	Dissenting Congregations.	Agricultural Counties.	Established Churches.	Dissenting Congregations.
Middlesex .	233	289	Sussex . . .	300	87
Chester . .	145	153	Monmouth .	118	72
Lancashire .	287	504	Gloucester .	290	117
Yorkshire. .	809	1,019	Suffolk . . .	486	132
Stafford . .	178	213	Wilts . . .	274	129
Warwick . .	209	108	Hereford . .	201	49
	1,861	2,286		1,669	586

Nor is the numerical disproportion all that must be borne in mind in carrying on the comparison. In the

manufacturing counties and towns, the dissenters' con-
gregations are often more numerous than those of the
Established Church, whilst in the agricultural counties
they are generally very small, and placed in remote
situations.

This single fact of the difference existing in the religious forms between the agriculturist and the mill artisans will show how much more accurate are the means
for ascertaining the particular condition of the one over
those of the other, and will explain one cause why all the
tables of mortality exhibit so great a preponderance in
favour of the agriculturist, greatly indeed above what in
truth belongs to him.

It is not denied that the rate of mortality is higher in
towns and manufactories, but the disparity is less than
is generally believed. The immigrations which are
continually going on from the agricultural districts to
the manufacturing ones, consist of those families which
would be precisely the parties to swell the bill of mortality in their own parishes, and they are little likely to
improve that of the situation in which they settle themselves. These families are generally those that have
numerous children, the parents of which have no means
of supporting them by agricultural labour. These therefore appear in the lists of births, but no further.

Again, the extensive immigrations into these districts
are uniformly driven there by want, and often suffer very
severe privations before they can obtain work ;—many of
them perish in consequence, especially the children, from
the change of locality, and hence swell enormously the
deaths in the towns ; but these have nothing to do with
the fixed population. Farther still, great numbers of these
families bring with them the older members, who have
hitherto lived in open and healthy situations, favourable

for the prolongation of life, but who sink at once beneath
the depressing influence of their new abodes. When
these several drawbacks are taken into account, the mean
mortality naturally incident to manufacturing districts
will be considerably lowered, for it would be a manifest
injustice to load these with the imputation of a destruction which is perfectly foreign to them. But still the
mortality will not be brought down to that in agricultural districts, in which it has been shown the elements for
fatal disease are much more rife, and where consequently
a rate of death should be exhibited according to this mode
of viewing the question as high, if not higher, than in
the opposite case. This remains to be explained.

In that portion of this work which has been devoted
to the examination of the social and domestic conditions
of the mill artisans, it has been demonstrated how
closely in some respects these approximate to the
modes of life in savage and half civilized states or
tribes; and in a previous portion of the present chapter
it has been said, that amongst people so situated, one
great cause of the excessive contraction in the average
duration of life, was to be found in the number of infants
who perished shortly after birth, and in the prevalence of
infanticide and voluntary abortion.

It has been stated that the majority of children delivered in Manchester, the offspring of the poor, are brought
into the world by the aid of public charity; that these
children are abandoned by their mothers in a few days
after birth to the care of strangers; that they are of
necessity badly attended to, badly fed, exposed to cold,
or are crammed with patent medicines or dosed with gin;
and the consequences are, that more than one-half of all
children born to the lower class perish before they have
completed their fifth year. This appears upon the face

of the bills of mortality, and their imperfection has been pointed out. In this case they only serve as an index to the enormous extent of infantile mortality—an extent equal, if not greater, than what exists in the most uncivilized nation on the face of the globe. This too, when compared with the average number of deaths before ten, explains at once one reason why the general rate of mortality is so high in these situations.

Manufactures since absorbed into mills have also the inevitable effect of bringing men together in masses, and hence the districts where they chiefly prevail may be looked upon as one vast town ; and this is another cause of the increase of mortality, and one too which, *de facto,* has nothing to do with the town being a manufacturing one. The rate of mortality, as far as can be ascertained, is about 1 to 35 to Manchester ; and though this at first sight appears excessive, yet, when compared to other great towns, it ceases to be remarkable.*

* From a parliamentary paper, containing a return of the number of burials occurring annually in Manchester, from 1821 to 1830, and returns obtained by the Board of Health, the following Table has been constructed .—

Year.	Interments of Churchmen.	Interments of Dissenters.	Total of interments.	Population.	Rate of Mortality.	
1821	1,561	1,726	3,287	152,683	46.45	
1822	1,285	1,044	2,329	156,663	67.223	
1823	1,585	3,230	4,815	160,664	33.36	mean
1824	1,428	3,219	4,647	166,117	35.74	rate;
1825	1,398	3,539	4,928	173,083	35.12	35.22
1826	1,548	3,804	5,352	180,052	33.64	
1827	1,604	3,235	4,839	186,462	38.53	
1828	1,615	4,106	5,721	192,874	33.73	
1829	1,479	3,719	5,198	201,691	38.80	
1830	1,590	4,383	5,973	212.913	35.64	
1831			6,736	224,143	33.27	

-This Table shews, too, very distinctly, the preponderance of Dissenters numerically, which is even considerably greater than the proportion it exhibits.

In Paris it is as 1 to 32 ; in London, 1 to 34 ; in Bir-
mingham, 1 to 40.

In making these calculations, and in reasoning upon
them, it must never be forgotten that, from the rapid
growth of the manufacturing towns, and from the fluctuating and uncertain nature of their population, they
have been built without the slightest regard to health
or convenience ; and the account given in Chapter III.
will show in how lamentable a condition Manchester was
found in 1832, in every thing having reference to the
health, decency, or comfort of its inhabitants.

When these various concurrent causes, adding to the
mean mortality of manufacturing counties and towns,
are taken into due consideration, and proper weight
attached to them, an explanation is afforded why, in all
tables of increase and decrease of population, these
counties always seem very unfavourably placed ; but
these concurrent causes have most clearly nothing whatever to do with manufactures as an occupation, and
their influence upon health and mortality.

The details in the beginning of this chapter have
shown, that during the last fifty years the entire population has been undergoing a rapid conversion from
an agricultural to a manufacturing character, or, more
correctly speaking, that mill labour has superseded
domestic manufacture : that in 1800, it was calculated
that manufacturers, strictly so called, were, to agriculturists, or mixed labourers, partly manufacturers and
partly husbandmen, as 6 to 5 ; in 1825, 8 to 5 ; and in
1830, as 2 to 1 : that if this examination is carried farther
back, the tables are turned, and agriculturists have the
numerical majority. Beginning in 1780, they were about
equal ; 1760, 6 to 5 ; 1740, 8 to 5 ; 1700, 2 to 1 ; and
so on, till the great body of the inhabitants were exclusively devoted to agriculture : that at the period

when this was the condition of society, the average mortality was fully 1 in 35; in 1780, when manufactures had received their first great impulse, 1 in 40; in 1810, when the bulk of the population was engaged in them, 1 in 52; in 1820, 1 in 57; and in 1830, 1 in 60. Hence it appears that during the transition of employment, the mean duration of life has been steadily improving, and that at the present time its value is double to what it was in 1700. How manifestly unjust—how manifestly absurd, to declare that manufactures are injurious to human life! On the contrary, it may be said that, were the population a fixed one, it would show a rate of mortality lighter than that in agricultural counties; although the health and physical vigour of the mill artisans are so greatly inferior to those of the husbandmen, that they may be said to labour under constant illness.

In thus speaking, it must be borne in mind that no account is taken of an immense body of farm manufacturers. This observation should be carefully remembered in connexion with the whole of this chapter.

As a particular example of the diminution of mortality, Leeds may be quoted. In 1801 the population of the township was 30,669. At that period there were few manufactories established, and the annual burials were 941, giving a mortality of 1 in $32\frac{1}{2}$. In 1831 the population amounted to 71,602, of which number nearly 9,000 are engaged in manufacture, chiefly woollen and flax, and the mortality has been reduced to 1 in $41\frac{1}{2}$.

CHAPTER IX.

FACTORY LABOUR IN GENERAL—PECULIAR DISEASES, &c.

Wages—Bodily Labour -- Attention — Temperature — Effects of
Heat—Vegetable and Animal Decomposition—Difference of
these upon Health—Effect of continued Labour in high Tem-
peratures—Smell of Oil, &c.—Inhalation of Dust—Knife
Grinders, &c.—Dust in Cotton Spinning—Effects of Breathing
—Does it produce Organic Disease ?—Dust proceeding from
Filing of Steel—Polishing Marble, and its Difference from
Cotton Flue—Habit--Bronchitis—Comparison of Mortality
between Weavers and Spinners—Error of the received Opinion as to the Injurious Effects of this Dust—De-oxygenation
of the Atmospheric Air in Mills—Production of Carbonic Acid
Gas—Qualities of the Gas, and the Consequences of Breathing it
—Its Specific Gravity, &c.—Change of Temperature—Summary
of their Conditions—Scrofula--Indigestion--Fever—Consumption, &c. &c.

BEFORE proceeding to examine the diseases to which
the manufacturing population are peculiarly exposed, it
will be useful to take a survey of factory labour in
general, and the conditions (if any) which render it so
noxious to health, as is universally imagined.

The persons engaged in cotton mills earn much
higher wages* than most other classes of labourers.

* Bricksetters, builders, joiners, painters, &c. &c., earn, it is
true, higher wages per day, and their labour never exceeds ten
working hours. A day's wages for these men may, as an ave-

Spinners of fine yarn can earn 25s. to 30s. per week ;
coarse spinners, chiefly women, 18s. to 21s. ; children of
nine years of age, and upwards, get from 3s. to 4s. 6d. ;
weavers, chiefly young women and girls, 10s. to 16s. ;
and various other rates of wages, none below 3s., are
paid to the batters, pickers, carders, stretchers, doublers,
reelers, makers-up, warpers, winders, &c., which form
the complement of workers in the mills, as at present
constituted. The average rate of wages for each individual may be fixed at 10s. per week ; this, of course,
includes the children, who in all instances form a great
proportion of the hands. This rate of payment is very
nearly the same as that which was obtained in 1816.
The usual hours of labour are from five o'clock in the
morning to seven o'clock in the evening, half an hour
being allowed for breakfast, one hour for dinner, and
half an hour in the afternoon. The time of labour has
also undergone very little change during the last twenty-
six years.

With respect to the amount of bodily labour gone
through by the operatives — generally speaking it is
exceedingly small, the steam engine doing the work. The
labour of spinners and stretchers certainly is fatiguing
at times, and from its length, twelve entire hours, it
is necessarily accompanied by great exhaustion. In these
processes the 'hands are hardly an instant at rest, except
whilst their mules are doffing, in which they sometimes
assist : and however hardy or robust a man may be, this
incessant exertion is overpowering. But in all other
cases, as in the carders, rovers, winders, piecers, weavers,

rage, be stated at four shillings. The great drawback is, that the
demand for their labour is fluctuating and uncertain, and at some
periods of the year they are in complete idleness. The manufacturer's employment is invariable.

&c., very little manual labour is required—none indeed worth speaking of. The only fatigue suffered is that brought on by the necessity for continued attention—a fatigue as injurious to health as that induced by physical exertion, if not excessive.

The mean temperature in the factories may be taken at 70° Fahrenheit. In dressing and finishing, a much higher temperature is necessary in the present mode of going through these operations. It is, however, likely that certain changes will be introduced, very shortly, which will very considerably modify this. Inquiries amongst the dressers have shown that, as a body, they are by no means unhealthy when their habits are moderately regular. They earn excellent wages, perspire during their work very copiously, and in place of supplying this waste by proper food, drink largely, a fact quite sufficient to account for their occasional illnesses and general emaciated appearance. Temperature in itself is in no wise injurious to health, provided it is not joined with close and imperfectly ventilated situations.*

The difficulty in the mills has always been the keeping up the requisite degrees of heat, with a free admission of fresh air; and some years ago the system was decidedly noxious. By means of steam-pipes traversing the rooms in various directions, and giving out certain known quantities of heat, the mischief has, in a great measure, been done away with; and in the best regulated mills, the temperature, though considerable, is in no farther degree oppressive or injurious than as its relaxing muscular tonicity.

* A number of girls work in the stoves at Mr. Monteith's printing establishment near Glasgow, the average temperature of which is 140° Fahrenheit: they enjoy excellent health.

Hot climates may be, and are healthy, when cleared from vegetable undergrowth, and free from swampy soils. Humboldt, and other travellers and observers, have examined this point quite sufficiently. Heat generates miasmata fatal to human life, wherever moisture, joined, as it universally is in tropical countries, with rank vegetation, exists. The littoral districts of New Spain, the cedar swamps bordering the great South American rivers, the jungles of Africa, and of the torrid zone in Asia, bear evidence how deadly an influence may be produced by vegetable decomposition, &c. &c. Beyond these, however, perfect salubrity is quite compatible with a very elevated temperature.

A wide distinction must be here made between animal and vegetable decomposition—a distinction little understood, and still less attended to. The gases which are evolved during the putrefaction of animal substances do not appear, from experience, to be fatal to life, but, on the contrary, in some respects, and to some extent, seem rather conducive to health. In a note, which will be found in the chapter on Infant Labour, some remarks have been made on this subject; and in illustration, M. de Noe's account of the Oyster Fisheries has been quoted. Here, although millions of oysters are putrefying under a burning sun, in the very midst of a dense and promiscuous mass of human beings, filling the atmosphere with a most intolerable stench, sickness is hardly known. In the process of grinding bones in this country for manure, a smell the most dreadfully offensive attends upon the operation; yet the men, who are constantly inhaling this odour, are exceedingly healthy. Butchers, tripe-men, tanners, candle-makers, &c. are all exposed more or less to the effluvium from animal matter, in various stages of decomposition;

ostlers, nightmen, are under similar circumstances, and
yet, all things considered, are far from being unhealthy.
Not only this, but many nations devour ravenously
putrid meat, and, in our own times, several species of
animal food are esteemed unfit for the table till putrefaction is very considerably advanced; and yet these are
considered as wholesome articles of diet.

It is often said that factory labour must be exceedingly
prejudicial to life, in consequence of the crowding together numbers of individuals in one room, or one mill,
from the effluvia which proceed from the bodies of these
individuals—none of them, probably, very cleanly, and
all in a state of perspiration, more or less profuse. This
opinion is not borne out by facts, where the crowding is
not extreme—and it never is extreme in modern factories. Many persons have drawn a parallel between
the factory and the Black Hole of Calcutta, and have
suffered their imaginations to run riot, in colouring a
series of dismal pictures similar to that so forcibly and
graphically described by Mr. Howell. There is no similarity in the two cases whatever; therefore deductions
drawn from the one are not applicable to the other.

The consequences of labour carried on for twelve
hours, in a heated atmosphere, which slightly accelerates
the action of the heart, are, that the muscular system
becomes languid, and a degree of irritability is produced, which exhausts the powers of the nervous
system, and excites feelings of great discomfort and
depression. Still this is not disease. It is true
that it is a condition closely bordering upon it, but it
neither is disease, nor would it lead to disease, if the
operative had a home stored with domestic comforts,
which he could well afford, and had habits which led
him to devote all his spare time to their enjoyment.

What is the fact? His home itself is often a sty, abounding in all the elements for exciting and perpetuating disease. In place of seeking by nutritious food and rest, to dissipate his languor and exhaustion, he flies for temporary relief to the excitement consequent on drinking ardent spirits—the very mode to add to his other evils, and to develop the seeds of disease lurking within him, generated partly by the nature of his occupatiou, and partly by his want of proper diet.

The exhalations from oil, &c. in a heated atmosphere, though sickly in their impressions upon strangers, there is no reason to believe are injurious to health; probably, indeed, the reverse, as it is a well-known fact that oilmen, and oil-porters, have enjoyed a singular exemption from the attacks of plague, and other epidemic and contagious diseases. So far has this been the case, that as a protection during the visitation of these scourges, it has been recommended to wear oiled dresses, or to anoint the body with oil several times a day. The copious use of oil for the purpose of lessening friction does away with the notion, that this going on so extensively in mills, between metallic bodies, might give rise to a state of atmosphere something, though remotely, analogous to that breathed by knife-grinders and pointers of needles, and which is exceedingly destructive. Every precaution, however, is taken to lessen the amount of this friction, which rapidly destroys the parts upon which it acts, and which, without these precautions, would speedily ruin the machinery.

Several writers who have devoted their attention to the influence of particular occupations upon health, have noticed the effects of inhaling particles of solid matter into the bronchi, &c. &c. No question exists, that when an atmosphere is surcharged with foreign matter, so finely pulverized as to float easily, the breathing such an atmosphere must be more or less injurious. The extent of the mischief which will result from this, however, must depend considerably upon the nature of the inspired particles.

The vivid sketch given by Dr. Knight,* has shown very decidedly that all the operations of steel grinding and polishing produce a species of asthma and phthisis in those engaged in them, which generally proves fatal early in life. The researches of Patissier,† in relation to cotton-spinners, led him to remark, " These workmen constantly inhale an atmosphere loaded with very fine cotton dust, which excites the bronchi, provokes cough, and maintains a perpetual irritation in the lungs. They are often obliged to change their employment in order to avoid phthisis." Similar observations have been made with regard to other branches of trade, such as stone-masons, bakers, furriers, feather-dressers, knitters, flax-dressers, &c. &c. In the words of Mr. Thakrah, " The dust largely inhaled in respiration irritates the air tubes, produces at length organic disease of its membrane, or of the lungs themselves, and often excites the development of tubercles in constitutions predisposed to consumption." ‡ These remarks refer more particularly to the filing, &c. of metals.

. In the production of yarn, the cotton has to go through several processes, some of which are attended by considerable quantities of dust, and minute filaments.

* *Vide* North of England Medical and Surgical Journal, No. II.

† Sur les Maladies des Artizans, p. 215.

‡ *Vide* Thakrah " On the Effect of the Principal Arts, Trades Professions, &c. upon Health and Longevity."

In the scutching and blowing department, especially where coarse and inferior cotton is used, spite of every precaution, much dust is diffused through the rooms. There are many contrivances to lessen this inconvenience, such as turning a strong current of air over the blowing machine, an aperture being made to permit the escape of flue outside—covering the machines with woodwork so as to isolate them in some degree, &c. &c. These succeed to some extent. After the first process of cleaning the cotton from foreign bodies, it is carried into the card rooms, and is here further cleaned, and advanced another step towards being converted into yarn. Here also, where coarse cotton is employed, there is a quantity of dust and filaments thrown off, and it is here perhaps that most inconvenience is felt. When, however, fine cotton, of the first qualities, is used, very little dust arises from it.

The system of better ventilation and attention to cleanliness, which is spreading among the mills, has already freed many of them from the greater portion of the atmosphere of dust, which, not many years ago, rendered it difficult to breathe in those divisions in which the first processes were carried on. Much remains to be done, and there is no doubt, that, as far as human invention can succeed in ridding the mills from dust and flue, this will be effected; for it is advantageous to have them as clean, &c. as possible.*

Many hands are of course employed in this labour—the carding of cotton, &c.—though but few, when compared to the entire complement of mill labourers: and it is here that, if evils do arise from the inhalation of foreign

---

* Since this was written, ventilators of the most powerful operation have been introduced into factories, producing a current of air sufficient to remove every impurity.

particles, they will of course be discovered, for all the subsequent processes are nearly free from this nuisance. In the weaving department nothing of the sort exists.

There can be no doubt but that in many instances this dust, and these cottony particles, lead to slight irritation of the mucous membrane lining the bronchi, and produce cough and expectoration; but it may be questioned whether they induce organic disease of the substance of the lungs, or even bring on ulceration of the air passages, terminating in bronchial consumption; although a disease has been named the "spinners' phthisis." It will be remembered, that Dr. Knight, in the paper already mentioned, has very clearly demonstrated—less by post mortem examinations, than by symptoms during life certainly—that the inhaling steel particles, which are plentifully evolved during grinding, polishing, &c. produces asthma, running into consumption. By a parity of reasoning, it has been wished to prove, that the cotton-spinner breathing an atmosphere surcharged with dust must be a sufferer in like manner. The comparison is not fair; and the results from it must be viewed with suspicion.

In the first place, this nuisance exists to any serious degree only in a few mills, and in the working a peculiar kind of material; and in the second, this dust, where it does exist even abundantly, is of a vegetable nature chiefly, and free from the irritating qualities of metallic particles, which must in general be more or less angular, and which cannot undergo any softening, before chemical decomposition resolves them into new compounds. In these particulars, the dust floating in cotton, flax, and silk mills, is widely different from that in cutlery workshops, marble and stone grinding, &c., and most assuredly is much less prejudicial. That this dust should excite a very troublesome irritation to persons who have never been exposed to its influence, except during the few minutes spent in the mills on a casual visit, need excite no surprise : but in the parties who have become accustomed to such an atmosphere it produces little or no inconvenience.

Dr. Kay, who advocates the opposite opinion, remarks very correctly, that " in this example, as in others, is displayed that peculiar law of structure, by which it insensibly undergoes changes which enable it to endure the presence of a foreign or noxious substance, without suffering the ordinary functional derangement ; and a great proportion of the operatives engaged in cotton spinning, suffer little, if at all, from the foreign particles which they inspire during twelve hours in the day. The diseases which arise from the circumstances which we have described are chronic and subacute bronchitis."*

The latter part of this quotation may be questioned as to its accuracy. In some few cases indeed, which have been brought under medical notice, a species of bronchitis, having a few trifling points of difference, when compared to the common symptoms of this affection, have been cited as proofs that they were the result of the inhalation of this dust. Symptomatology is however too uncertain a science to be worthy implicit credit, and is deserving little consideration when viewed singly, and none whatever when its dicta are opposed to the results of general observation. These cases differ so little from others occurring under circumstances where this agent could not have been applied, that it is quite obvious they are not dependent upon it; but rather that cases of common bronchitis have been rendered

* *Vide* North of England Medical and Surgical Journal, No. III.

occasionally more obstinate in their character in consequence of these cottony particles being brought incessantly into contact with the inflamed and diseased surfaces.

If the inhalation of this dust was, as is asserted by these authors, followed by consumption, whether laryngeal or pulmonary, which is on all hands acknowledged to be almost uniformly fatal, there would unquestionably be found a higher rate of mortality among spinners than among weavers, the one being exposed to this inconvenience, the other being nearly, if not quite free from it. This datum, if it can be correctly ascertained, will be at once conclusive. Fortunately such is the case, as it is given in a return from the mill of Mr. Ashton, and is undoubtedly correct.

" In thirteen years, during the first six of which, the number of rovers, spinners, piecers, and dressers, (*that is, those connected with the dusty part of the processes*) was one hundred, and during the last seven, above two hundred, only eight deaths occurred, though the same persons were, with rare exceptions, employed during the whole period. Supposing these deaths, for the sake of convenience, to have been nine, then by ascribing three to the first six years, and six to the last seven, the mortality during the former period was 1 in 200, and during the latter, 1 in 233. The number of weavers (*that is, those unconnected with the dusty part of the processes*), during the first six years, was two hundred, and during the last seven, four hundred ; and in the body of workmen forty deaths occurred in thirteen years. By ascribing thirteen of these deaths to the first six years, and twenty-seven to the last seven, the mortality during the former period was 1 in 92, and during the latter, 1 in 103."*

* Moral and Physical Condition, &c. p. 104.

Thus, then, it appears, that the mortality amongst those persons who were removed from the supposed noxious agent—dust, was more than double that which occurred among those who were exposed to its influence ; and this disparity is the more remarkable, when it is considered that in the body of spinners, which exhibits such a low rate of mortality, a great number of children are included from eight to twelve years of age—a period when many deaths occur ; whilst, on the contrary, the weavers consist chiefly of young men and women from fifteen to twenty-five, a decade as little fatal as any in the course of human life.

Nothing can be more conclusive as to the question— Is the atmosphere which is breathed by the factory labourer necessarily injurious to his existence, in consequence of its being loaded with the *débris* of cotton ? Public opinion says, yes ; examination into the fact says, no ; though it may be admitted that the catarrhal affections to which he is so much exposed are occasionally aggravated by this cause.

Another circumstance supposed to influence the salubrity of mill labour is, that numbers being congregated into one room—by the process of respiration, the air being rapidly deoxygenated, is rendered unfit for the purposes of respiration.*   Wherever numbers of human beings are crowded into a limited space, the respired air is rapidly freed from its oxygen, that portion of its constituent parts which alone possesses capabilities for supporting animal life ; and its place becomes occupied by a gas produced by certain chemical changes carried on within the lungs, named carbonic acid gas— a gas destructive to life, and incapable of supporting

---

* This deoxygenation is aided at the present day by the extensive use of gas as an illuminating agent.

flame. This change in the nature of the respired air is fatal in two ways,—one, by removing the oxygen, and the other, by substituting the gas just mentioned ; but to be injurious in a very marked degree in either of these ways, the place must be confined, and the temperature pretty nearly the same with that of the surrounding atmosphere,—as elevation of temperature produces a continual current of fresh air, which it is very difficult to shut out, even were this desired.

Before, however, that degree of saturation with this obnoxious gas is reached, which would be immediately fatal to animal existence, the atmosphere of a room may be so far impregnated as to produce very depressing effects upon the vital activity of the system, which is attended with some peculiar consequences; and these have been well hinted at by Cabanis, in conjunction with some other circumstances which have been noticed. " Dans les ateliers clos, surtout dans ceux où l'air se renouvelle avec difficulté, les forces musculaires diminuent rapide-ment ; la reproduction de la chaleur animale languit ; et les hommes de la constitution la plus robuste, con-tractent le tempérament mobile et capricieux des femmes. Ajoutez que, si la nombre des ouvriers est un peu considérable, l'altération progressive de l'air agit d'une manière directe et pernicieuse, d'abord sur les poumons, dont le sang reçoit son caractère vital, et bientôt sur le cerveau lui-même. Ainsi donc, sans parler des émanations malfaisantes que les matières manufac-turées ou celles qu'on emploi dans leur préparation exha-lent souvent, presque toutes circonstances se réunissent pour rendre les ateliers également malsains au physique et au moral."*

* Rapports du Physique et du Moral de l'Homme, par P. I. G. Cabanis. Vol. II. p. 83.

An atmosphere thus impregnated acts indeed as a slow poison, and produces a particular impression upon the sensorium, apparently through the medium of the blood, which loses its florid colour; and when circulated through the brain in this condition, lowers all the powers of life in direct proportion with the extent of deterioration; and this is one cause of the low degree of vital energy possessed by the mill artisans. In former times, when the interior economy of mills was imperfect, and the rooms were low and small, the baleful influence of this poisonous gas operated most powerfully upon those engaged in them. Latterly, since the great improvement as to ventilation, loftiness of rooms, &c., this influence is decidedly lessened, and, in the best constructed mills of the present day, can hardly be said to exist.

This gas, carbonic acid, is heavier than common air,* and as fast as it is evolved sinks down to the floor, forming a stratum more or less dense, according to the facilities allowed for its escape. It is thus, in some degree, removed from the influence of ventilation, as generally managed, namely, by apertures or windows placed high in the walls of the room. This plan is the best* and most efficacious for regulating temperature, merely as the heated air rising, according to its specific gravity, escapes freely from any opening offered it, and is replaced by a current of cold air, which rushes in to

* A very simple experiment is sufficient to show this—"When a jar is perfectly filled with this gas, take another jar of smaller size, and place at the bottom of it a lighted taper, supported by a stand; then pour the contents of the first-mentioned jar into the second, as if you were pouring water. The candle will be instantly extinguished, as if it had been immersed in water.—*Dr. Henry's Chemistry*, Vol. I. p. 341.

occupy its place. Not so with carbonic acid gas : it remains undulating on the floor, or falls slowly through any casual aperture, or flows down the stairs, but very little escapes through a common ventilator. The Grotto del Cane is a curious example of this, the depth of the stratum of gas generally being about two feet. Its existence at the bottom of wells, mines, &c. &c., is another proof of its density being greater than that of common atmospheric air, the mine or well being quite free from it, except within two or three yards at the bottom. It may be questioned whether the use of cast-iron floors, now so common in mills, does not interfere with the dispersion of this gas, however advantageous they may be in other respects.

This evil is, however, undergoing a beneficial change, from the increased use of machinery requiring a less number of hands in particular rooms ; and might be still more effectually removed by directing a current of air along the floors, and leaving openings sunk through the walls.*

The transitions from a heated temperature to the common day, and *vice versâ*, especially during certain portions of the year, are circumstances which inevitably expose the mill labourers to colds and catarrhal fevers. This effect is aided by their very light and imperfect clothing,—often issuing from the mill but half-clad, and without shoes or hat. This might to a great degree be remedied by the labourers themselves, by a greater atten-tion to their personal comforts.

From this cursory examination of the conditions of factory labour in general, it will be apparent, that there is

---

* The powerful ventilators now in use in the best regulated mills carry away this noxious agent very completely.

nothing connected with them necessarily fatal to life; but that some of the agencies to which the labourers are exposed exert a depressing influence upon their muscular and sensorial systems: that there is nothing in the structure of the mills, as to temperature—nothing in the material upon which they are engaged—nothing in the processes, which are, *per se*, prejudicial. On the contrary, from an extensive inquiry, it appears that the average rate of mortality has been and is diminishing since the mills have absorbed such an increased amount of population; but that, although life has been benefited, considered as to its duration,—yet, that the standard of health has been seriously diminished. The former is demonstrably the result of lessened vital energy, rendering the human system less susceptible of acute fatal diseases; and the latter is owing, first, to the use of steam, which, by requiring certain local advantages, of necessity crowds men into limited spaces, a circumstance ever unfavourable to health; secondly, from the unintermitted attention demanded by machinery; thirdly, from protracted hours of labour; and, fourthly, from the bad habits of the labourers themselves.

The diseases of the manufacturing population take their peculiar character from the causes mentioned, and are almost uniformly of a slow and very protracted kind.* Few amongst the population can be said to enjoy perfect health; all are more or less ailing, and are deprived of every chance of restoration by the impossibility of removing themselves from the influence which is ever around and within them.

* " We have no reason to believe that in the cotton mills urgent diseases are often produced, or the immediate mortality great. Disorders of the nervous and digestive systems are frequent, but not severe."—*Thackrah on Health, &c.* p. 106.

In the chapter on Infant Labour, the situation of the factory child has been dilated upon, and shown to be exposed to every thing which can injure its constitution. In reference to this, Mr. Green, in his evidence before a Committee of the House of Commons, remarks : " There is no disease to which children, both from the constitution of their frames, and the various unfavourable circumstances to which they are exposed, are more liable than scrofula, in all its multitudinous forms. To the production of this disease, one of the most influential circumstances is, I am persuaded, breathing an impure air ; and by purity of air I do not mean any thing that can be determined by chemistry : but I refer to the fact that scrofula chiefly prevails in the children of the inhabitants of densely peopled towns and crowded cities."

Scrofula may be defined a disease, or rather the name for a group of diseases, arising from imperfect or depraved nutrition, and exhibits itself in a variety of forms, all evincing that the processes of absorption and deposition are going on badly, and that the series of vessels devoted to these purposes is conveying a fluid unfitted for healthy growth, the result of imperfect elimination. This is a disease to which, *à priori*, it might be supposed the manufacturing population, in its younger branches, would be very liable,—all the conditions of their labour, localities, and modes of living, favouring the production of its peculiar diathesis. Such, indeed, observation tells is the fact: but this by no means so universally as is believed.

The records of the Royal Infirmary at Manchester, containing a classification and list of diseases, are, in many points, of somewhat doubtful authenticity, no regular and systematic plan of registry being in use. Independently of surgical operations, consequent upon accidents, the majority of cases of amputation, &c. &c. are from scrofulous diseases in the joints and other parts. If a judgment were formed from this circumstance alone, it would appear that the greater number of patients seeking assistance were scrofulous. That a very considerable portion of these patients, under sixteen years of age, is affected by this disease, is perhaps true, but its effects are not marked as such; and again, vast numbers of the worst cases which fill the wards are brought from out-districts, generally in the anticipation that some operation may be needful. Still, scrofula must be ranked as one of the diseases of the operative manufacturer; but it exists to an equal extent both in the one engaged in factories, and in the hand-loom weaver, who, although removed from a part of the depressing agencies of the mill-spinner or weaver,* has to contend with an enemy still more destructive—actual want! In early life, rachitic affections prevail largely; but has been spoken of in connexion with infant labour.

One of the most frequent ailments of the mill artisans, however, is derangement in the digestive organs, attended by a host of troublesome symptoms, and followed by a tissue of mischiefs, which place it in advance of all other affections preying upon the manufacturing population. The diet of these people is innutritious and badly cooked. Their habits, their dram-drinking, their undrained houses and streets, are all fruitful sources of

* "For the last sixteen years, I have been in the habit of putting to the patients the question, 'What trade are you of?' especially when the case was that of a distorted limb or joint; to which question the answer has almost never been, 'Work in a cotton factory;' but almost constantly, 'A hand-loom weaver,' or other trade."—*Factory Commission—Appendix to Medical Report,* p. 281.

evil, and tell most decidedly upon the functions of the *primæ viæ*, altering their secretions, and producing effects in the highest degree injurious to bodily health, and reacting very powerfully upon the functions of the brain.

It may be very safely stated, that one half the diseases among adults spring from this cause. The food they take is hastily swallowed, almost unmasticated: it is often coarse, and not very easily digested; it wants the stimulants of solidity and proper nutritive qualities; and, pushed into the stomach as it is, does not undergo complete chymification; hence portions are forced downwards into the intestines, and become so many sources of irritation. The constant repetition of this disturbs the healthy function of the mucous membrane lining the whole of these passages. Its secretion is changed, and it becomes exceedingly irritable, in some instances exciting the muscular coat of the intestines to frequent, irregular, and spasmodic action, giving rise to griping and cholicky pains, which are very distressing. In other examples, an opposite state of things is the consequence: the bowels are torpid, and many days, and sometimes upwards of a week, pass over, and no alvine evacuation takes place.

In both these instances the appetite fails after a time; the sufferers lose flesh, become pale and languid, and this very often attended by hypochondriasis,* which increases a hundred-fold their miseries, aggravating every paroxysm of pain to a degree almost unendurable. This mental accompaniment is one of the peculiarities of indigestion; and, in the case of the labouring poor who suffer under it, hurries them to seek relief from ardent

* " Hypochondriasis, from indulging too much the corrupt desires of the flesh and spirit, is in fact the prevalent disease of the highest paid operative."—*Philosophy of Manufactures*, p. 386.

spirits, which are a very poison when systematically or largely swallowed during the continuance of these attacks.

Little wonder can be excited that, harassed by the miserable sensations to which this condition of health gives birth, the degraded labourer should have recourse to this temporary relief. He either knows not, or cares not, that it is injurious, but follows up too truly the rest of his improvidences by thinking only of to-day! Medical aid, it is true, is at hand; but to seek that he must lose his work, and a difficulty might arise as to his resuming it. He therefore struggles on till the disease takes a favourable turn, or he is so far reduced as to be incapable of going to the mill. The singularly miserable aspect presented by many of the operatives, shewing, as it were, an epitome of every thing that melancholy can impress on the human face, is owing to these bowel affections. Beyond their own immediate seat of disease or derangement, they call into play a crowd of painful feelings in all parts of the body, and are the originators of many of those anomalous diseases classed under the general term—nervous, the majority of which are dependent upon the chylopoietic viscera.

However troublesome this class of diseases may be,— and it would be impossible to point out any maladies attended by a more harassing train of consequences,— they are not necessarily fatal. To what extent derangements in the digestive organs may run, compatible with life, it is very difficult to say: not many years have elapsed since their importance became understood—a circumstance which may be explained from the change in the diet and general habits of society, rendering it not improbable that, as an extensive class of disease, they are only of recent origin. So long as the lower orders were engaged in active out-door occupations, and were supported by a simple and nutritious diet, there is no reason to suppose that they were subject to these morbid conditions of the bowels.

In the higher classes of society, a tribe of diseases, having their origin in too nourishing and stimulant a diet, which produces a precisely similar train of suffering, has attracted considerable attention. It is, indeed, a new feature in the history of medicine, to find the two extremes of the social confederacy labouring under the same maladies, running through a similar course, and producing the same peculiar feeling of morbid irritability, intermitting with the most profound melancholy. If the situation of the pampered man of wealth, who is the victim to dyspepsia, is pitiable, how shall that of the operative be described? Language wants force to depict its evils: unmitigated, as it is, by all those foreign aids which can be procured by individuals differently circumstanced, he is condemned to labour on, a prey to bodily sufferings, and the most deplorable mental anxiety—alternately drowning his troubles in the delirium of intoxication, or standing, a miserable and woe-worn figure, before his machine or loom.

Fever occurs in manufacturing towns, as in all other localities, but is neither more common nor more severe in its attacks. It generally assumes a low and somewhat typhoid character, and very often is attended by slight ulcerations in the bowels—a condition which has been ably described by several recent pathological writers. The manufacturing towns, from the denseness of their population, might reasonably be supposed to be peculiarly liable to epidemic febrile visitations. When it is recollected in what state the homes, streets, &c. are found, it is indeed a source of wonder that the most destructive pestilences do not periodically rage among them. Sporadic cases of fever are of course common ; but looking at these towns and districts generally, they will be discovered to be exceedingly free from contagious diseases—adding another proof to those already given, that the low and depressed state of vital activity, universally characterizing this population, removes it beyond their influences.* Many speculations have been thrown out as to the purifying qualities of smoke, gas emanations, &c. &c., but no proofs are in existence which endow these with any importance.

Consumption has been supposed to be another disease of great extent and mortality in this population. Connected as it appears to be in some degree with a scrofulous diathesis, and exposed to so many causes of mischief in the respiratory organs, as the mill artisans are, this disease is doubtless common. The imperfect clothing, the sudden changes as to temperature, &c., are powerful agents in keeping alive bronchial irritation, which occasionally runs into ulceration, or the formation of tubercles in the lungs. Still pulmonary consumption does not merit consideration, as a peculiar affection among the operative manufacturers. Neither does it appear that the deaths from this disease are increasing, in any thing like an equal ratio, with the increase in this class of workers. Coughs and asthmatic affections are very prevalent from the same causes, but do not necessarily shorten life, or lead to organic changes beyond a slight thickening of the mucous membrane lining the air passages.

On the whole, it may be said that the class of manufacturers engaged in mill labour, exhibit but few well-

* *Vide* Second Factory Commission Report, p. 56, &c. This population was remarkably exempt from cholera during the late visitation of that disease.

defined diseases ; but that nearly the entire number are victims to a train of irregular morbid actions, chiefly indicated by disturbances in the functions of the digestive apparatus, with their consequent effects upon the nervous system ; producing melancholy, extreme mental irritability, and great exhaustion. Their existence does not seem shortened ; on the contrary, a general improvement in the value of human life is the result of the changes which have operated on the condition of the labouring community.

The nature of the labour of the factory artisan, and the imperative necessity for his regular attendance, explain what might at first sight appear a contradiction between many of the foregoing observations and Dr. Mitchell's very curious table of the comparative amount of sickness in different occupations per annum.

	Days' sicknesses.	
Staffordshire Potteries, to the age of 61 .	9.3	each man.
Silk mills	7.8	—
Woollen mills	7.08	—
Flax mills	5.01	—
Cotton mills (Glasgow)	5.6	—
East India Company's servants . . .	5.4	—
Labourers in Chatham dock-yard . . .	5.38	—
Lancashire cotton mills	5.35	—
Lancashire ditto, under 16 years of age .	3.14	—

The sub-acute character of the diseases of manufacturers is also strongly demonstrated by the fact, that of 1046 patients admitted into the Manchester hospital in the year 1832, and whose occupations were registered, only 208 belonged to the factory classes.

CHAPTER X.

EDUCATION—RELIGION—CRIME—PAUPERISM.

It has been said that "knowledge unemployed will
preserve us from vice, for vice is but another name for
ignorance; but knowledge employed is virtue." This
assertion is, however, in so far fallacious, that it assumes
vice to exist alone with ignorance, and to be alone
compatible with it. The history of all ages and the
experience of every-day life are sufficient proofs that
this is a position which cannot be maintained, unless by
the term knowledge be understood both moral and
intellectual acquirement—and these, too, so proportioned
and determined, as to maintain an equal balance, a
nicety of adaptation difficult to point out, and still more
difficult to reduce to settled rules.

The ignorant man, indeed, is improvident in proportion to his ignorance; for being unaware of the evils

which result to him individually, and to the good of
society in general, he has no check to restrain his
irregular and inordinate appetites; knowing nothing
also of the resources open to his exertions, he makes no
advance in civilization or refinement, and is much under
the influence of example, and much more easily led
away from the path of private duty and public propriety.
The ignorant man, not understanding the principles
which guide the conduct of the legislature, the particular
acts of municipal bodies, the relation of master and
servant, is consequently a bad servant and a turbulent
citizen; and having no data on which to reason, necessarily forms erroneous conclusions upon most of [the
phenomena, whether moral or physical, which come under
his notice.   Hence ignorance is a great evil.

Education is a word applied to a series of acts having
for their objects, first, the development and proper
direction of man's social instincts; this may be termed
the education of morals : and, secondly, the cultivation
of mind, considered in reference to its peculiar attributes;
this may be termed intellectual education.

The intention of educating the labouring community
ought to be, and no doubt is, to increase the individual
happiness of every separate member; to elevate him in
the scale of society, and to add to the harmony and
contentment of the whole social union.

Moral education is that which, by acting upon man's
feelings and principles, his natural instincts, his duties
as a father, son, husband and brother, and upon his
religious aspirations, has the most immediate and direct
influence upon his character and happiness.

This is the education which is of the most importance
to the labouring man.   Circumstanced as he often is,
verging upon positive want, a most demoralizing agent,

he requires all the aids which can be given to preserve him from habitual vice. He is at perpetual warfare with himself, inasmuch as his appetites and desires are more varied and more extensive than his means and opportunities can satisfy. Hence it is that morals, as applied to his domestic affections and duties, are of such mighty importance to his well being.

If the education which is afforded him does not aim at these ends, its proposed advantages are illusory, and its effects may be positively injurious. If the poor man's home is not rendered happier by it, he is better without it. He had better be suffered to remain in ignorance, that other classes have certain specific advantages, denied him, if at the same time he is shewn that he has the capabilities, the physical and political strength to aim at a summary mode of changing his condition. If his instincts and social affections are not roused and determined to their legitimate objects, his comfort is only more widely ruined; for he becomes discontented with a lot which he inherits as a birthright, and with which he might have struggled on through existence, miserable indeed in the estimation of the looker-on, but rendered more miserable a thousand times by having superadded the gnawing sense of his inferiority, which, had he been suffered to remain in his original state of obtuse ignorance, would never have disturbed his peace.

Home ever has been and ever will be the school for moral education. It is here alone that man can develop in their full beauty those affections of the heart which are destined to be, through life, the haven to which he may retire when driven about by the storms of fortune. It is here that he may have about him, if his condition is not supereminently wretched, feelings and emotions

R

of the most ennobling influence ; it is here that he may
hold communion with himself; and it is here, and here
alone, that he will be enabled to retain his pride of self,
and his personal respectability.

Moral education then is that, the offices of which are
to cultivate man's inherent sense of justice, to direct his
religious aspirations, to make him charitable, humane,
and honourable in his dealings ; to bring into play his
social virtues and his domestic affections ; to render him
a good father, son, husband, and citizen. To secure the
noble ends of moral instruction, it must be cultivated at
home ; and the way in which its primary influence will ·
be perceived, is in increasing the happiness of himself
and family.

It may be safely asserted, that the means hitherto in
force have not been well calculated to the great purposes of true education. The error has lain, and it is one
as yet but partially and imperfectly acknowledged, in
the giving of mere mental instruction—the acquisition
of fundamental learning.

It is, however, insufficient to teach a child to read or
write ; it is insufficient to teach it texts from the Bible ;
it is insufficient to teach it mathematics, chemistry, or
history ; it is insufficient to teach it a language beyond
its own. These do nothing towards teaching its moral
duties, and it is upon these the excellence of its character and future life must depend. As accessories, as a
means to an end, and as extending the sphere of man's
knowledge, these are excellent. As fitting him for improving or modifying his condition, they are excellent ;
as elevating him another step above the brutes around
him, and as giving him a more correct estimate of himself, they are excellent ; but they should be considered as
subsidiary to morals, for without morality knowledge is

pernicious, as it extends more widely the capabilities for being mischievous.

Mere intellectual education cannot improve the moral condition of the labouring classes—it cannot render them better men or better citizens; but it can teach them their own power, and it is doing so at a period when that tuition is pregnant with danger to themselves.

So long as the homes of the factory labourer are what they are—so long as drunkenness and riot, so long as all the ties of natural affection and parental subordination are unacknowledged and unfelt—so long as children are deprived of the force of beneficial example—so long as they are, both at home and abroad, exposed to vicious example, so long will intellectual cultivation not prove the remedy for the manifold miseries incident to their present condition. Many of these have their origin in the conduct of the interested parties themselves, and many of them are the consequence of a system of labour and of payment capable of great improvement.

The benevolent founder of Sunday schools was prompted, no doubt, by feelings of the purest humanity. In the agricultural districts in which, compared with manufacturing towns, morals were in much higher perfection in ratio with intellectual acquirements, their effects were beneficial. The child of the agricultural labourer has a purer sense of religion than the child of the artisan born and bred in a great town; its domestic habits are formed at home, in which home, however, no means or opportunities for the acquisition of learning are afforded. To the child so circumstanced the Sunday school was an invaluable boon in some respects.

Its introduction into the large manufacturing towns, in certain points of view, was equally valuable, as the incessant occupation of the factory child entirely prevents it from acquiring the simplest rudiments of knowledge during the week-days.

The Sunday school to this child, therefore, gives the only possible means of gaining instruction intellectually. In another point of view it is of equal consequence to it ; it prevents the desecration of the sabbath, which, were it not engaged here, would inevitably follow the want of its customary labour. It thus becomes a moral restraint, and it may perhaps admit of question whether this be not the chief benefit derived from it.

The Sunday school may be thus looked upon as the first step towards the establishment of moral feelings in the bosom of the factory child : it removes it from home —a home having little within or around it breathing a healthy or social atmosphere. It exhibits the day of rest in its proper light—an abstraction from habitual labour, and it conduces materially to personal cleanliness.

Sunday schools are not exclusively appropriated to the child of the manufacturing labourer ; a very considerable portion of their attendants are the children of shopkeepers, petty tradesmen, and people engaged in various other occupations. Here one mischief arises from them : these, which of themselves are freed from many of the evils of the social condition of their companions, derive any thing but benefit from their association, indiscriminate as it is. It is here that great improvement may yet be made in the constitution of these schools. As they now stand, the moral good they produce on the one hand, is counterpoised by a correspondent extent of evil on the other; and their influence on the whole community has not been operative in the moral regeneration of the factory districts as could have been wished.

Want of due classification may be looked upon as the

one leading error: the selection of teachers and monitors, another. Vulgar habits and coarse minds should never have a place in the superintendence of any portion, however minute, in these schools.

The number of children who receive a limited education in these schools, is very considerable. This argues well on the part both of their promoters, and of those who attend them.

The evidence in the Factory Report Commission is on this head, as well as some others, singularly meagre, or rather exceedingly defective. From inquiries instituted by the Statistical Society of Manchester, there are it appears about 36,000 children taught in the Sunday schools of that town, of whom five-eighths are factory children, as near as can be judged—a fair proportion, considering the occupation of the inhabitants. In Stockport, 4,932 children are educated in Sunday schools, of whom one-half are connected with factory labour.*

The following Table, though obviously inaccurate in many particulars, is curious. For example, it has been ascertained that in Manchester alone, somewhere about five-eighths of 36,000 children are connected with factories, and taught in Sunday schools. It does not follow as a matter of course that *all* can read ; but it is certainly true that the majority can ; and yet, in the Table below, 11,000 factory people, capable of reading, are given to the whole of Lancashire. The same observation applies to Cheshire :—Stockport furnishing 2,668 factory Sunday school learners, and the whole county only 3,000 factory people capable of reading.

* The Statistics of Dr. Ure, in his "Philosophy of Manufactures," are often of a very singular kind. The population he gives to Stockport is one illustration.

If this return is to be looked upon as an accurate one, what becomes of the educational benefit, so loudly vaunted as resulting from Sunday schools; since it appears that in the magnificent and admirably conducted Stockport great Sunday school, not less than 40,850 scholars have been inscribed on its registers, and, in the language of its own Report for 1833, a great part of these children have received a religious and moral education in its walls? How happens it, then, that if near 30,000 factory children have received the elements of education, reading being the first of these, only 3,000 factory people were found capable of reading? Another curious fact shewn by the Table is the comparative education of factory labourers in different counties.

We have again to repeat that the Table must be considered not as a complete tabular view of the state of education amongst the parties to whom it has reference; and it must be remembered that the mind of the mill artisan is little disposed to intellectual pursuits.*

* "The mind (of the mill artisan) gathers neither stores nor strength from the constant extension and retraction of the same muscles. The intellect slumbers in inert supineness, but the grosser parts of our nature attain a rank development. To condemn man to such a toil as this, is, in some measure, to cultivate in him the habits of an animal : he becomes reckless; he disregards the distinguishing appetites and habits of his species; he neglects the comforts and delicacies of life ; he lives in squalid wretchedness, on meagre food, and expends his superfluous gains in debauchery."—*Moral and Physical Condition of the Working Classes,* p. 22.

FACTORY EDUCATION TABLE.

	Numbers taken from the Returns.				Proportion in the hundred.			
	Read.	Cannot read.	Write.	Cannot write.	Read.	Cannot read.	Write.	Cannot write.
ENGLAND.								
Lancashire	11,393	2,344	5,184	8,553	83	17	38	62
Cheshire	3,092	344	1,630	1,806	90	10	47	53
Yorkshire.	9,087	1,616	5,194	5,509	85	15	48	52
Derbyshire	2,490	314	1,200	1,604	88	12	43	57
Staffordshire . . .	3,530	718	2,603	1,645	83	17	61	39
Leicestershire . .	351	92	174	269	80	20	40	60
Nottinghamshire .	948	127	455	616	88	12	43	57
Norfolk, Suffolk, Essex	1,914	433	608	1,739	81	19	26	74
Wiltshire	3,045	527	1,364	2,208	85	15	38	62
Somersetshire . .	2,040	229	591	1,678	89	11	26	74
Devonshire	755	34	401	386	96	4	51	49
Gloucestershire . .	4,556	379	1,983	2,952	92	8	40	60
Worcestershire . .	21	—	16	5	100	—	77	23
Warwickshire . .	105	15	81	39	88	12	68	32
Total . . .	43,327	7,172	21,484	29,009	86	14	43	57
SCOTLAND.								
Aberdeenshire . .	4,336	305	2,133	2,508	93	7	46	54
Forfarshire	4,879	237	2,425	2,691	95	5	47	53
Perthshire	1,601	96	1,054	643	94	6	62	38
Fifeshire	1,558	38	862	734	97	3	57	43
Clackmannanshire	213	6	754	65	97	3	70	30
Stirlingshire . . .	795	23	547	271	97	3	66	34
Lanarkshire . . .	7,815	317	4,454	3,678	96	4	54	46
Renfrewshire. . .	5,664	199	3,165	2,698	97	3	54	46
Ayrshire	867	2	594	275	100	—	68	32
Bute	430	4	310	124	99	1	71	39
Mid Lothian . . .	98	3	96	5	97	3	95	5
Total	28,256	1,230	16,394	13,692	96	4	53	47

It is amongst this population, gathered together as it is in masses, that a general plan of education should be introduced. It has been, and is yet, a disgrace to Great Britain, that whilst palaces and halls have been built and richly endowed for the sons of her higher ranks, the people, emphatically so called, have been left uncared-for, and that, to the present day, there are but few kingdoms in Europe which do not put us to shame in this respect. The educational institutions of Germany are open before us as an example of what may be effected by a well-organised system either of voluntary or compulsory education. Were a plan of primary schools, well developed, and introduced into the manufacturing districts, and made to include all children from six to twelve, a vast moral improvement would be the immediate result.

Mechanic institutions, intended for the instruction of "children of a larger growth," have certain advantages and disadvantages, similar to those of Sunday schools.

The mental improvement must again be looked upon as subordinate to the moral restraint which their members voluntarily impose upon themselves. If a man spends time, and a limited portion of his earnings in the institute, both the one and the other must be abstracted from the demands of home. But as it so generally happens, that a very small amount of the operative's actual earnings are devoted to domestic wants and enjoyments, it necessarily follows that his money must be spent, and his time engaged in the pursuit of debasing pleasures, if they can be so called; viz. in the beer-shop, the gin-vault, or the political club; any time or any money, therefore, which a wish for instruction may induce him to devote to the institution, is one step gained towards a better order of things. They are doubtless worthy of every encouragement, but it is far from desirable that they should be too exclusively made up of operatives ; in fact, the greater number of masters and other respectable and superior members there are, the better it is for the true advantage of these societies.

There is one circumstance connected with these institutions, which those who augured that they would effect a complete moral revolution in the habits of the artisan must deeply deplore ; and this is the gradual divergence which has been going on from their original object and intentions. Few, indeed, of their numbers are from the class they are chiefly intended to benefit.

The great moral evils which press upon the manufacturing population, are—first, the causes producing the separation of families, and the consequent breaking up of all social ties ; secondly, the early introduction of children into the mills ; and thirdly, the neglect to which the infant members of the family are exposed.

To remedy this last evil—one not less in its consequences than the two others in the determination of character—a means happily has been devised, and partially adopted, which promises the best results.

Neglected, as the great majority of the infants of the factory and hand-loom labourers are by their parents throughout the day ; left in charge of a mere child, or, what is still worse, a hireling nurse ; badly fed, badly clothed, badly treated ; their young affections blighted and seared in the bud—the establishment of schools for very young children would obviate these evils, and be of the most signal benefit.

The error into which infant schools have fallen, and which, from a want of correct understanding as to the noble purposes to which they may be directed, and a corresponding want of correct knowledge of the moral evils under which their little charges labour at home, is the wish and endeavour to cultivate too much the intellect. This is an error, and, still further, it is an absurdity; for no purpose of real utility can be effected by it. The great objects of the promoters and superintendents of these infant asylums should be, to stand *in loco parentis* in all those attachments and moral associations which are inherent in young minds, and by so doing, lay the foundation for a structure which, though it may never be finished; and though it may be injured and defaced by occurrences to which it will be subjected, will, nevertheless, still show itself at points like the beautiful proportion of a Greek temple, half buried amidst the ruins of a coarser and later period of architecture.*

It is much to be wished that the master manufacturers would rouse themselves universally to organize juvenile schools amongst their hands. They are the only parties who can do so effectually; and no mill owner could more worthily perform the duties which abstractedly he most certainly owes to those in his employ, than by establishing, or aiding in the establishing these schools, which should embrace every child, the parents of which were manifestly unfitted for its charge, either by moral delinquency, or by being engaged in the factory.

Some of these men have,† indeed, forwarded these

---

* " Great numbers of young men and women, but perhaps more of the latter, have received, with reading and writing, religious instructions and impressions in Sunday schools, and though these are often weakened and obscured in after life, there is still a preparation for good."—*Report of the Ministry to the Poor—Manchester*, p. 10.

† Mr. David Dale, near Lanark, Mr. Grant, of Ramsbottom, and many other intelligent masters, in *country* situations, have by judicious arrangements for education and religious instruction surrounded themselves by moral labourers.

institutions, as well as shown in other points a disposition to assist and guide the moral conduct of their
hands ; their number is, however, exceedingly small.
It must be hoped that the discussions which have arisen
concerning the moral and physical evils attendant upon
the factory system, will not be without their influence
upon them. As a class, they have a most extensive
power of doing good; and as a class they have, either
by direct example or by negligence, extensive power of
doing harm. Of one thing they may be assured, that
by forwarding the interests and happiness of the demoralized artisan, they will in equal ratio add to their
own ; and that if they continue to neglect or overlook
these for selfish purposes, they will have cause for
repentance..

The number of children brought under the system of
infant schools, when all things are considered, is full as
great as could be expected. Its practical advantages
want explaining to the parents ; probably the provident
societies now establishing will do something towards
this—their influence cannot be better directed.

The diffusion of correct information on the common
arts of life, with facts and moral examples drawn from
authentic and pure sources, in the shape of very cheap
periodicals, will undoubtedly have their influence upon
the minds of all classes. It is a vast advantage to what
may be termed the accidental reader and inquirer, to
have information brought to him at short intervals, and
in an attractive form,—a thing aimed at by all the pub-
lications of this class.

The diffusion of these, however, amongst the lower
orders of the population in manufacturing towns, amounts
to nothing. It is true enough that the lowness of their
price brings them within the reach of most of the operatives, and it is equally true that many of them can

read, but they do not purchase the weekly magazines; the vast number sold being taken by the middle classes of society. Their place is occupied by sectarian and political tracts, which, by their exciting nature, seem to harmonize better with the depraved taste existing amongst them. Very little interest or curiosity is shewn by this class of the community for the generality of subjects discussed and illustrated by the weekly periodicals. They do not come home sufficiently to their feelings and situations, they do not apply themselves with sufficient closeness to their peculiar passions and wants, and they are in consequence neglected.

The literature which will succeed at present in extending itself amongst them, must come down to their moral and intellectual level—must take a much lower tone, and must be coarser and ruder in its details: facts clearly demonstrated by an examination of the works which are read and studied by them. By the neglect of this, they have as a body been left to the writings of individuals who have written for some particular purpose, totally independent of moral aim; and it is desirable that the field should be now occupied by something equally homely, equally stirring, but directed to better purposes.

The results of the various efforts which have been made, and which are still making, to educate this portion of the community, are extensive and surprising, and, were intellectual education alone wanting, highly satisfactory. Not many years ago, very few of the thousands that were congregated in these districts could read, and still fewer write. Now, the majority can at least read. No human being whose time, for twelve to sixteen hours per day, is occupied by exertions for procuring a livelihood, can devote himself to extend the sphere of his knowledge beyond some of its primary elements; and to do this they must be brought to his door, and be offered to him, or they will never be sought for by him.

It is in vain to imagine and theorize upon that disposition of the human mind, which, having had its impulses once stirred, will be led to seek for information at the sacrifice of needful repose, or the grosser pleasures of sense. It neither is, nor will it ever be, the case generally. Isolated examples may indeed be found of men struggling through the severest and most oppressive difficulties in this pursuit; but they are isolated examples—nothing upon which to found data applicable to the mass. Till the factory system is revised—till morals are established—no intellectual education will render them better husbands, better fathers, or better citizens; still it is a step gained—a step which, if followed by an attention to their wants by those who have the means of alleviating them, may, and it is fervently hoped will, have the most happy and beneficial result.

The little regard paid to religion by the mass of the manufacturing population in towns, is a painful circumstance connected with their condition,* as it has been truly said, by Dr. Chalmers, that the masses of mill artisans live in practical heathenism. A disregard for the common observances of religious worship, and the spending the Sabbath in drunkenness, is almost universal in the lowest classes. The proportion of these degraded beings, who possess no knowledge whatever of the most simple portions of Christian faith, is truly astonishing. The Report of the Ministry to the Poor in

* " Religious ceremonies are exceedingly neglected; with rare exceptions, the adults of the vast population of 81,147 contained in districts (Manchester) Nos. 1, 2, 3, 4, spend Sunday either in supine sloth, in sensuality, or in listless inactivity."—*Moral and Physical Condition of the Working Classes,* p. 64.

Manchester, says :—" The wide open fields at the outskirts of the town, and places in town less frequented by
the walks of man, are, on the Lord's day, occupied by
herds of boys and young men, and even by men more
advanced in life, gaming. The dram-shops, Tom and
Jerry shops, swarm the Lord's day over (except for an
hour or two in service time), and overflow it at night . . .
Very many of the people whom I visit believe that they
have no power to do the will of God—that they must wait
until they have received assistance from the Spirit of '
God—until God enables them, and makes them willing to
repent. They believe their children equally powerless .
to do good. This belief, and the habits which it has
produced, makes them neglect the moral culture of
themselves and children."—P. 16. Dr. Kay, who was
connected professionally with several charitable institutions, which led him into the homes of these people,
says, that the men spend the Sabbath day in idle
and drunken negligence; and our own observations,
continued for many years, have abundantly satisfied us,
that religion is little cared for, and its forms, in a great
measure, unattended to.

Inquiries made amongst these classes have shewn,
that often there is no belief in the superintending care
of a beneficent Creator—none, of a state of future
rewards or punishments; and that materialism has
placed them, in these respects, upon a level with the
beasts that perish. In numerous other examples, where
even some knowledge was found on religious subjects, it
failed in producing its salutary influence upon morals,
in consequence of apathy and indifference.

Thus, deprived of the most ennobling characteristic of
the human mind, what wonder can be felt that it is a wild
waste, overgrown with noxious weeds, which choke and

destroy the seeds of a better harvest, scattered as they are
so thinly and so rarely over its surface. The savage,
roaming through his native wilderness, bows down with
reverence before the objects he has been taught to worship; and however degraded these are, they are such as
his condition leads him to fear or to love; and he looks
forward to the " spirit land" as his place of rest. Thus,
he is religious in the only way in which his untutored
mind and limited observation will permit, and thus far he
is superior to that portion of the operative manufacturers
which acknowledges no God — which worships no
image—which regards no hereafter. The savage, indeed, from his familiarity with the operations of nature,
in all their wild wonders, is impressed with her power,
and yields obedience to the dictates of a whispering
consciousness that there is—that there must be—a *cause*
for all he sees around him. But how differently placed
is the factory labourer! He knows nothing of nature—
her very face is hidden and obscured from him, and he
is surrounded and hemmed in by a vast circle of human
inventions. He is at perpetual warfare with the world
and with himself, and his bad passions are consequently
in constant play. Thus combating—the pure and holy
impulses of religion can find no home with him, but,
like the dove hanging with trembling wing over the
agitated waters of the deluge, they seek a refuge in the
ark of some more peaceful bosom, and leave him occupied solely by his own impure sensations.*

The immoralities which stain the character of the

* Many manufactories in detached situations, and under the
superintendence of religious masters, must not be included in the
above condemnation. We are speaking of the many—the inferences of the Factory Commissioners, and others, are drawn from
the few.

manufacturing population, have been brought under review; these admit of no classification—no statistical inquiries can reach them. Vice, licentiousness, and depravity, which are of universal extent, can only be pointed out, and their operations watched by individuals who are led into their haunts, either by curiosity, a desire to learn in order to amend, or by professional and private duties. Crime, however, open violations of the existing laws, which subject the criminal to punishment, is more in view, and a tolerably accurate account may be given of it.

As civilization advances, and as countries become populous, a change takes place in the character of crime. In the early ages of society, human life was little considered; and hence, injuries to the person characterize this portion of its history. In an opposite state of things, offences against property chiefly prevail; bloodshed and murder giving way to criminal acts of minor enormity; whilst, at the same time, crimes, in proportion as they lessen in enormity, become numerically greater, and of more universal prevalence.

The following table, which has been drawn up with great care, and the results of which have been verified by examination of the authorities, very distinctly shews the varieties in the criminal character of different countries, when viewed in relation to their particular social systems.

Countries.	Population.	Crimes as to Person.	Crimes as to Property.	Personal crimes to Population 1 in	Property do. to Population 1 in
Netherlands .	6,676,000	231	935	28,904	7,140
England . . .	12,422,700	531	15,616	23,395	799
France . . .	32,000,000	1,821	17,735	17,573	1,804
Spain	17,732,000	3,610	2,313	3,804	5,937

In the language of the intelligent author from whose pages the foregoing table is taken:—" Crimes against property have regularly increased with the increase of commerce and manufactures, and the consequent concentration of the population into large towns. The above table shows this too plainly to be misunderstood. Spain, the most ignorant, degraded, and uncommercial of all countries pretending to civilisation, is, in respect of crime against property, *three times* less vicious than France, and more than *seven times* less vicious than England.

This fact is a fearful one, and speaks volumes. England is more than twice as criminal as France, in this department of offences. We also find a striking difference between the north and south of France.* In the former, according to Mr. Charles Dupin, the increase of manufactures and trade is attested by the mercenary nature of the crimes there committed, as compared with the southern districts of the same country ; where offences against the person are substituted for offences against property, and are perpetrated with a black and savage atrocity, which almost baffles conception.† Ireland, again, especially the south, where manufactures have not penetrated, exhibits much violence and bloodshed, but comparatively little of dishonesty or larceny ; while our own country, whose civilisation we are so apt to vaunt, *far* exceeds all others in the career of mercenary crime, and has increased many years back, and is still increasing rapidly, in this painful pre-eminence in guilt."‡

By a parliamentary paper, lately laid before the House, it appears, that crime, during the last twenty

* " Forces Productives et Commerciales de la France."
† " Causes Criminelles Célèbres," &c. Paris, 1828.
‡ *Enquiry*, &c. p. 24.

years, has been progressing in much greater ratio than
the increase of population, but that this progression has
equally characterized the agricultural and manufacturing
districts.   Since the late distress has so widely spread
over many of the agriculturists, there is every reason to
suppose criminal acts are full as frequent as amongst
manufacturers.

The mass of crime which prevails amongst mill
artisans, originates from a variety of causes, totally
independent of manufactures ; and the author just
quoted has mistaken the reason of the dereliction which
he so correctly describes.   The table which he gives
to illustrate his opinions will serve another purpose
just as well.   The average amount of crime as to population in eight manufacturing counties, is 1 to 840,—
in the eight agricultural counties, 1 to 1,043 ; a disproportion much less than might have reasonably been
inferred, when it is remembered how differently the two
situations compared are circumstanced.

In the one, there is a thinly-scattered population—in
the other, densely populous districts, resembling, in fact,
a continued town.   In the one, an abstraction from all
opportunities of committing petty crimes—in the other, a
thousand incitements offered for the commission of larce-
nies.   An examination of all towns will show, that they
are placed in conditions equally as unfavourable as Manchester in this respect.   Crime is no more common in
manufacturing towns and districts, than in other equally
populous localities ; and when the detail which has been
given, as to the general immorality pervading this population, is considered, astonishment should rather be
excited, that crimes of greater enormity are not of more
frequent occurrence.   That crimes are more numerous in
towns and great cities, is sufficiently well known ; but

with regard to England—when her agricultural divisions are found having one criminal in every 1,044 of their inhabitants, and when her manufacturers exhibit one in 840, the difference is much less than might have been fairly presumed.

Pauperism in the class of manufacturers employed at steam machinery, is far from being of very extensive prevalence. These individuals, brought as they are into close contact with each other, and leagued together by combinations, have also, from the force of these circumstances, formed themselves into sick-clubs, having funds for their support or assistance during illness.

Most of the large mills have a particular club or union of their own; and often the spinners, weavers, &c., have each a separate one. These excellent institutions deserve every encouragement and protection, as they tend to do away with some of the evils attending upon the general improvidence of this class.

That parochial relief is administered very largely in manufacturing towns and districts, is certain; but this originates and depends upon the character of the movable population, congregated there *—not upon the actual manufacturers themselves. The immigrations which are continually taking place—the surplus number of hands—and the little respect paid to parents in their old age, and when they are unable to procure a livelihood, are circumstances driving many to the poor-rates.

An inspection of the past and present state of Man-

* Thus in Stockport the number of families receiving relief in 1833 was 651, and the amount distributed 2,447*l.*; of these 65 families were connected with factories, and received 297*l.*, the remainder being divided amongst other poor not engaged in factory employment.

chester, and a comparison of these with the condition of other towns, as to the amount paid by the parish, will show very distinctly, that the major part of the population is supporting itself. Neither are the parties who claim relief from this fund, those connected with manufacture particularly; on the contrary, but very few who depend upon these are burdensome. This arises from their unvarying occupation; a circumstance widely dissimilar from the condition of other manual labourers, who are, in many instances, necessitated to pass a considerable portion of their time in idleness, and, of course, in poverty, and who have no resource, but to seek their subsistence from foreign aid.

The most decisive evidence on this point is to be found in the Tables of Revenue and Commerce lately published by Government. From these Tables it appears that the amount levied for the relief of the poor, compared with the population, is less in Lancashire, the great seat of manufactures, than in any other county in the kingdom, being only 4s. 8d. per head.

	s.	d.	
Cumberland	5	8	per head.
Westmoreland	9	3	
Oxfordshire	18	0	
Sussex	20	11	
Middlesex	10	1	

Hyde, a township exclusively manufacturing, into which machinery was introduced in 1801, when the population amounted to 830, paid at that time in poor-rate 533l.; whilst in 1830, when the population had increased to 7000, the poor rate was only 550l.

CHAPTER XI.

COMBINATIONS.

Labour the Poor Man's Capital—Considerations on this—Its fluctuating Value—Its Rate of Exchange—Peculiar Nature of this
Capital——Want of Confidence between Master and Men—Combination, Evils of—Effects—Consequences to the Men, and to
particular Districts—Extent of Combinations—Their Tyranny—
Their Universality—Delegates—Their Character—Seeds of Disunion existing in Combination described—Effects of Turn-outs—
Evil to the Men—Master less injured—Stationary Nature of their
Property—Its Advantages—Union of Regulations—Consideration as to the Fate of Cotton Manufacture, if entirely dependent
on Human Labour—Moral Influence of Combinations—Vitriol
throwing—Murder, &c. &c.—Conduct towards the Masters—
Combinations of Masters, &c.—Conduct of Delegates—Conduct
of Masters—Importance of Confidence—Consequences of existing state of things—Gluts—New Hands, &c.—Benefit of Mutual
Regulations—Steam Engine—Application and Extent of its
'Powers—Proper Conduct of Masters and Men—Morality of the
Operatives, exhibited in Combinations—Domestic Manufacturers.

It has been argued by those who are favourable to
combinations amongst workmen, that their labour is
their capital ; that it is the fund upon which they live ;
and that they have the same right to turn it to the utmost
advantage as any capitalist has to turn money to the best
account. Viewed abstractedly, this is true—a man's
labour is his capital ; it is the fund from which he

derives his means of sustenance ; and he has as much, and as clear a right to dispose of it in the most advan- tageous manner, as of capital of any other sort.

Labour, or the physical strength necessary for labour, to be converted into capital, must have a rateable value put upon it. It is the unrefined ore or cotton rag, the respective values of which are entirely conventional. And it is so with labour. Of itself it is nothing, by itself it is nothing—it must be stamped or moulded to bring it into a state fit for useful exchange.

Such is the mere physical capability of the working man. It would not prevent him dying of inanition. Its value is given to it by the demand, and the person or community so calling it into demand, has, in the first instance, an obvious right to rate it as may seem at the particular juncture its fair equivalent.

So far, then, the labour of the artisan is not, *per se,* of value, but its value is given to it by certain causes independent of any voluntary act of his own. The value once given, it becomes his fixed capital, and it is here the comparison commences.

In making this acknowledgment, it must be borne in mind, that if it be capital, it is of necessity liable to the same fluctuations as affect other species of capital ; now, from fortuitous circumstances, doubled or trebled in value ; then reduced to a like amount, or so far lower, that it ceases to be worth the possessor's while to employ it.

Labour being the poor man's sole possession, his property, deserves an equal portion of legislative protec- tion with property of any other kind ; and in return, it should be content to be placed under the same restraints and regulations, which are placed for the benefit of all parties upon other kinds of property.

If in periods of great public distress, the monied men of the kingdom were permitted, unrestrained by legal shackles, to advance at will the rate of interest, they would quickly absorb the greatest portion of the national wealth; if, in times of manufacturing depression, the workman was permitted to raise at will the price of his labour, he would quickly absorb the wealth or means of the manufacturer. In the one instance the few would be enriched at the expense of the many; in the other, the many would be enriched at the expense of the few; but, in both instances, it is quite clear that the advantages gained would be no compensation for the evils which must necessarily disorganize society.

The exchangeable value of labour must at all times depend upon many contingencies, just as the exchangeable value of the manufactured article does. The middle man, as the master manufacturer may be called, placed between the labourer on the one hand, and the consumer on the other, is necessitated to accommodate both parties, and to regulate their mutual operations. If the labourer take the arrangement into his own hands, he will naturally enough keep up the price of his own article—labour. To suppose that he will keep this well balanced, so as to enable the master manufacturer to make a profit on his capital—money; and the consumer to supply himself at a rate, advantageous, when compared with other markets, is an absurdity. He will do no such thing—he is selfish from his very circumstances and condition, and has besides that, none of those general views and extended information which are requisite for preserving a just equilibrium. He would, in the first place, ruin his master by preventing him fairly competing with his neighbours; he would ruin himself by thus lessening the immediate amount of manufacture ; and he would ruin his country as a commercial one, by disabling it from carrying on its manufacturing operations in a way to rival other countries.

On the other hand the master-manufacturer, if permitted to regulate the value of labour, would undoubtedly reduce it below its just level. It is asserted that the minimum price of labour should be that which affords to the labourer a comfortable subsistence. The value of a man's labour, however, in many instances, is far below what would support him. The proposition would be more tenable, were it said, that every member of a community who labours in his vocation, and is productive as far as circumstances will permit, has a claim for support upon the community at large, which, in some shape or other, derives benefit from him ; but to saddle him upon a particular portion of the community, would be alike unjust and partial.

Nothing should be expected from the master-manufacturer beyond this—that he should not enrich himself at the expense of his labourers ; but after securing that which he has a right to do—a proper return for his outlay of capital, risk, and other contingencies, then that the surplus should be considered due to the labourers, and paid over to them in such a way as to interfere the least with their independent use of it.

Experience has long ago taught one lesson, that wherever power was possessed by man over man, it was liable to abuse, and that some regulation was essentially necessary to remedy a state of things apparently natural to him, in whatever state of civilisation he is placed. It is equally for the benefit of master and men, that they should either make these regulations for themselves, or should wisely submit to any legislative enactments intended to save them from each other, and from their own partial and unjust opinions.

There is always a great difficulty in legislating for the protection of particular interests, arising chiefly from the impossibility of government acquiring correct information. Each party is alike strenuous for their separate interests, and each alike interested in perverting or distorting the facts of one another. Could they once be convinced that their interests are mutual, they would be by far the best legislators for themselves; but from the various combinations which exist, and from the exasperations of feeling which have grown up between them in consequence of these, very little hope is left that they will ever cordially unite in mitigating, on the one hand, the condition of the labourer, and, on the other, in upholding the just interests of the manufacturer.

The total want of confidence which at present marks the relations of the master manufacturer and his hands, have been brought about chiefly by unadvised combinations on both sides.

It may be truly stated, that they are in organized opposition, in banded societies, for the purpose of injuring the interests of each other, from a mistaken and groundless hope that such injury would benefit themselves. It could do no such thing; and they only heighten the unavoidable misfortunes incident upon their separate states, by a course of proceeding at variance with every thing just and charitable, and which, by its demoralizing agency, is rapidly unfitting them from ever regaining a position, with reference to each other, which is alone compatible with their best interests.

Combination is justifiable only when a disposition

is plainly shown to take certain advantages which may be more or less injurious to either party. On the one hand, the master may wish and endeavour to exact more work from his hands without increasing their wages, and thus add to his profits at the expense of their labour. Here he may find himself thwarted in his purpose. His men scatter themselves amongst his neighbours, or refuse to work, knowing that he cannot afford to let his machinery and stock in trade remain idle.* Under these circumstances, if his neighbours do not embrace his cause, he is compelled to take back his hands upon their own terms, having possibly to make certain sacrifices, as to mill regulations, as a propitiation.

The passive combination of the men here gains them their object; and in this particular instance, perhaps, the conduct of the individual master might be wrong. But this triumph by no means leaves them in the same relative situation which they held before. Their natural order is to some extent reversed, and the men have learnt a dangerous power. Farther still, the character of the master is lowered in their estimation; they have no faith in him, and are eternally jangling and disputing upon points of discipline. On the other hand, this power having once been acknowledged, the men, in their turn, become more unreasonable, and during a run of trade, or seizing upon some other favourable juncture, demand either a lessening of the period of labour, or an increased rate of payment for that which they already go through. The master demurs; his hands strike, and he finds himself on the very verge of ruin in consequence. He holds out if he can; and the men, having their own

* " There are many cotton mills in Manchester of which the interest on sunk capital amounts to from 5,000l. to 10,000l."— *Philosophy of Manufactures,* p. 281.

sufferings to contend with, in the end return at their old prices, or an increase so small, as to be a straw in the balance compared to what they have lost during their wilful idleness.

It is quite obvious, that occurrences of this nature, so detrimental to the interests of the men on the one hand, and the masters on the other, must lead to the adoption of some measures having for their intention the equalization or protection of both against caprice, avariciousness, and unreasonable and untimely demands. Unfortunately, each party made their own arrangements. The men under the belief that they were all powerful, and the masters in self-defence, with the farther understanding that they would assist each other. On both sides funds were collected, delegates and secretaries appointed, and labour and monied capital came into direct collision.

A history of the privations borne by the workmen in some of these insane contests would present an awful picture of human suffering, and a picture, not the less awful, of rapid demoralization. So far have these gone sometimes, as to threaten the ruin of an entire and flourishing town or district, and have involved in it not only the interests of the two conflicting parties, but the race of shopkeepers and others dependent upon them for their support. The most extensive emigrations have taken place, poor-rates have been doubled, and society disorganized.* Of the truth of these remarks the silk trade of Macclesfield affords a notable example.

* "The effects arising from combinations are almost always injurious to the parties themselves. As the injury done to the men and their families is almost always more serious than that which affects their employers, it is of the utmost importance to the comfort and happiness of the former class that they should themselves entertain sound views upon this question."—*Babbage*, p. 296.

These struggles have uniformly been most disastrous
to the men, and must ever be so. It is in vain that in
their rage, worked up into madness by heartless demagogues, by hunger, by the sight of their famishing
children, they have taken the law into their own hands,
and dreadful proofs have they given how unfit were they
to wield it for their own benefit. Incendiarism, machine
breaking, assassination,* vitriol throwing,† acts of diabolical outrage, all have been perpetrated for intimidation
or revenge ; but in all cases with the like result, or when

---

* The deliberate assassination of Thomas Ashton, son of Mr.
S. Ashton, one of the principal cotton manufacturers in the neighbourhood of Manchester, during the strike in 1831-32, was an act
of the most atrocious villany. Returning from the mill early in
the evening through a bye-road, he was shot through the chest
within a very few yards both of the mill and his father's house. A
victim less deserving his untimely fate it would have been difficult
to have selected, for he was distinguished by his general kindness
to the men, and endeared by his amiable qualities to his friends.
The crime would seem to have been perpetrated by three people
in company, who had been seen lurking about during the early
part of the evening. The men lately tried and condemned as the
perpetrators of this heinous deed were accused under circumstances of an exceedingly suspicious character.

† The crime of vitriol throwing is a novel feature in the annals
of the country. It consists of putting into a wide-necked bottle a
quantity of sulphuric acid—oil of vitriol as it is commonly called—
and throwing this upon the person of the obnoxious individual,
being either directed to the face or dress merely, or of throwing a
quantity upon any work offensive to the party. The caustic
nature of this fluid renders it a formidable weapon when it is
applied to any exposed part of the body, and in several instances
loss of sight has resulted from it, and in a vast number of others
very great suffering has resulted from its application. It is immediately destructive to the texture of cloth from its corrosive qualities. This demoniacal proceeding was exceedingly prevalent
during the turn out of 1830-1, many of the masters not daring to
stir out during the evening.

partial success has attended them, it has been but temporary.

The extent to which combinations exist amongst workmen is only fully shewn when a general strike in a particular branch of trade takes place. Then they are seen ramifying in every direction, embracing all trades alike, each having their separate rules and code of laws, but all uniting in one point, to support the operative, when he either voluntarily abstracts himself from employ, or is driven out by some new demand on the part of his master. Each trade has a sort of corporate board for the management of its funds, the protection so called of its particular interests, and this board is paid for its services out of a specific allowance made by every workman who is a member of the union or combination. The sums thus abstracted from the pockets of the deluded artisan have been very considerable, the regulations being compulsory in the extreme.

" I was not aware," says Mr. Stewart, in the first Report of the Factory Commission, " until I was engaged in the investigation at Glasgow, that the operatives there have so completely organized their association, as not only to prescribe the wages to be paid to the members of the association, but to all other persons, from whatever quarter they may come : that, further, no male worker not entered with them *is allowed to work at all* without their consent and the concurrence of the association, and never without making a payment to them at the beginning, and continuing a weekly payment at the same rate as their own afterwards ; that females, however able, are not allowed to become spinners, or to be engaged as such ; and that it is hardly in the power of a piecer, that is, of an assistant to a spinner, to learn the business of a spinner, unless he is related to a spinner, who will bring him

forward; that, in short, the object of the Glasgow Association is to make their company a close corporation,
accessible only to those whom they choose to admit, and
not only to prevent all others from becoming spinners
by their regulations, but, by a system of intimidation,
which they successfully carry into execution, absolutely
by physical force."

No workman is allowed to act according to the dictates of his own feelings—he is compelled to become a
member, or subject himself to a course of annoyances
and injuries which have repeatedly ended in death.
This arbitrary and tyrannical assumption of power is one
of the greatest evils attending upon the system of combinations amongst the operatives. However well-disposed the industrious and economical workman may be,
he is placed upon a level with the most profligate and
idle, who are in general the stirrers up of these strikes;
he is condemned against his own judgment to abstain
from working; to be satisfied with two or four shillings
per week from the union fund for the support of his
family, in the place of earning amongst them two or
three pounds—to remain in idleness for weeks in succession, to the utter ruin of his habits—and is deprived
of all stimulus to be a good and industrious citizen, by
the certainty that he is liable to be turned out of employment from causes over which he has no control,
and which not unfrequently he cannot comprehend.

Mr Chappel, a manufacturer in Manchester, relates,
in the Report of the Factory Commission, a common
and illustrative case—" I will relate the circumstances
of the last turn-out, which took place on the 16th of
October, 1830, and continued till the 17th of January,
1831. The whole of our spinners, whose average
weekly wages were 2l. 13s. 6d., turned out at the insti-

gation, as they told at the time, of the delegates of the Union. They said they had no fault to find with their wages, their work, or their masters ; but the Union obliged them to turn out. The same week, three delegates from the Spinners' Union waited upon us at our mill, and dictated certain advances in wages, and other regulations ; to which, if we would not adhere, they said neither our own spinners nor any other should work for us again. Of course we declined, believing our wages to be ample, and our regulations such as were necessary for the proper conducting our establishment. The consequences were, they set watches on every avenue of the mill, day and night, to prevent any fresh hands coming into the mill ;—an object which they effectually attained by intimidating some and promising support to others (whom I got into the mill in a caravan,) if they would leave their work. Under these circumstances I could not work the mill, and advertised it for 'sale without any application, and I also tried in vain to let it. At the end of twenty-three weeks, the hands requested to be taken into the mill again on the same terms they had left it, declaring, as they had done at first, that the Union alone had forced them to turn out."

When it is borne in mind how great a proportion of the labourers employed in factories consists of females and children, the evil presents itself in a still more striking point of view. In nineteen cases out of twenty these can have nothing to do with the originating the turn-out, which is equally, however, operative upon them, a regular complement and series of hands being necessary for the working of a mill. They are thus subjected to starvation and idleness, both exercising a most powerful influence upon their moral and social character—an influence of the most debasing quality.

The operations of manufacturing yarn from the raw material, it is true, is distinct from the manufacturing it into cloth—so far the spinner and the weaver are completely separated; they are, however, often carried on simultaneously in the same mill, the same steam-engine serving for both purposes. Occasions have occurred when the spinners have turned out, leaving the weavers in employ; and *vice versâ*, the weavers have turned out, leaving the spinners in employ, each supposing itself to have separate causes for complaint or satisfaction. The great turn outs have, however, involved both, or when they have been partial, the injury, though less, has still been felt by the whole—the members of the same family or household being indiscriminately composed of spinners, weavers, and their dependents.

It has repeatedly happened that the disputes which have ended in a general turn out have had reference only to a very small portion of the hands—spinners of a particular class for example, such as coarse or fine yarns, in the demand for which some change has come on, which may have necessitated the master to reduce the wages paid for its manufacture; but so complete and determinate has been the organization amongst the whole union, that thousands have deserted their occupation, and submitted to every sort of suffering incident to the deepest poverty.

Many writers, at various times, when the public mind has been disturbed by these disastrous divisions, have stated that the funds of the unions have, to a very considerable extent, shielded the turn-outs from sufferings. When a turn-out is but partial—that is, when the hands of a particular mill, or of a limited portion of one of the great division of labourers, from causes peculiar to themselves, have struck, this statement is to some degree true; but in the general turn-outs, when from ten to eighteen thousand men, women, and children, have to receive assistance from these funds, they are but a drop of water in the bucket, even though assisted in the most extensive way by the shopkeepers, and by advances from every other trade.

The appointment of delegates, individuals chosen from amongst the workmen, and invested with power to arrange disputes and to manage their funds, is a practice deserving the severest reprobation. By withdrawing the body of the workmen from confidential intercourse with their masters, the interposition of these middlemen, like the Tribunes of ancient Rome, increase the evil a thousand-fold. Living as they do upon a liberal allowance from the wages of the starving operative, their motives are open to suspicion of the most injurious tendency, and the character of most of them does any thing but remove these. Selected at moments of party excitement, of rancorous feelings, of raised expectations—the brawler, the factious man, the specious scoundrel, have too often become the dictators of the misguided people, and to maintain their own evil pre-eminence, they have spared no pains to distort and garble facts, to blacken and destroy the reputation of the masters, and to keep open the breach from which they alone could derive advantage. For a considerable period subsequent to the first organization of the unions, the men were misled by the numbers which formed them—and their calculations based on numerical strength deluded them into the belief that they were all powerful.

This hallucination, for it deserves no other term, was carefully fostered by the delegates, who, finding

T

themselves elevated into petty kings, wielded their authority with as much complacency and despotism as other potentates. For a time, it is possible, from the narrow and selfish view they took of matters, they were equally deceived by the universality of the combinations, and indulged the hope that they should be able to crush the masters, and make them subservient to their dictates.

Combinations have, however, within themselves the seeds of discord and disunion—the elements of dissolution. Could they be brought to conform to fixed and general laws, and to act simultaneously, they would indeed be irresistible. Great bodies of men, dependent although they may be upon some one branch of national industry, have nevertheless separate and well-defined interests. During the first burst of enthusiasm, brought about by what they think emancipation from thraldom, these may be forgotten or thrown aside, and all may join heart and hand in the promotion of what they suppose the cause. If at this time any man of commanding talents, and great energies, were to arise amongst them, he might become the agent for prolonging this state of things. Men gifted with the requisite talents and influence have, however, as yet, fortunately for the welfare and commercial existence of the kingdom, never arisen. Trumpery demagogues have indeed pushed themselves into short-lived authority and leading; none have, however, been found, who have not soon displayed their entire inability to rule or direct the storm, which merely bore them on its surface. No sooner were the effects of the vast drain upon their money resources felt—no sooner the first excitement passed away—than the natural interests and importance of each separate town or body were again brought into play, and want of general cordiality and unanimity of acting soon rendered the great combinations partially inoperative.

The scenes which were the result of these combinations of labour against capital and due subordination, all who have witnessed will join in condemning as tending to the destruction of social order, and the security of life and property; and though the arm of the executive may have fallen heavily and indiscriminately upon the disturbers of the public peace, every man having a correct knowledge of the results which would have necessarily emanated from them, may deplore but cannot condemn it.

No estimate, at all approaching to accuracy, can be made by persons living in districts or towns which have never been visited by one of these turn-outs, of the social disorganization which attends upon them. In 1805-6, when power-looms were introduced, the total suspension of trade, and the turbulent and distracted state of the hand-loom weavers, with the consequent violations of rights of property, in the destruction of machinery, are still well remembered. But this display of hostility by no means interfered with the rapid spread of the power-loom; on the contrary, it only afforded a more decided stimulus to it.

The manifestation which had been made, previous to this epoch, of the difficulty of keeping in due subordination human power, made steam doubly welcome to the manufacturers, by placing under their control an agent, which their sagacity clearly foresaw would, in the course of time, render them to a very great degree independent of it. And events have justified their prognostications: but they failed then, and have since failed, in convincing the men, that they were pursuing a line of conduct, which, if permitted to proceed to extremities, must ruin them by ruining the manufacturers; and by driving away capital,

for ever deprive themselves of the benefits invariably
resulting from its judicious employment: and in showing
also that their opposition to improvements in machinery,
which were gradually lowering their wages, only tended
still farther to accelerate their progress.

One great evil which has ever attended both partial
and general strikes that have continued for any length
of time—and some of these have extended over six
months—is, that the means of the turn-out have been
quite exhausted long before he again got to work.
The pittance he received from the Union did but little
towards his support, and hence he was necessitated to
get into debt, and pay a most extortionate price for the
common necessaries of life. These engagements were,
of course, to the retail dealers in provisions, who were
themselves not unfrequently ruined by a system of
credit, far too extensive for their limited capital. In all
cases, however, the long arrear had to be paid up whenever work was obtained, and this absorbed the greater
portion of his wages for many months, — thus prolonging the distress which had already well nigh overwhelmed him. This has been one great cause of the
squalid wretchedness so generally found in the houses
of the operatives.

It is obvious, from the preceding details, that combinations of workmen against masters—of labour against
capital—have uniformly, in the manufacturing districts,
been injurious to the men to a much greater extent than
to the master.* His capital, it is true, was for the time
injured, but he had means of supporting himself during

* " I have seen a great many turn-outs, and have invariably
found that the result was the lowering the wages of the operative."
—Mr. Harter, Evidence on Silk Trade. Second Factory Commission
Report.

these struggles. The nature of his investment prevented him from carrying away his capital and enterprise to other localities, and other ways of employing them; and in this has consisted one great cause of the stability of manufacturers. Building and machinery could not be removed nor converted into portable property, without a ruinous sacrifice. Often, indeed, the manufacturer has been heard to deplore this as his greatest hardship, which was in point of fact his greatest advantage, for it prevented his abstraction, and by forcing him to submit to a temporary inconvenience, he was sure, in a short time, to be right again.

The same fact—and it is one which strongly illustrates the almost paradoxical proposition, that men rarely know what is their real advantage — induced the workmen to believe, that by thus having the property of their master fast in its present position, they could the more easily make him compromise himself. It had, in point of fact, exactly the opposite effect in both cases. On the side of the master he was chained down, and thus compelled to wait for a revulsion in the popular mind; on that of the workmen, in spite of all the precautions they could adopt, new hands were invariably introduced, or means taken to secure their introduction, when the storm was blown over; added to which, the mill-owner, thus deserted by his men, turned his attention and efforts to the improvement of his machinery, and acquired a practical knowledge of its operations, and capabilities for alteration, which, under a different state of things, he might possibly never have acquired.*

The general combinations, which include nearly the whole of the manufacturing population, and which are

* *Vide* Babbage, p. 298—Manufacture of Gun Barrels, &c.

so mischievous in their effects, have numerous minor and subsidiary cooperative unions. The spinners, weavers, piecers, finishers, &c. &c. each combine in their own class, and have each distinct rules and regulations for their direction; subordinate, however, to the general confederations into which their distinct interests merge. The same evils in a minor degree attend upon these; the divisions amongst them being founded chiefly with regard to the amount of wages received, and the differences in the amounts of contributions paid into the general fund. They are, however, quite distinct in their separate corporate capacities, acting quite independently of one another, and assimilating only in being parties in the general combination.

Independently of associations for the fancied protection of the general and separate interests of the several classes which compose the mill artisans, and which relate to general questions connected with their interests, every mill has its peculiar arrangements. These are regulations as to hours of work, fines for imperfect work, regulations as to the engine, &c. &c., and are commonly made in conjunction with the master, and are indeed necessary for the interests of both, as they serve as mutual checks, and as restrictions upon the conduct of the overlookers, engine men, &c., and are thus found mutually advantageous.

In looking back at the history of the cotton manufacture, and in examining the rise and growth of combinations amongst workmen, it may be asserted, that but for the application of steam, it must either have been destroyed by those who should most have fostered it, or that it would have been so restricted in its operations, and so burdened with expensive details, that it would never have progressed so as to become the staple trade of the country, and this, too, quite independent of the additional power gained by it. To what extent hand manufacture might have gone, it is not easy even to guess; but it is quite certain that it might have gone vastly farther than it has ever yet been pushed. If the power now engaged in manufacture were derived from hand labour, an immense amount of production would be the result. There is no reason why double the amount of hands should not be engaged in it, or treble, or any amount that would be sufficient to throw off as much work as would equal the present joint production of steam and hand labour.

Such a mass of labourers, if brought into intimate communion with each other, would, however, be utterly unmanageable. Trade would be liable to fluctuations which must ruin it, and its entire control would be vested in the workmen. If combinations have been ruinous to some masters, and injurious to trade at some junctures, with the aid of steam, in some degree an independent power, what would have been their effect if it must have entirely submitted to their caprice?

The moral influence of combinations upon the character of the manufacturing population has been exceedingly pernicious. It has placed a barrier between the master and the hands which can never be removed, but with the utmost difficulty. Suspicion has usurped the place of confidence; with an utter alienation of all friendly feelings—mutual fear—hatred, and a system of espionage totally subversive of every thing honourable in their intercourse.

Nothing can more strongly mark the demoralization brought about by the agency of turn-outs, the result of combination, than the acts which have been committed by the men, and openly boasted of. * Cutting away cloth from the looms of those better disposed individuals who preferred working for the support of their families, to starving in obedience to a fiat to strike—a system of inquisitorial visitation ruinous to neighbourly kindness— the darker crime of vitriol throwing, more cowardly and treacherous than the stab of the Italian bravo—the waylaying and abusing obnoxious individuals—and the stain which must ever rest upon them, indelibly marked, and branding them with infamy—that of murder.*

The demonstrations of vengeance, carried into effect in some instances, have at times forced the masters to arm themselves—to garrison their houses and mills, and have placed a whole district in a state of siege, with all the disorganization of social ties incident to civil warfare. No man was safe—no family secure from midnight disturbance; shots were fired into the rooms where it was believed the master had his resting-place. By day he had to use every precaution to avoid falling into the hands of an infuriated mob—his family reviled—loaded with the most opprobrious epithets—hooted and hissed wherever opportunity offered; no wonder that feelings of bitterness were roused against those who thus wantonly violated all the forms of decency and justice.

Another moral evil of equal magnitude to the labourer, resulting from combinations, is, that it renders himself and family improvident, and this is the very bane of all his comfort. Whatever the cause may be which renders a man's labour of doubtful continuance, or which

---

* " They set watches in the streets, and abuse any body that comes in the most shocking manner, even to taking their lives if it were necessary. Some years ago, there were several people almost destroyed by vitriol being thrown upon them by combined men."—*Wm. Graham, Esq. of Glasgow, in Report of Committee on Manufactures*, p. 335.

occasionally, and at uncertain intervals, throws him out
of employ, it invariably injures his industrial character.
The same remark has been used before, when speaking
of the hand-loom weavers, whose occupation was irregular and fluctuating. It was very truly observed by
Mr. Galloway, in his evidence, that " When employers
are competent to show their men that their business is
steady and certain, and that when men find that they
are likely to have permanent employment, they have
always better habits and more settled notions, which will
make them better men and better workmen, and will
produce great benefits to all who are interested in their
employment." In these respects the combinations and
" strikes " have been ruinous to a degree. A consciousness that there is this uncertainty with regard to the
continuance of his work, removes from the labourer all
stimulus to work diligently, and earn for himself an
honest reputation. He feels that he is no free agent in
the matter, and loses, in consequence, much of that
personal respect for himself, without which he possesses
but half his moral stamina.

The repeated evils brought upon the masters by the
combinations of their hands, made it imperatively necessary that they should be met in a similar way. No
master could cope single-handed with a combination of
his own men,* who were leagued together to prevent
any sufficient supply of new hands, and were liberally
supported by their co-mates. The interests of the
masters having become more generally understood, and
that of one identified with the rest, they in turn refused
to employ any operative who made himself conspicuous

* " We have, once or twice, ourselves attempted to stand out
against our men, but we have been obliged to take them in."—
Wm. Graham, Esq. in Committee's Report on Manufactures, p. 335.

in the combinations, and gradually feeling their own
strength, dismissed all those who could be detected as
belonging to the obnoxious unions. Not satisfied with
this, however, they refused to engage a workman who
had been dismissed or had voluntarily withdrawn himself
from the service of another master, provided he did not
bring with him a certificate as to character. This point
gained, the masters had the destiny of each operative in
their keeping. If he disbehaved himself he was straightway
dismissed, and found himself, unless under very peculiar
circumstances, utterly excluded from all chance of getting
occupation in that town or district, and had no little
difficulty in procuring it even if he removed. For a
time he received a pittance from the joint funds, which,
spite of all the vigilance exercised for its suppression,
still existed.

So long as masters confine themselves to the legitimate objects which should govern their unions, viz.
protection against the unfounded and unreasonable
demands of their workmen—the cultivation of their
own undoubted authority, with the interior regulation of
their mills—their efforts will be hailed and cordially
seconded by every man who has a knowledge of the
miseries incident to the want of these, and who looks
forward to a regeneration in the moral and social condition of the operatives. It is much to be feared, however, that these combinations may not end here. The
terrible lessons which have been taught the masters will
lead them to exert every device, to strain every nerve,
in order to annihilate the influence of the men beyond
simple and subordinate agents to their tractable and
gigantic servant the steam-engine; and in doing this,
both the interests of the men, and that of the public,
would inevitably suffer.

If experience could have taught the men wisdom, they would long ago have learnt that riot could serve no good purpose; and that now the masters are banded together, and know their interests to depend upon the exclusion of turbulence from their mills, it must be fatal to any party who indulge in it. They cannot prevent the introduction of new hands, they cannot prevent improvements in machinery ; and though their wages must suffer, and though their labour must go on increasing to acquire even the wages they now earn, there is no human power to interfere with or thwart it.

The moral effects of combinations amongst the masters are, the keeping alive those suspicions which have so long been the bane both to the happiness of the labourer and to their own. Ever disposed to view all attempts at change as innovations upon what he erroneously conceives to be a matter under his own control, the workman murmurs and finally rebels, if he finds that these changes are tending to increase his hours of labour without an adequate compensation. As he finds, however, that his rebellion has ceased to be beneficial, that his master assumes a higher tone, and, spite of all his efforts, contrives to carry on the operations of his mill, partly by the introduction of new hands, and partly by improving his machinery, he will surely discover that he had better, in place of becoming a turn-out, endeavour, by exertion, by economy, by domestic habits, by acquiring feelings of providence and anxiety for something beyond to-day, remedy, as far as is in his power, the change in his circumstances. If masters will combine steadily, and aim at inculcating subordination, respect for proper authority, and to these add their anxious endeavours to effect these desirable alterations in the present characters of their workmen, which can alone render them permanently quiet, they will deserve well of their country. If they succeed in establishing their own power upon the wreck of the labourer's independence and morality, they will have nothing to congratulate themselves upon, and must ever live on the surface of a volcano, which at any moment may be roused into destructive action.

Intellectual education, by partially expanding the views of the operative, has as yet done little towards improving his correct judgment, and enabling him to detect the mischief that may lurk beneath the disguise of apparent sympathy when painted in glowing colours. Opportunity has been taken of this by their delegates, &c. &c., and they still succeed to a certain extent in some situations in keeping up their injurious influence, driven as they have deservedly been from the mills of those masters who are anxious to preserve order, and establish a good understanding between themselves and their men: they have either been compelled to work for the inferior employers at a less wage, or have sought some other business ostensibly, but still trusting to derive subsistence from the occasional ebullitions on the part of the prejudiced and irritable workmen, and in some instances they are successful.

The bad passions of the men are easily roused—they have no faith in the justice of their masters; and though a state of things is gradually encompassing them, which must force them to succumb, or entirely ruin themselves, no sooner does some improvement in machinery of extensive operation lower the value of labour, and render certain changes necessary either in wages or hours of work, than bickerings and heartburnings arise, which, however, for some time, have subsided peaceably. The example shown to the men during 1830 and 1831, when the masters one and all stood out to resist certain demands, did much towards breaking the spirit of insubordination; and if they remain firm and decided, and mutually assist each other, they will eventually succeed in putting an end to combinations and their concomitant evils.

The establishment of schools by the masters; the taking a personal and positive interest in the welfare of those immediately under them; the showing them that they are sincerely anxious to assist; and pointing out the way in which their wages may be made amply suffi-cient to cover all their wants; will in time produce their effects, in all out districts—in the towns the process of regeneration must be slower. The men are much less under the influence of the masters, their hands making only a part of a great and demoralized population.

The improvement which has taken place in the great body of masters within the last few years, is perhaps the best guarantee for improvement amongst the men. The immense amount of capital invested in manufac-tures will prevent them unnecessarily doing any thing which can involve in danger the returns for this outlay. They are, too, fully aware that their locality is determined, and that, however turn-outs may plague and harass them, that they are fixed and sta-tionary. A general turn-out, even for a limited period, is attended with enormous pecuniary sacrifices, but fall-ing as it does upon great masses of capital, or upon high reputation and credit, it is comparatively harmless. Any lengthened idleness, however, in this capital, is ruinous in a high degree, both to the trade itself and to the masters. This is one of the most powerful reasons for inducing them to cultivate the confidence of their men, and for joining in an union which will enable them to protect themselves, by refusing to yield to clamour, and in arranging certain amounts of wages to be paid by them as a fixed rule.

The higher the character of the master ascends, and the greater his wealth, and the gradual clearing away from amongst their body mere men of straw, who can submit to no rules on account of their necessities, and the approximation to one general standard, will enable them in time to lay down such rates of wages as will be universally applicable ;. some time must necessarily elapse before this can take place.

The great manufacturers, who also invariably possess the best machinery, can afford to make goods at a something less price than the secondary men. If a strict combination were therefore to take place amongst them, and they were determined to sell as low as possible, and keep their wages down, they would speedily ruin the inferior manufacturer, who having a limited capital, second rate machinery, and an absolute necessity for quick returns, could not meet them in the market. A tacit agreement seems to exist, by which the operative and manufacturer at present benefit at the expense cf the public, and this enables the inferior man to make a profit under all his disadvantages. The outcry as to the ruin of the trade is a positive absurdity—it may be confidently asserted that those manufactories which are extensive, and upon the most approved arrangement as to machinery, are making fair returns, and the proprietors could afford to work them, and sell their produce at a diminished price.

If the workmen could be brought to understand some of these truths, a better chance would be given for a union taking place between them and the masters, and both would succeed in keeping up a remunerating price for their separate capitals ; whereas the men, on the one hand, by injuring the property of their masters, compel them to reduce their wages as a compensation, or to demand such excellence of work, and to cut off so much for fines, that it amounts to the same thing as reduction; whilst, on the other hand, the master, finding his hands thus turbulent and unruly, turns all his energies to improvements in his machinery, and endeavours, by throwing off an increased quantity of work, to make amends for the incertitude in his labourers.

This state of things often produces gluts, which injure, again, both masters and men. Another advantage would be gained by a mutual understanding: during turn-outs great numbers of new hands come into the town or district where it exists, generally hand-loom weavers, or operatives from other kinds of manufacture, or individuals from the mining districts; and, rather than have their mills remaining totally idle, the masters engage these, spite of the violence and resistance of the old hands : but then they are ignorant of the details of spinning or weaving, and of the particular kind of labour required; much has to be taught them; a great deal of work is spoiled, and much loss sustained for a time. The men, finding their places partially occupied, and their obstinacy and turbulence yielding before continued privations, gladly return at the old prices: many of necessity cannot be taken in, as it would be a manifest injustice to discharge the hands they have, even though inferior in capability for producing good work.* Thus they are compelled to seek work somewhere else, or to lower their wages, and have been instrumental in introducing a greater number of hands than can find present employ, and hence the

* " In the spring of the year, when the looms were full of goods, the weavers thought they could do what they pleased, and struck for higher wages; but after remaining out of work for three or four months, they came to terms. I had in the meantime got hands from the cotton trade."—*Factory Commission Report. Evidence of Mr. Harter.*

foundation for other reductions of wages before any very long period.

The most important benefit which the men would derive from coalescing with their masters, and agreeing to some certain rules for their mutual regulation, is that they would very soon think each other trustworthy, and those feelings of hostility and bitterness which now exist between them, and which are kept up by combinations — delegates — secretaries — would be done away with. It will be in vain for the men to expect to do this so long as they submit to the dictates of parties interested in keeping up mischief between them and their masters.

The moral revolution which this would at once produce would be an excellent basis on which to rear a superstructure of social arrangements, which might snatch the men and their families from their present degradation. One thing is quite certain, that if they do not adopt some plan of this nature, they will miss the opportunity, and will condemn themselves to a life of servitude to an iron master, who is already more than threatening them.* Let them remember that already the steam-engine, though applied to the same purposes as human labour for so very few years, performs as much work, in simple power, as many millions of human beings! Let them farther remember, that each steam-loom is nearly four times as effective as the hand-loom; that improvements are hourly taking place in its applicability of machinery—giving it endowments —approximating it with the most delicate operations of the human hand ; and let them remember, also, that the moving power never tires ; that to it eight, ten, twelve,

---

* *Vide* Chapter on the Influence of Machinery on the Value of Human Labour.

fourteen, or twenty hours are alike! To endeavour to arrest its progress would be madness: they cannot turn back the stream of events—the onward current of mechanism—their efforts would be equally impotent and ruinous. They may, however, compete with it on more equal ground if they choose, and may prevent the accelerations of its career by working steadily, orderly, and systematically. Every effort which they have made to retard or destroy the progress of machinery has only hurried on the march of improvement; and if they persevere in such a course of proceedings, they will become its victims, bound hand and foot, and resembling, in their condition, the serfs—the *glebæ ascripti* of a former period. Their attempts to break up the social confederacy by violence and outrage, and thus bring on such internal disorder as would deprive the nation of its manufacturing pre-eminence, would be not less fatal to themselves than to their masters.

Let the masters, then, combine — let them elevate their own character let them become great and wealthy; for greatness and wealth, when joined to correct knowledge of the wants of those around them, are the best masters. Let them, by every means in their power, aid the moral and social regeneration of their men; and let them be met frankly and fairly. Let the mill artisans be assisted to shake off habits which destroy them physically and morally; let them cultivate home; let them become good husbands and good wives; and they will, in a single generation, produce offspring who will, in their turn, inherit their good qualities. Let them discountenance agitation, combination, and political quacks. Let them become a sober and orderly race: let them, if they will, appeal to the legislature for enactments to regulate their labour, if excessive—and by so doing they will be their own best friends. With economy and foresight, the means they possess are sufficient to supply their wants, and the requisites of their stations; and were these doubled, without economy, they would be no real gainers. Let them bear in mind that all the members of their family have a resource in the mill; and though the individual earnings may be in some instances small, yet that collectively they are considerable. Let families reunite: let them eschew the gin and the beer shops, the political clubs and union rooms, and they may yet be a happy and contented population. But, if they do not, one thing is certain—that they will be, ere long, ground down to the earth, and present the most humiliating and miserable spectacle the world has ever yet seen, save only the slave-gang and the Indian miners under the deadly yoke of the early Spaniards.

The system of combination is one strongly characteristic of automatic manufacture. For the economic use of the steam-engine, certain local advantages are required, and the same if water be made the moving power. Hence it follows, as it has been already remarked, that the manufacturing arts in the present day assemble the operatives in condensed masses, and thus combination assumes an importance far higher than is usually bestowed upon it.

This principle of union is a striking feature between domestic and factory manufacture. The hand-loom weavers, whether of silk, cotton, or worsted, comprising a far greater number of hands than the factories, have rarely combined. They are a far more moral and conscientious body of people than the factory labourers: even in the midst of the darkest and most hopeless poverty, they have toiled on nearly in silence, whilst the turbulent and demoralized town and country steam spinner, whilst rolling in comparative wealth, has been committing outrages of the most wanton and vicious description. No evidence can be stronger than this of the unhealthy moral condition of one vast section of our population.

" Proud of the power of malefaction," says Dr. Ure, " many of the cotton-spinners, though better paid, as we have shown, than any similar set of artisans in the world, organized the machinery of *strikes* through all the gradations of their people, terrifying or cajoling the timid or the passive among them to join their vindictive union. They boasted of possessing a dark tribunal, by the mandates of which they could paralyse every mill whose master did not comply with their wishes, and so bring ruin on the man who had given them profitable employment for many a year. By flattery or intimidation, they levied contributions from their associates in the privileged mills, which they suffered to proceed in order to furnish spare funds for the maintenance of the idle during the decreed suspension of labour. In this extraordinary state of things, when the inventive head and the sustaining heart of trade were held in bondage by the unruly lower members, a destructive spirit began to display itself among some partisans of the Union. Acts of singular atrocity were committed, sometimes with weapons fit only for demons to wield, such as the corrosive oil of vitriol dashed in the faces of the most meritorious individuals, with the effect of disfiguring their persons, and burning their eyes out of the sockets with the most dreadful agony."*

This atrocious system of violence was exceedingly common in Stockport, Manchester, Oldham, Hyde, Stayley Bridge, and Duckenfield, some time ago. The

* Philosophy of Manufactures, p. 283.

most vindictive and ignorant of savage nations have never exhibited any cruelty or depravity more glaring than this, and the simple fact tells more forcibly the immoral and degraded state of the factory population than the most graphic description or the most minute detail.

. It has been said that the vast body of hand-loom weavers and domestic manufacturers have been hitherto in a great measure free from combination. It is with pain, but without surprise, that we find that of late their unparalleled distress has given rise to many discussions, and that the most strenuous efforts are making to unite them, scattered as they are over a wide extent of territory, into one general and efficient community. Committees have been already formed at Preston, Manchester, Wigan, Bradford, Warrington, and are likely to extend to Scotland, and into the ribbon, stocking-weaving, and bobbin-net district.

CHAPTER XII.

The Feudal Barons and the Master Manufacturers—Nature of the
Truck System—Its injustice—The Cottage System—Its extent
—Advantages and Disadvantages—Moral Evils, &c.—Remarks
on the Proper Conduct of Masters and Men.

Two very important features of the concentration of
labourers in particular localities, brought about by the
application of steam and water power to the manufacturing arts, are the truck and the cottage systems.
The approximation which these show of the condition of
the labourer, under the factory system, to the times of
feudal tenure and vassalage in England is singular.
Then every baron had his set of dependents and retainers,
generally gathered around, or in the immediate neighbourhood of, his castellated mansion, for the convenience
of mutual protection. There is likely to be a much more
rapid return to this state of things than a superficial
observer would discover amongst ourselves.

It has been said, and said truly, that the extremes of
civilisation meet. More than one proof of this remark
may be found in the foregoing pages, and the master

manufacturer and the old feudal baron, however different they may appear, occupy a similar social position.

Hitherto it has happened that the master has been, to some considerable extent, governed by his retainers. Concentration gave power; but as the necessity for the hands daily diminishes before automatic industry, the governing power is reversing, and in many country districts the change is already complete.

An inspection of Belper, Cromford, Hyde, Duckenfield, Stayley Bridge, the villages and hamlets around Oldham, Bolton, Manchester, Stockport, Preston, Glasgow, &c. &c., will show many magnificent factories surrounded by ranges of cottages, often exhibiting signs of comfort and cleanliness highly honourable to the proprietor and the occupants. These cottages are generally the property of the mill owner, and the occupants are universally his dependents.

This dependence is in many cases of the most absolute kind; no power ever enjoyed by the feudal lord was so operative. It is true that the life of the dependent no longer lies at the mercy of the superior: what may be termed his social existence is however at his disposal. Around many mills a fixed population has arisen, which is as much a part and parcel of the property of the master as his machinery. The rapid improvement in this last has put an end to the necessity for new labourers, and thus little colonies are formed under the absolute government of the employer.

Combination amongst the great body of the operatives has as yet checked, or rather overpowered, the growing superiority of the master; and in towns where the hands have no dependence upon the master beyond working for him simply, this superiority is not strongly marked. Every new machine, however, is a step in advance, because every new machine renders him, as far as it goes, independent of his labourer; whilst in equal rate it increases the dependence of the latter.

This dependence has been at times very singularly displayed in what is called the truck system, which the legislature has more than once endeavoured to put down, and always in vain. This system consists in the payment of the wages of the labourer, not in money, but in goods—the master being the seller, and engrossing the market for all the necessaries.

This is a species of traffic which is injurious alike to the character of the master and his men, and one, the abolition of which it would be very desirable to see for both their sakes. It is unjust to the labourer in many ways ; it assists in the ruin of his feelings of independence and free agency, and keeps down his provident wishes, inasmuch as he has no opportunity of being provident.

It has been urged by some writers,* that the men should unite and establish shops for their own supply of the necessaries or comforts of life, such as tea, coffee,

---

* "When the number of workmen living upon the same spot is large, it may be thought desirable that they should unite together, and have an agent to purchase by wholesale those articles which are in most demand, such as tea, sugar, bacon, &c. and to retail them at prices which will just repay the wholesale cost, together with the expense of the agent who conducts their sale. If this be managed wholly by a committee of workmen, aided perhaps by advice from the master, and if the agent is paid in such a manner as to have himself an interest in procuring good and reasonable articles, it may be a benefit to the workman."—*Babbage*, p. 308.

There are innumerable difficulties in the way of Mr. Babbage's scheme, advantageous as it appears at first sight, and in practice it would be found totally useless. It was fairly tried by Mr. Strutt's work people, under the most favourable circumstances, and failed signally.

sugar, soap, &c. &c.   There is no question that the
retail dealer, the petty shopkeeper, gains a very large
profit by his sales, partly by overcharging, and partly
by adulterating his articles, and that so far the men
would improve their situation if they could do away
with this.   A little acquaintance with their characters
and feelings would dissipate any notion of preconceived
advantages, which they would derive from an establishment of a joint stock concern, in the majority of instances, and besides it is impracticable from many
causes.   They will suffer the least from an adherence to
the old plan, both in a pecuniary and in a moral point
of view, and the retail dealer will be by simple competition brought to something like a moderate demand for
the employment of his capital.

The case, however, is widely different with regard to
the masters.   They have indeed urged that the men are
still free to purchase at their shop, or elsewhere, as best
suits their convenience.   The statement is fallacious,
and unworthy consideration; the men are not, cannot
be free agents in the matter.   Abundant means are in
the hands of the master to compel them, by indirect
measures, to confine themselves to his shop; and in very
numerous instances no such reserve is shewn, but the
men are presented with a ticket to nearly the full
amount of their wages, and this is alone negotiable at
these shops.   It has happened repeatedly that the workman, wanting a few shillings for some other purpose,
has consented to take a sum considerably less than was
his right, rather than have articles which he either did
not want, or that he wanted something else more indis-
pensably and immediately—and this was his only mode
of procuring the needful sum at an immense sacrifice.
What more striking proof of utter dependence can be

found than this on the part of the labourer? It is carrying power a step beyond the oppression of the warlike baron, or the Russian noble over his serfs.

If the master's object were the advantage of the labourer, and if the labourer could be induced to give him credit that it were so ; and if the master employed a portion of his capital in the purchase of wholesome goods, and retailed them at a lower price than the common shopkeeper, which he could well afford to do, and still have a fair return ; some of the objections against the system would fall to the ground. But it is just the reverse; the price charged by the master is invariably as high, and in many instances much higher, than his humble neighbour, and his goods are very generally inferior, and retailed out so arbitrarily as to increase the other mischiefs. Many masters, in all branches of manufactures, are in the habit of killing cows, sheep, pigs, &c., very extensively, and distributing the meat amongst their men, at a price universally above the market average ; many are dealers in coal ; and, in short, every commodity required by the operative, some or other of these masters deal in.*

The evils of this system are so apparent, and its injustice so gross and glaring, that nothing but a very low estimate of morality can be possessed by those masters who are engaged in it. They drive all competitors at once from the field, ruining numbers of decent retailers, and forcing them a step downwards in the

* " If the manufacturer kept this shop merely for the purpose of securing good articles at fair prices to his workmen, and if he offered no inducement to them to purchase at his shop, except the superior cheapness of his articles, it would certainly be advantageous to the men. But, unfortunately, this is not always the case."
—Babbage, p. 309.

social scale, by converting them into labourers, and obliging their families, who were most probably living at home in domestic privacy, and preparing themselves for decent members of society, to take refuge in the mill, —a situation certain to do away with many of those probabilities. They thus prevent any middle class betwixt themselves and their operatives from springing into permanent existence—a class to which the industrious, economical, and well-disposed workman might aspire— they smother all disposition for social amendment, and thus both directly and indirectly keep up and increase the improvidence and indifference of the labourer. The establishment of a middle class between them would be exceedingly beneficial to the character of both :—to the man, by shewing within his reach a condition in life elevated above that which he now holds—to the master, by establishing a barrier which would prevent him troublesomely and vexatiously interfering with the details of his inferior.*

Another system rapidly progressing, and very much resembling the truck system, of which in fact it may be viewed as an off-set, is the cottage system. A master having in his employ several hundred hands, whose habitations are scattered at considerable distances from each other and from the mill, erects ranges of cottages in its immediate vicinity, forming a part, indeed, of itself. These cottages are probably better built, more commodious, in every respect more comfortable, than those which the labourers previously inhabited. By bringing them nearer their work, they escape exposure to the

* Dr. Ure was much struck at seeing one or more shopkeepers doing very well in a few country mill villages. A little inquiry would have developed that the connexions of these shopkeepers could not fail to make them prosperous.

weather in their progress to and from their work; they have also an opportunity of securing longer hours of rest by the saving of time which was occupied by these progresses:—and yet the system is a bad one, and one decidedly injurious to the men. This system of cottage building, it is true, is not universal: in towns where masses of labourers are already collected, and when considerable expense would attend upon it, it is very little practised. It is chiefly in the out-districts; and it is a striking proof of the advantages to the master, that the great manufacturers are gradually creeping to the outskirts, or into localities a few miles from the great towns.

The extension and influence of this system may be very distinctly seen in the now populous township of Hyde and Newton, Duckenfield, &c. about seven miles from Manchester, and three from Ashton.

The population of these districts in 1801 scarcely amounted to three thousand, whilst in 1830 it had increased to twenty-six thousand nearly—a rate of increase unequalled. The rapid growth of such a population in this neighbourhood is of course owing to the concentration of a number of manufactories, favoured, as their position is, by an abundant supply of coal and excellent means of transport. This population, which is the resident one, by no means indicates the number of hands employed; on the contrary, great numbers are furnished by the surrounding townships.

An examination of the dwellings of this population would show how very large a proportion is in the hands of the manufacturers, either as owners, or general tenants.

It may be urged, that the masters, in consequence of the increase in the number of mills, and the consequent difficulty of collecting hands from a distance, have been forced to build, nobody else, indeed, being found who would speculate upon such property. This is very true, and quite unanswerable. They have been forced to build, and are still building; but it does not lessen the evils attendant upon the system.

The demoralizing effects of crowding together promiscuously the labourers in factories, have in large towns been materially aided by the nature of their habits, and the vices which large towns afford facilities for pursuing. So long as the operative, after having completed his day's toil, was separated from his fellows, and had to seek his isolated cottage, some of these evils were avoided. It freed him for a time at least from bad example, removed him from immediate contact with the gin-shop or tavern, collected his family generally under one roof, and gave him an opportunity for cultivating his social affections, and keeping down the overwhelming force of demoralization, which too often destroyed the town labourer. By affording him the cheering influences of a pure atmosphere, the sights and sounds of natural objects,—the out-district labourer presented for a time some moral and physical traits, which made him superior to the town operative.

The Beer Act has unhappily destroyed one of these advantages. The race of keepers of public-houses in the rural districts was, generally speaking, one something superior to his immediate neighbours—a small farmer or shopkeeper, and reputable householder. Since that period, however, a great change has been working in the licensed victuallers. The small sum required for a license threw it open to a labourer, and the idle and profligate took immediate advantage of it. Numbers of beer-houses were speedily seen occupying sites where, as a matter of trade, very little advantage could be derived from them. Every way-side, every' clump of cottages, showed, as it was termed here, its " Tom and Jerry shop." It cannot be denied, that prior to the introduction of these, an organized system for evading the excise laws was developing itself, in a very singular, and yet in a very effective form. The public-house at this period, (prior to the passing of the Beer Act) it has been said, was a house of good report, where, though immorality and drunkenness would at times show themselves, still they were checked and kept in some sort of discipline.

The bringing together numbers of the young of both sexes by the factory system, generated irregularities, which had no adequate field for their display; drinking became more habitual, and the more it was indulged, the more it required indulgence. To meet this demand of demoralization a number of houses were opened in the vicinity of the manufactories for the sale of beer, which, however, as the parties were unlicensed, subjected them to a penalty. To evade this, no beer was sold, bu abundance was given. The mode in which this transfer was managed, to the advantage and compensation of the giver, was, that a straw was the matter in barter; the drinker bought a bit of straw for the price of a pint of beer, and this pint was given in with the bargain. Odd as this may seem, it was carried on very extensively, and exists yet to some degree, though it has been displaced partially by the opening of beer-houses, which cost little, and free their owners or occupiers from the risk of punishment. By lowering the value of public-house property, and by lowering in an equal degree the character of the holders of these houses, great moral injury has been done, without one single advantage to the poor man to compensate for it. It was a law based upon most erroneous and mistaken principles—holding out to the labourer an apparent addition to his comfort, but which has signally and unhappily failed.

The masters, many of whom have 80, 100, 200, or more of those cottages surrounding, or in the immediate neighbourhood of their mills, are immense gainers by the arrangement. The cost of building a range of houses such as these, say 100, will not, upon the most liberal average, be more than 5,000*l.* ; indeed it may be estimated at vastly less, for the generality of them, taking the very best, 50*l.* per house will over and above cover the outlay. Now for the outlay of 5,000*l.*, the capitalist draws an annual income of 800*l.*, or 13½ per cent., and completely covers himself in little more than six years. This profitable return is burdened with no drawback ; no rent is lost, every pay-night it is deducted from the wages. One cannot wonder, therefore, at the universal practice of manufacturers building cottages, favourably placed as they are.

Besides this disproportionate rate of interest, he derives other great advantages from thus congregating his men under his immediate control. In the first place, it enables him without difficulty to perpetuate the truck system ; for he invariably builds two or three shops, and houses calculated for taverns or beer-houses; and if he has no direct dealing in them, he abstracts an equivalent rent ; and his hands are expected, and do spend a considerable portion of their earnings there, so that they suffer precisely the same injury as if their master was the retailer ; and they know it. Again, he derives benefit in another way : it enables him to shorten the hours allowed for meals—to begin earlier in the morning, to continue later at night—and this too with the concurrence of the hands, who do not often understand the difference sufficiently between mill labour and walking on the road in the open air; and yield up an hour at least per diem, which is added to the profits of the cottage building.

It is argued by those who advocate the system, that there are many circumstances favourable to the men in it—that generally a school-house is built, and every disposition shown by the master to forward the comfort and domestic enjoyments of the men—that the houses are commodious, clean, whitewashed, and in every respect vastly superior to the habitations for a similar class of labourers in the town. Any one who will take the trouble to inspect them, will at once acknowledge the truth of these assertions; but, in opposition, it must be borne in mind, that all these advantages in the domestic condition of the hands are sources of large pecuniary profit to the master, at their expense. It is said the rent, 3s. per week, is not more than the tenant would have to pay for a cottage *as near* the mill, to any other landlord. This is not denied—but the argument is unfair. The landlord who has cottage property charges probably the same per centage in towns and populous neighbourhoods; but he is liable to loss of rent continually—to have his houses empty for weeks and months together—to have his tenants leaving his houses, almost in a state of dilapidation, &c. &c. so that, although he has the same nominal rent, and is so far on a par with the manufacturer, he seldom calculates upon receiving, or ever does receive, on an average, more than six per cent. at the utmost—rarely indeed so much. It is, therefore, obviously and clearly a misnomer to say that the one derives the same profit as the other; whereas the manufacturer receives without risk or trouble, or even collecting, $13\frac{1}{2}$ per cent., whilst the common capitalist has very considerable difficulty in securing his five or six per cent.; and that has to be waited for and got together with incessant exertion.

It would be highly gratifying if the masters, in extending this system, which might have been the agent of much good to the men, had not shown their rapacity so plainly. Had they contented themselves with fair interest, and accommodated their hands with these cottages, it would have been well—it would have been gratifying to every one desirous of seeing a change in the intercourse between them. They might have, indeed, contented themselves with even a less amount of interest than that paid by building property in general, and still have been gainers, by having the opportunity of lengthening, in a very limited degree, the hours of labour, and by many other incidental advantages which they gain, by bringing the men in such immediate contact with the mill. But when this system is made a source of great revenue—and when to this it superadds the truck system, with all its vices—it can neither improve the condition of the labourer, nor add to the honourable name of the master.

The truck system and the cottage system are both departures from the proper track and duties of the master—both bring him into collision with his men upon points with which he ought never to interfere. His duties are so strongly marked that he should never suffer a question which can, for a moment, in any way make him diverge from their proper performance, to be entertained. He has a large capital employed; and for the purpose of turning it to profitable account, he requires the assistance of a certain number of labourers, the expense of the hiring of which is added to the cost of the peculiar manufacture he brings into the market. This payment of labour should be of that extent, and no farther, as will enable him to compete with other traders ; and should be greater and smaller as the article he produces sells at greater or less price than all the expenses of its production, such as raw material, building, machinery, labourers, &c. leaving to the speculator, or producer, a fair profit for time and capital expended. This constitutes the profit of the manufacturer ; and this done, he is bound to pay his labourers in money their part of the expense of production—namely, for their labour. But ·the truck system and the cottage system go beyond this. The master pays or gives an acknowledgment to the men for their quota of profit, which he declares to be that which the present state of the market enables him to make ; but he is not content with taking his share in the first instance, for he taxes their wages, and though nominally not reducing them, subtracts twelve per cent. at least from their gross amount.

One mode in which these systems are prejudicial to the interests of the workmen is, that it gives the masters an opportunity of lowering their wages in times of trade depression, or at their own caprice, and that too in an underhand way, which they can with difficulty resist. Sixpence a week in addition to the rent of their houses, and a halfpenny or farthing a pound or yard. on the articles of their consumption, are innovations not so great as to arouse their attention or indignation ; but it gives a large sum to the masters, and the temptation thus held out is too great to be resisted. Hence a·series of frauds upon the men—for frauds they decidedly are, of the most injurious tendency.

A manufacturer employs six hundred hands, the entire sum of whose wages for six months, at an average of ten shillings per head, is 7,800*l.* This he pays as the value of their labour, after having allowed for every

x

other item, and his own profit. If his men are subjected to the truck and cottage systems (and remember
the first amount which he declares, is one left to his own
conscience, and is not improbably much below its fair
value), he levies upon their capital a tax of nearly 500*l.*,
and this over and above the customary profits made
upon the articles with which he supplies them, namely,
houses and goods, and all this without risk.

It has been previously urged that combinations of the
masters are needful and desirable when · founded upon
justice and *equity ;* but this perversion of both cannot be
sufficiently condemned.

The capabilities which the labouring man has to
improve his condition, under the numerous evils to
which he is subjected, cannot receive a more striking
exemplification than from the fact, that the hands who,
in addition to their other disadvantages, are farther
exposed to these two systems, are in many respects
decidedly improved in their social and moral organization ; and nothing can show more clearly what might
be done by masters, than what interest based upon
injustice has led them to.

This injustice comes with double force upon the
operative, as it injures him indirectly, and in a way
which he does not understand, and in a way, too, that
he cannot resist. He perhaps does not feel its operation
so onerous as in reality it is, and struggles on, com-
plaining against a rate of wages, which is hardly adequate
for his wants and expectations, combining, too, against
them, paying a further sum on this account, while the
actual cause of his misfortunes lies shrouded and
covered by so specious a show, that he never dreams of
imputing them to it.

The moral evils of the truck and cottage systems are

analogous. By reducing the labourer to a mere machine —by destroying his personal independence—by cutting off his claim to self-respect—they degrade him to a condition of mere slavery, compared to which the West Indian negro may indeed congratulate himself on his good fortune, for his is a state in some respects to be desired in preference. The name of slave is a bye-word for conjuring up a frightful catalogue of miseries and degradations; but the slave has no master like the steam-engine. He is not compelled by this inexorable task master to work for twelve or fourteen hours uninterruptedly; and be it remembered that the factory labourer works in an atmosphere of equal temperature with the slave—and shall a name make such mighty difference, when the moral and physical conditions of slavery are equally in force in both instances? for so it is when the master takes under his control the hard won wages of his labourers, and again converts them to his own use, leaving them to suffer any degree of hardship which will not drive them to desperation.

Both systems necessarily render the men improvident and reckless—destroy all forethought—paralyze every better feeling within them, and thus brutalize and degrade them in exact ratio as they are made dependent and hopeless of amelioration or amendment.

It is hardly possible that the masters will ever sufficiently comprehend that to make money is an evil, or that they will possess such honourable feelings as will lead them to sacrifice a positive advantage over the men, when it is entirely in their power. Even were it so—even were masters disposed to consult these things, it is not likely the world, or at all events their men, would give them credit for it. Let them, therefore, wash their hands of all temptation; let them show, by not having, that they do not wish to have unfair advantages; and though they may lose something for a time, they will eventually be large gainers; for it will be the first great step towards improving the moral and social condition of the mass of the labourers,—by rendering them economical, introducing household virtues, withdrawing them from unnatural stimuli, and inducing them to seek their support from solid and wholesome diet. All these things may be effected at a rate of wages inferior to that which they now contrive to squander, and yet starve; to labour incessantly, yet seem to labour for a pittance unequal to supply their wants. It is indeed difficult to say what is the minimum upon which a provident man and his family can subsist: one thing is obvious to every inquirer, that an amount of earning which appears to one family totally inadequate to live upon even decently, when all about is squalid beggary, and every thing shows the extremity of want—yet that another family, equally if not more numerous, will, with the same amount of wages, appear clean, well fed, well clothed, cheerful, and happy.

It is not on the amount of a man's earning, simply, but on his capability of turning this to the best account, that his comfort depends. Great wealth is no safeguard against occasional distress, if not properly economized and managed; neither are liberal wages any reason why those earning them should not be pauperized. The same family, to the present writer's positive knowledge, have at one period earned 5*l.* per week. Trade has become depressed—prices have fallen—and in a year or two their earnings have been reduced to 2*l.* 10*s.* But were they poorer? By no means. Riches and poverty are merely terms of comparison. Were they worse dressed? No!

Worse fed? No! Did they become burdensome to the parish? No!—How then? They learnt to reduce their superfluous expenditure; to cut off all unnecessary sources of outlay; to live more regularly, and they were, in every respect, as well to do in the latter period as in the former.

Thus it will be, if the artisans engaged in factories can be roused from their present habits—if they make home what it should be; if the earnings of families are brought into a joint fund; if domestic discipline is re-established; if they become good husbands, fathers, brothers, and wives; if they limit the demands of their appetites to their means of supply; throw aside ruinous combinations; become peaceable, orderly, and well-behaved citizens; devote their earnings to legitimate purposes, and eschew alike evil and folly. They have within their power, by so doing, means to be comfortable, happy, and perfectly independent; and to defer, or perhaps do away with the frightful consummation of the factory system which is so rapidly approaching.

CHAPTER XIII.

THE INFLUENCE OF MACHINERY ON THE VALUE OF
HUMAN LABOUR—SUBSTITUTION OF AUTOMATA FOR
HUMAN AGENTS—ITS EXTENT AND ULTIMATE CON-
SEQUENCES.

It has been observed by Mr. M'Culloch, " That the
operatives are in great measure the architects of
their own fortunes ; for what others can do for them is
trifling indeed compared with what they can do for
themselves. That they are infinitely more interested in
the preservation of public tranquillity than any other
class of society ; that *mechanical inventions and disco-*
veries are supremely advantageous to them; and that
their real interests can only be efficiently protected by
displaying greater prudence and forethought."*

The influence of machinery upon the value of human
labour is a subject of paramount importance. It has
hitherto been very partially examined, whilst the consequences certain to attend upon it, should make its consideration one of great and unprejudiced care. The
remark in the foregoing quotation from M'Culloch,
" that mechanical inventions and discoveries are supremely advantageous to them," *i. e.* the manufacturing
population, is far too general and sweeping ; and an
attentive examination of the subject would have sufficed

* Edinburgh Review, No. XCI.

to satisfy the author that he was suffering imperfect data to mislead his judgment, and was hazarding an assertion unsustained by facts, whether of observation or reasoning.

"One very important inquiry," says Mr. Babbage, "which this subject presents, is the question, Whether it is more for the interest of the working classes that improved machinery should be so perfect as to defy the competition of hand-labour, and that they should thus at once be driven out of the trade by it, or be gradually forced to quit it, by the slow and successive advances of the machine. The suffering which arises from a quick transition is undoubtedly more intense, but it is also much less permanent than that which results from the slower process; and if the competition is perceived to be perfectly hopeless, the workman will at once set himself to learn a new department of his art. On the other hand, although new machinery causes an increased demand for skill in those who make and repair it, and in those who first superintend its use, yet there are other cases in which it enables children and infirm workmen to execute work that previously required greater skill. In such circumstances, even though the increased demand for the article, produced by its diminished price, should speedily give occupation to all who were before unemployed, yet this very diminution of skill required, would open a wider field for competition amongst the working classes themselves."*

This is a tolerably fair statement of the general bearings of the question, but does not take into full account either the condition of the workmen, or the history of machinery, as applied to manufactures, when put into motion by steam or water power.

* Babbage, Economy of Manufactures, p. 336.

In the first place, the object of every mechanical contrivance is, to do away with the necessity for human
labour, which is at once the most expensive and troublesome agent in the production of manufactured articles.   This point has not yet been fully attained : but
already facilities for increased production have been
given, which, from diminution in the first outlay,
from the use of steam power and machinery, and the
immense quantity produced lowering its market value,
have rendered it necessary that workmen should individually turn off a vastly increased amount of work, to
keep them on a level with the state of things brought
about by the two former causes.   Those who are employed, are at present enabled to do this; and their
earnings have kept on the whole more steady than
is generally imagined, notwithstanding the fact, as
stated by Mr. Marshall, that the same quantity of work
is now performed for 1s. 10d. for which 16s. were paid
in 1814.

Again, from the simplification in the processes of
manufactures, and from whatever power is required
being given by steam, the family of the mill artisan,
from nine years of age and upwards, are able to earn
something; so that when all things are considered, it is
probable that, as far as pecuniary matters are concerned, he is as favourably placed as at any former period
of his history.

It has been remarked by Mr. Babbage, that " if the
competition between machinery and human labour is
perceived to be perfectly hopeless, the workman will at
once set himself to learn a new department of his art."
Were this possible, the necessary consequences of
mechanical improvement would signify nothing ; but it
is impossible, and a reference to his own table on hand-

loom weavers will sufficiently show that there are at present insurmountable difficulties in the way of the conversion of a great body* of operatives from one industrial condition to another.

Whoever is in the habit of visiting the workshops of the machine-makers, and the mills of the great cotton manufacturers, from time to time, cannot fail to be struck with the incessant improvements in the application of machinery. These improvements, though they may not enable the master to dismiss any of his hands, prevent the necessity for engaging fresh ones, though he doubles the productive powers of his mill.

The rapid growth of the staple branch of manufacture —the cotton trade, has caused vast immigrations into those districts in which it is principally carried on. The depression in the agricultural counties has pushed these immigrations beyond the demand ; the repeated turnouts have brought sudden accessions of new hands in great numbers—thousands of Irish have deserted their native and miserable homes, in search of employment at the loom ; these circumstances, one and all, have brought into the trade a surplus quantity of men, and that at a period when the necessity for them is daily lessening.

The time, too, must come, though it cannot come very quickly, when the trade will reach its maximum. Great Britain will long retain her pre-eminence as a manufacturing country, in consequence of the progress she has already made, which places her immeasurably in advance of the whole world. Her wealth, the industry of her

---

* On this point the evidence given before the Select Committee on Hand-loom Weavers, in 1834, has already been referred to. Almost every page shows clearly that there is no hope of the artisan changing his trade.

people, the enterprise of her merchants, the possession of coal, the skill of her machinists—these will long secure her the lead. In retaining this, however, the population engaged in the manufacture will have to suffer greatly. Other nations, in their turn, will devote their energies to the same purpose ; and though their present inferiority as to roads, canals, skill, and enterprise, combine to render their competition not very formidable, this will not long continue.

Already the United States, France, the Low Countries, and Switzerland, are striding in the same track, and already do something to lessen the value of English manufacture. They are as yet only in their infancy. It is a trade, however, which can advance with great rapidity, when energetically taken up ; and the period is not very remote when powerful rivals will dispute the ground with Great Britain, and compel her manufacturers to adopt measures, and to lower the value of human labour to a level, so as to enable them to meet upon equal terms the foreign trader. The surplus hands would readily enable them to lessen the rate of wages ; but the certainty that any considerable reduction would be followed by immediate immense losses from turn-outs, extended stoppages, and various other impediments which would ·be thrown in their way, makes them prefer the slower process of mechanical improvement, by which, though they may triple production, they require no new men.*

But these improved applications of mechanism will not end here. Whenever the pressure of foreign or domestic competition becomes more severe, the masters will be necessitated to avail themselves to the utmost of

* *Vide* Appendix—Extent of Foreign Competition.

every thing which can assist in lowering the price of their products, and human labour must and will be pushed to the wall. Many great changes will, of course, take place before this inevitable result is gained, and reductions in wages for quantity will be constantly progressing; but the ultimatum is less remote than those interested in it are aware of; for let it be remembered that all mechanical applications, and the moving power derived from the expansive nature of steam, have as yet but arrived at one point in their career, and this point says nothing as to what may be done. There can be no question whatever that many processes, for which the human hand is at present indispensable, will very shortly have machines adapted to them; these, if they will not quite displace the workman, will render one man capable of producing, or rather of superintending, the production of quantity now requiring ten or twenty labourers. This is no theoretical opinion—the whole history of the cotton manufacture attests its truth, and collateral proofs are abundant in other branches of manufacture.

It does not follow that improvements in existing machinery, or every new machine, should at once throw out a number of hands. Those, however, who argue that machinery never has that effect, and never will have it, either wilfully delude themselves, or take a very limited and imperfect view of the subject. It must have one of two effects,—the objects of every change, improvement, and addition, being to lessen the amount of labour required for production;—these effects must be either to render fewer workmen necessary to produce a given quantity of manufacture, or so far lower the price of the manufactured article as at once to increase the demand for it so considerably, as to absorb the same number of men as are already engaged in it. In many instances, in fact generally, the latter has been the case hitherto, and would, perhaps, continue to be so, were Great Britain entirely to monopolize manufactures. But this cannot be ; and, as it has been before stated, the maximum must be attained. All these improvements having therefore one end, all tending to the same point, namely, the cheapening of labour, the time must come when its value will be so small as to make it nearly worthless to the possessor.

The triumphant appeal made by those who consider the acquisition of wealth to be the sole end of national and commercial policy, to the rise and progress of the cotton trade, overlooks the history of the manufacture in connexion with the labourers. No man can be so blind as not to see that physico-mechanical science has increased enormously the wealth of Great Britain, and has placed her in a commercial position far in advance of all other countries. Of this every man who has considered the subject for a moment must be aware ; and every Englishman may well be proud of the magnificent inventions which have contributed to raise the importance of his country. " Machines have been invented which enable one man to produce as much yarn as two hundred and fifty, or three hundred even, could have produced seventy years ago—which enable one man and one boy to print as many goods as a hundred men and a hundred boys could have printed formerly. * * * The 150,000 workmen in the spinning mills produce as much yarn as could have been produced by 40,000,000 with the one-thread wheel ; and yet there are those who look on it as a calamity, that human labour has been rendered so productive." *

" When this new career (adaptation of mechanism)

* History of the Cotton Manufacture, p. 302.

commenced, about the year 1770, the annual consumption of cotton in British manufactures was under four millions of pounds' weight, and that of the whole of Christendom was probably not more than ten millions. Last year the consumption in great Britain and Ireland was about two hundred and seventy million pounds; and that of Europe and the United States together, four hundred and eighty millions. This prodigious increase is, without doubt, almost entirely due to the factory system, founded and upreared by the intrepid native of Preston (Arkwright). If, then, this system be not merely an inevitable step in the social progression of the world, but the one which gives a commanding station and influence to the people who most resolutely take it, does it become any man, far less a denizen of this favoured land, to vilify* the author of a benefaction which, wisely administered, may become the best temporal gift of Providence to the poor—a blessing destined to mitigate, and in *some measure to repeal the primeval curse* pronounced on the labour of man—' in the sweat of thy face shalt thou eat bread.' Arkwright well deserves to live in honoured remembrance among those ancient master-spirits who persuaded their roaming companions to exchange the precarious toils of the chase for the settled comforts of agriculture."

" In my recent tour, I have seen tens of thousands of old, young, and middle aged, of both sexes, many of them too feeble to get their daily bread by any former modes of industry, earning abundant food, raiment, and domestic accommodation, without perspiring at a single pore, screened

---

* We are not aware of any individuals who have vilified this extraordinary man, except his contemporary brother manufacturers, who did all in their power to injure him—more especially the Lancastrians.

meanwhile from the summer's sun, and the winter's frost, in apartments more airy and salubrious than those of the metropolis in which our legislative and fashionable aristocracies assemble. *In those spacious halls the benignant power of steam summons around him his myriads of willing menials*, and assigns to each the regulated task, substituting for painful muscular efforts on their part the energies of his own gigantic arm, and demanding in return only attention and dexterity to connect such little aberrations as casually occur in his workmanship. The *gentle docility** of this moving force qualifies it for impelling the tiny bobbins of the lace machine with a speed inimitable by the most dexterous hands directed by the quickest eyes. Hence, under its auspices, and in obedience to Arkwright's policy, magnificent edifices, surpassing far in number, value, usefulness, and ingenuity of construction, the boasted monuments of Asiatic, Egyptian, and Roman despotism, have, within the short period of fifty years, risen up in this kingdom, to show to what extent capital, industry, and science, may augment the resources of a state, while they ameliorate the condition of its citizens. Such is the factory system, replete with prodigies in mechanics and political economy, which promises in its future growth to become the great minister of civilisation to the terraqueous globe, enabling this country, as its heart, to diffuse along with its commerce the life-blood of science and religion to myriads of people still lying ' in the region and shadow of death.' "*

Mr. Baines remarks, that the history of cotton spin-

* Like other potent genii, steam occasionally puts off its gentle docility, blowing up factories, steam-boats, &c. &c. We presume the author whom we are quoting is ignorant of this.

† Dr. Ure's Philosophy of Manufactures, pp. 17, 18.

ning is almost romantic ; and Dr. Ure, taking the hint, has exhibited in the foregoing extract that mingling of truth, exaggeration, and poetical description, usually forming a romance. Dr. Darwin, in his " Botanic Garden," has preceded Dr. Ure—the former speaking of a " watery god," and the latter of the " benignant power of steam ;" the substance, however, is the same in both cases. Dr. Darwin alludes to the Cromford Mills, on the Derwent.*

" An extensive cotton mill is a striking instance of the application of the greatest powers to perform a prodigious quantity of light and easy work. A steam engine of 100 horse power, which has the strength of 880 men, gives a rapid motion to 50,000 spindles, for spinning fine cotton threads : each spindle forms a separate thread, and the whole number work together in an immense building erected on purpose, and so adapted to receive the machines that no room is lost. Seven hundred and fifty people are sufficient to attend all the operations of such a cotton mill ; and by the assistance of

* " ——— Where Derwent guides his dusky floods
　　　Through vaulted mountains and a night of woods,
　　　The nymph *Gossypia* treads the velvet sod,
　　　And warms with rosy smiles the wat'ry god;
　　　His pond'rous oars to slender spindles turns,
　　　And pours o'er massy wheels his foaming urns ;
　　　With playful charms her hoary lover wins,
　　　And wields his trident whilst the monarch spins. '
　　　First, with nice eye, emerging naiads cull
　　　From leathery pods the vegetable wool :
　　　With wiry teeth, revolving cards release
　　　The tangled knots, and smoothe the ravell'd fleece :
　　　Next moves with iron hands the fingers fine ;
　　　Combs the wide card, and forms the eternal line.
　　　Now with soft lips the whirling can acquires
　　　The tender skeins, and wraps in rising spires."

the steam engine, they will be enabled to spin as much thread as 200,000 persons could do without machinery, *or one person can do as much as* 266." *

" Watt," says M. Charles Dupin, in his address to the Parisian operatives, " improves the steam engine,— and this single improvement causes the industry of England to make an immense stride. This machine represents at the present time the power of 300,000 horses, or of 2,000,000 of men, strong and well-fitted for labour, who should work day and night without repose to augment the riches of a country not two-thirds the extent of France. A hairdresser invents, or at least brings into action, a machine for spinning cotton—this alone gives to British industry an immense superiority. Fifty years only after this discovery more than 1,000,000 of the inhabitants of England are employed in those operations which depend directly or indirectly on the action of this machine. Lastly, England exports cotton, spun and woven by an admirable system of machinery, to the value of 400,000,000 of francs yearly. The Indies—so long superior to Europe—the Indies, which inundated the west with her products, and exhausted the riches of Europe—the Indies are conquered in their turn. The British navigator travels in quest of the cotton of India; brings it from a distance of 4,000 leagues; commits it to an operation of the machine of Arkwright, and of those that are attached to it; carries back their products to the east, making them again travel 4,000 leagues; and in spite of loss of time, in spite of the enormous expense incurred by this voyage of 8,000 leagues, the cotton manufactured by the machinery of England becomes less costly than the cotton of India spun and woven by the hand, near the field

* *Vide* Farey's Treatise on the Steam Engine.

that produced it, and sold at the nearest market. So great is the power of the progress of machinery!"

To all in the foregoing quotations relating to the ingenuity of the contrivers, the increase of trade, and the additions made to our commercial resources, we fully subscribe—and dull indeed must be that mind that does not glory in the fact, that British science and British skill have made his country the manufacturer of the world. This is one view of the adaptation of machinery to the arts; but it is an exceedingly partial view: it sees magnificent mills—prodigies of science—millions of exports,—a vast accumulation of private wealth, and a prospect teeming with the wonderful results of automatic industry. We clothe a great part of mankind with cottons; and a similar series of improvements which have enabled us to do this with one fabric, will enable us to do it with woollen, silk, flax, and linen trades, to some very considerable extent.

With this knowledge before us—with an intimate acquaintance with the history of manufacture—we do not hesitate to affirm, that these vast resources have been gained at too costly a price, and that we are in danger of losing them, not by force or competition from without, but by the pressure from within.

Writers who have hitherto examined the bearings of machinery on human labour, have failed to take an enlarged and general survey of the past and present condition of the operatives. Satisfied by observing that every improvement in mechanism bearing upon the arts has freed the human labourer from toil, and, in many cases, increased the wages earned by him, they have not looked beyond that. " *It is, in fact, the constant aim and tendency of every improvement in machinery to supersede human labour altogether, or to diminish its cost,* *by substituting the industry of women and children for that of men, or that of ordinary labourers for trained artisans.*"* Add to this Mr. Poulett Scrope's remark— that "*every means of economising human labour and facilitating production is a benefit and a blessing to mankind ;*"† and we have before us the essential principles of those political economists who advocate mechanical contrivance. They amount to this,—that the end and aim of mechanism is to do away with the necessity for human labour, and that this is to be a benefit and a blessing to mankind. " The blessings which physico-mechanical science has bestowed on society, and the means it has still in store for ameliorating the lot of mankind, have been too little dwelt upon ; while, on the other hand, it has been accused of lending itself to the rich capitalists as an instrument for harassing the poor, and exacting from the operative an accelerated rate of work."‡ The abuse of science has nothing to do with the argument ; as far as the capitalist is concerned, he finds a productive power of boundless capabilities at his command, and he uses it as a matter of course.

It is not a little singular that Mr. Scrope should, as an illustration of his remark, repeatedly assert that " Great Britain offers no choice (to the labourer) but starvation or the workhouse, because the wages of all are, by excessive competition, reduced below the level of comfort ;" and that Dr. Ure should constantly point out the fact—that machinery must drive away adult labour ; and even quote triumphantly examples of the where and the how this has been effected. From this, it would appear that Mr. Scrope's economising of human

---

* Philosophy of Manufactures, p. 23.
† Letter II. to the Hand Loom Weavers, p. 22.
‡ Philosophy of Manufactures, p. 7.

labour has, according to his own showing, ruined the
human labourer, and in place of " being a benefit and a
blessing " to him, it has left him no resource but starvation—the workhouse—or Canada ; whilst, according to
Dr. Ure, the " blessings" of physico-mechanical science
to the operatives are to throw the adult population into
idleness.

The value of the opinions of the gentlemen quoted
above, as to the benefits of automatic industry upon the
labouring population, admit of an easy and unquestionable test—namely, the condition of that population
whilst automatic industry has been developing itself.

The first fact which meets us is—that the poor rates
of the kingdom have risen, during the progress of mechanical adaptation to processes hitherto demanding
human labour, to the enormous sum of nearly 8,000,000*l.*
sterling per annum. The second fact is—that a tide of
demoralization has swept over the land, displaying itself
in the agricultural districts by incendiarism and other
forms, the details of which have been rendered familiar
to the public by the Report of the Poor Law Commission,* and in the manufacturing districts, in the shapes
we have already spoken of. The third fact is—that
from the impossibility of finding adequate remuneration
for labour, no less than 351,056 persons have left our
shores for Canada between 1812 and 1832; and that
from the 7th of May, 1833, to the 24th of September,
1834, upwards of 30,000 emigrants departed from the
port of Liverpool alone. The fourth fact is—that there
are one million of human beings dependent on hand-
manufacture, who are literally starving in the midst of
the magnificent edifices housing the steam engine and
its workers, without the slightest hope or chance of

* *Vide* Report, *passim.*

improving their industrial condition.* The fifth fact is
—that two millions of hand-loom weavers in Hindostan
have been driven from their labour by machinery here,
multitudes of whom have perished by famine.† The
sixth fact is—that there are hundreds of thousands of
domestic manufacturers connected with the bobbin-net,
woollen, silk, flax, linen, and iron trades, now suffering
extreme privations, and who will shortly be driven from
their peculiar province of industry by competition with
steam-production. The seventh fact is—that the absorption of the household manufacture of the kingdom
into factories has completely deranged the social system
of our labouring community. The eighth fact is—that
the breaking up of the industrial occupations of the
people has led to so much idleness and dissoluteness,
that the legislature (overlooking the cause) has determined to cover the country with workhouses, a measure
which takes us back two centuries in the career of
civilisation.‡ The ninth fact is—that crime has pro-
ceeded at a fearful pace ; the commitments in 1811
(as early as data are in existence)§ being 5,337, and in
1832, 20,829. The tenth fact is—that discontent,
violence, and organized unions, threatening the very
safety of manufactures, universally characterize the
artisans of the present day. The eleventh fact is—
that drunkenness || and irreligion have made fearful
advances amongst the depressed operatives.**

* *Vide* History of the Cotton Manufacture, p. 239.
† Minutes of Evidence. Select Committee on Hand-loom
Weavers, p. 311.
‡ Poor Law Amendment Act.
§ *Vide* Table, Progress of Crime, in Appendix.
|| *Vide* Table of Spirits consumed in Great Britain, in Appendix.
** *Vide* Minutes of Evidence before Committee on Hand-loom
Weavers, *passim.*

These are truths too notorious to be questioned, and they do not depend upon the opinion of this man or that man. Those who maintain that the economising of human labour—the end and aim of mechanical contrivances—is a blessing to the operative, overlook the simple fact that if he cannot dispose of his labour he must perish; and, consequently, that every improvement in machines lessens the value of his fund of subsistence.* It needs no declamation as to the evils of Poor Laws, Taxation, or Currency, to lead us to the cause of the depressed condition of the labouring population—a depression which all admit : it arises from there being no market for their labour in Great Britain. Already steam power is at work more than equivalent to the entire adult labour of the kingdom ; and the numbers engaged in various manufactories as aids to automatic machinery produce more than could be produced by the united labour of the whole of the inhabitants of the British empire.

When speaking of steam power, the attention of the reader must not be confined to the operation of that power as exhibited before him in connexion with textile manufactories. It is at work in every branch of industry, pushing aside the human agent, and causing that overplus of hands which has by competition so rapidly reduced wages. Mr. Gordon, an eminent engineer, thus enumerates some of the applications of this plastic power, when treating of the substitution of inanimate for animate power in locomotion.

"Considered in its application to husbandry, the

* The advantage to the poor man, according to Mr. Baines, is, that his wife can purchase a printed calico gown for 2s. 6d. This is a fact he repeatedly insists upon. It seems to us a very poor compensation for poverty, expatriation, or the workhouse.

cottager looks forth upon the neat paling which fences his dwelling ; it was sawed *by steam*. The spade with which he digs his garden, the rake, the hoe, the pickaxe, the scythe, the sickle, every implement of rural toil which ministers to his necessities, are produced *by steam*. Steam bruises the oil-cake which feeds the farmer's cattle; moulds the ploughshare which overturns his fields ; forms the shears which clip his flock ; and cards, spins,. and weaves the produce.

" Applied to architecture, we find the Briarean arms of the steam engine every where at work. Stone is cut by it, marble polished, cement ground, mortar mixed, floors sawed, doors planed, chimney-pieces carved, lead rolled for roofs and drawn for gutters, rails formed, gratings and bolts forged, paint ground and mixed, paper made and stained, worsted dyed, and carpet wove ; mahogany veneered, door-locks ornamented, curtains and furniture made, printed, and measured; fringes, tassels, and bell-ropes, chair-covers and chair-nails, bell-wires, linens and blankets,—china and earthenware turned ; glass cut, and pier-glass formed ; the drawing-room, dining-room, kitchen, pantry, closets, &c. —all owe to steam their most essential requisites.

" Should the question be asked, What has enabled the inferior proprietors to wear two. hats a year instead of going bare-headed, or sporting the bonnet which their fathers wore ; what has clothed them in suits of excellent broad cloth, and given them to ruffle it with the first-born of the land; which has donned for their wives, ladies' apparel ; made their boys rejoice in a plurality of suits ; and, in the bridal hour, busked their daughters in robes, delicate in texture as the spider's web, beautiful in colour as the rainbow's hues, and for elegance such as never in her grandame's younger days, even Duchesses wore : which plaited her bonnet, tamboured her net, wove her laces, knitted her stockings, veneered her comb, flowered her ribands, gilded her buttons, sewed her shoes, and even fashioned the rosette that ornamented their ties ? The answer is—*Steam*." ·

It is urged by those who maintain that physico-mechanical science blesses the labouring classes, that the cheapness of the product has a necessary and constant tendency to increase the consumption of the article produced, and so to employ an increased number of operatives,—and the cotton trade is appealed to. The extraordinary growth of this trade, now become the staple of the country, is indeed one of the most wonderful events recorded in history. The wages earned are, as we have seen, even yet good; and it is contended that this trade is an undeniable evidence of the soundness of the opinions of those who applaud every advance in the arts. To the commercial part of these opinions we have already assented : were we disposed, however, to assent to the whole, looking no further than the cotton trade, the past and present state of that trade would at once assure us, that the mass of human labourers must, at no distant date, be utterly ruined.

But we should not look on the body of workmen connected with textile manufactures now, as affording an index to the operation of mechanical contrivances, upon human industry. The number of hands engaged in the cotton, wool, silk, and flax trades, has been stated by Dr. Ure to amount to 344,625. Granting that the wages of these workers are moderately good, we must set against them the wretched penury in which a million of human beings, now dependent on hand-loom weaving, are placed, together with an equal number at least connected with other handicrafts whose

labour has been partially displaced by automatic industry.

It has been remarked, that the rapid extension of
particular branches of trade, although carried on by new
agents, will nevertheless still find employment for the
human labourers; and Mr. Baines has endeavoured to
illustrate this position by making a guess at the number
supported by the cotton manufacture in 1760 : these he
states to have amounted to 40,000. There are no data,
however, on which to found the estimate; it is consequently purely conjectural. Basing his observations on
this calculation, he proceeds to show how vastly population and the persons employed in cotton manufacture
have increased since that period. Of the increase of
population in the manufacturing districts we have already
spoken, as well as of the number of individuals connected with the cotton trade. This statement should be
accompanied by other details; and then, in place of
Mr. Baines charging authors and members of parliament
with stupid ignorance for thinking that any evil has
attended the progress of machinery, he would be aware of
his own assumption and the narrow views expressed by
himself.

It might seem that, if 40,000 only were connected
with this branch of industry in 1760, and that now not
less than 220,000 are employed in cotton factories,
the assertion as to the absorption of labourers was supported by facts; but it must be borne in mind, that the
manufacture of cotton yarn and calicoes, whilst it required a great number of hands, completely destroyed
the coarse and heavy linen, cotton, woollen, and flax
fabrics, which had been carried on as a part of the
domestic economy of the great bulk of the cottage population of Great Britain. Against the increase in the

number of hands engaged in the cotton trade, is to be placed the multitudes of domestic manufacturers who were deprived of their household labour by a new producing power, and, thus viewed, the increase dwindles down into insignificance. One spinner produces as much in one day now as would have required a year's time to produce a century ago; and hence spinning, once an universal cottage labour, has become completely engrossed by factories. The mechanists will say,—very true, we have abolished cottage spinning, but we have increased the manufacture of cotton alone from 3,000,000 lbs. in 1760, to 303,656,837lbs. in 1833, and we have made the great staple trade of the country. The answer is — undoubtedly : but how many cottage hearths have been quenched, how many industrious families have sunk into pauperism, during this transition ? So far as the extended commerce of the nation is concerned, there is no dispute; but whilst we acknowledge the magnificent results of machinery, we contend, that the state of our labouring population has been in a great measure overlooked.

In the weaving department the consequence of mechanical adaptation is now beginning to be felt in its full force. Hitherto the depression which has crept over this department has resulted from competition with steam-looms, from cheap yarn, from this yarn being exported, and hence compelling the English merchant, in order to compete with the foreign manufacturer, to bring down the price of cotton cloth below his; and from the amazing productiveness of spinning machinery constantly choking the market, whilst human labour being driven from this department, and having no other resource, has been forced to keep itself on the loom. Hence it is that the hand cotton manufacturers have kept on the increase—

the number actually employed far exceeding the factory
labourers—and that the former are in a far greater proportion adults than the latter; yet the hand labourers
are charged with being the authors and perpetrators of
their own ruin!—for ruined every man who has inquired
into their condition acknowledges them to be.

But the time is near at hand when this resource for
industry, dreadful as it is, will be withdrawn from the
operatives.   During the last three years the power loom
has been rapidly on the increase, and every new mill
which is built contains them, and additions to old mills
of weaving rooms are going on in every direction.*
" The power-loom factories now generally weave only
their own yarn, spun to suit their peculiar fabric; and
hence they generally command a better profit on their
capital than establishments in which the same capital
is expended in either the mere spinning of power-loom
yarn, or the weaving of what is purchased."†   This is
a very sufficient reason for the rapid spread of power-
looms—it economises both capital and labour; and an
examination of the mills at Stockport will exhibit the
perfection at which this system of conjoined spinning
and weaving has arrived.

There cannot be a question, therefore, that the multitudes of adults now dependent on hand-weaving must be
pushed from the market; no extension in this department can absorb the operatives, because the power-loom

* "The number of power looms had very materially increased of
late years in and about Bury, Stockport, Bolton, Ashton, and in
Cheshire.   Did not know any person who was now building a
spinning-mill without addition of a power-loom mill.— *Evidence of
Mr. Greg* (a very eminent manufacturer) *before the Select Committee
of the House of Commons on Manufactures, Commerce, &c.   Report*,
p. 677.

† *Vide* Philosophy of Manufactures, p. 331.

does not require adult labour; whilst it is so greatly more productive, that the very cheapness of its produce must, when it is in general use, completely supersede hand-manufacture in the home and foreign market. The wage of this class of labourers cannot be lowered—it has reached its limit; and the next step must be famine or outrage.

" The throstle on which the warp is usually spun may be considered to be a complete *automaton*, capable, on a good construction, of furnishing a very uniform yarn; but the mule on which the weft is always spun has been, till recently, only *half-automatic*, and has partaken, therefore, in a certain degree, of the irregularity of hand-work, varying, with the skill and steadiness of the workman. The improved self-actors of Messrs. Sharp, Roberts, and Smith, are likely to remove the above cause of irregularity in calico and fustian wefts, and therefore they place a weaving factory, which works in train with them, in a condition to produce fabrics of invariable excellence. This new mechanical union of automatic spinning and weaving promises to have two admirable results: it will, in the first place, put an end to the folly of trades unions, so ruinous to the men, and so vexatious to the masters; and, in the second place, it will secure, for a long period to come, the monopoly of coarse cotton fabrics to Great Britain."*

According to this statement, which is quite correct in its mechanical details, arrangements are in progress to enable automatic industry to produce coarse cotton fabrics, which have been the chief production of the hand-loom, and which have supplied the foreign market, this quality of fabric being chiefly manufactured for exportation. There can be no question but that machinery will speedily reach this point, and then we shall find that

* Philosophy of Manufactures, p. 331.

automata have done away with the necessity for adult
workmen.   Girls tend the throstle which produce the
warp; boys tend the mule which produce the weft;
girls tend the looms which produce the cloth;—mechanism dresses it, and mechanism dyes it.   This point
reached, according to Dr. Ure, Mr. Baines, Mr.M‘Culloch, Mr. Scrope, and others, the very perfection of
manufacture has been attained.   A vast series of automatic machines will be seen revolving in palaces, pouring out produce in endless profusion ; but the question
deserves being asked—Where is the adult labourer?
Even now we find him toiling in damp, unwholesome
cellars, perishing of want; or, if better paid, leagued
with his fellows, and holding machinery at bay, with the
deadly resolve of not yielding one step further.

  " This combination of weaving and spinning in one
establishment has lately given a fresh. impulsion to our
cotton trade, and is likely to render it paramount over
all competition, enabling it to furnish supplies of cheap
clothing to many millions of new customers in every
region of the globe.   New factories will hence arise,
requiring multitudes of new hands, presenting prizes in
the lottery of life to the skilful and steady operatives,
and enabling them to become managers or masters."*

  A knowledge of the actual condition and prospects of
the cotton trade would convince Dr. Ure that his imagination had overleaped every thing like truth and probability in the latter part of the above paragraph.   That
new factories will spring up it is true, but that they will
require multitudes of new hands every page of his own
book shows to be false, abundant proofs of which will
be given shortly. If the 150,000 spinners of the present
day superintend the production of as much yarn as

* Philosophy of Manufactures, p. 332.

would have required the labour of 40,000,000' men a
century ago, what is to prevent 1000 doing that which
is now done by 150,000?   Not only is there nothing to
prevent it, but it will actually be done, if no great
convulsion overturn the present system.   If one power-
loom is six times as effective as a hand-loom, why should
not the power-loom be doubled in capability in ten years?
These things are yet in their infancy.   The introduction
of steam-power, of automatic labour, of power-looms,
are events of the present generation ; and there is not a
fabric but will shortly be transplanted from the hand to
steam.*

"The prizes in the lottery of life," which, Dr. Ure
remarks, automatic manufacture present to the operative,
are degradation and poverty.   A familiar acquaintance
with the growth and progress of the cotton manufacture
would have shown him, that so far is there a likelihood
of the steady workman becoming a master, that the trade
is rapidly assuming the character of a great monopoly ;
and that the next important change in the commercial
condition of those connected with it will be a combination of large proprietors, and the ruin of the small
manufacturers.

The correctness of our opinions is attested by every
page in the history of mechanism.   The increasing
powers of the steam-loom are shown in the following
statement, furnished by a manufacturer, as the advance
which has already been made.

---

* The progress of steam-looms will appear from the following
statement :—

	1820.	1833.
In England	12,150 . . .	85,000
In Scotland	2,000 . . .	15,000
	14,150	100,000

" A very good *hand-weaver*, twenty-five or thirty years of age, will weave *two pieces* of 9-8ths shirting per week.

" In 1823 a *steam-loom* weaver, about fifteen years of age, attending two looms, could weave *seven* similar pieces in a week.

" In 1826, a *steam-loom* weaver, about fifteen years of age, attending two looms, could weave *twelve* similar pieces in a week — some could weave *fifteen* pieces.

" In 1833, a *steam-loom weaver*, from fifteen to twenty years of age, assisted by a girl about twelve years of age, attending *four* looms, can weave *eighteen* similar pieces in a week—some can weave *twenty* pieces."*

From this document, it appears that in 1823 an adult hand-loom weaver could produce, *at the utmost*, not *one-third* as much as a girl at steam-loom : that in 1826 he could not produce *one-sixth* as much; and that in 1833 he could not produce *one-ninth* as much. This plain and simple fact is sufficient to show the nature of the contest between human and automatic industry ; the one stationary, as to capability, the other doubling or trebling its productive powers almost yearly.

We have said that one cause of the lowness of wages earned by the hand-weaver was the export of yarn. They themselves have attributed their poverty to ruinous competition amongst the masters : to some extent they are right, and as this particularly illustrates the consequence of mechanical production, we shall devote a short space to it.

In the sketch of the progressive change marking manufacture, forming the first chapter of this work, it was shown that the increased production of yarn or

* *Vide* History of the Cotton Manufacture, p. 340.

twist was the beginning of the great series of mechanical inventions, which the splendid genius and perseverance of Arkwright made operative. " In the year 1770, the cottagers in our township were entirely employed in spinning and weaving woollen, linen, or cotton, except a few weeks in harvest. The father of a family would earn eight shillings or half a guinea at his loom, and his sons, if he had one, two, or three, alongside of him, six or eight shillings each per week; but the great sheet-anchor of all cottages and small farms was the labour attached to the hand-wheel : and when it is considered that it required six or eight hands to prepare and spin yarn of all of the three materials, I have mentioned sufficient for the consumption of one weaver. This shows clearly the inexhaustible source there was for the labour of every person from the age of seven to eighty years (who retained their sight, and could move their hand), to earn their bread, say 1s. to 3s. per week, without going to the parish.*

" From 1770 to 1778 a complete change had gradually been effected in the spinning of yarns,—that of wool had disappeared altogether, and that of linen was also nearly gone :—cotton, cotton, cotton, was become the almost universal material for employment,—the hand-wheels were all thrown into lumber-rooms,—the yarn was all spun on common jennies,—the carding for all numbers up to forty hanks in the pound was done on carding engines."

The invention of the jenny and the mule, and the erection of spinning factories, aided by water-power,

* How different a picture is this from that of the cottager's condition of the present day ! These descriptions are particularly valuable, as coming from one of the very body the author is speaking of.—*Vide* Appendix.

speedily destroyed cottage-spinning, whilst it· benefited the cottage weaver; — spinning was therefore
abandoned without reluctance or alarm.   As these
machines multiplied, they very soon overstocked the
home market with yarn, notwithstanding the number of
weavers which flocked to a profitable employment.
The patent of Arkwright, which had restricted the use
of the best spinning machine, was set aside in 1785,
after a trial in the Court of King's Bench; and the
immediate result was a most extraordinary extension of
machine spinning.   Factories sprung up in Lancashire
and other counties, and the home market could not
work the yarn up, nor make any return for its production.
Capital had rushed into the trade, ·which had made
Arkwright and others princely fortunes; and the consequence of over production was a fall of profits, and a
necessity for seeking out foreign markets.

The impulse given to the cotton trade whilst these
mechanical improvements were proceeding, may be
clearly seen in the following Table :—

COTTON IMPORTED FROM 1701 to 1800.

Years.	lbs.	Years.	lbs.
1701	1,985,861	1764 . . .	3,870,392
1701 to 1705 } (average) . }	1,170,881	1771 to 1776 } (average) . }	4,764,589
1710	715,000	1776 to 1780 } (average) . }	6,766,613
1720	1,972,805		
1730	1,645,472	1790	31,447,605
1741	1,645,031	1800	56,010,732
1751	2,976,610		

From this Table we learn that from 1780 to 1790
the quantity of cotton consumed in this country increased nearly five-fold, and not far from one-half in
the next succeeding decade.

BRITISH COTTON EXPORTED FROM 1701 to 1800.
OFFICIAL VALUE.

Years.	£	Years.	£
1701	23,253	1764	200,354
1710	5,698	1766	220,759
1720	16,200	1780	355,060
1730	13,524	1787	1,101,457
1741	20,709	1796	1,662,369
1751	45,986	1800	5,406,501

" Within the first fifty years of the century, the quantity of cotton wool imported seems to have little more than doubled; within the last twenty years it multiplied more than eight-fold. The rate of progression, therefore, was ten times as great in the latter period as the former.

" Within the first fifty years the value of the cotton exports nearly doubled; within the last twenty it multiplied fifteen and a half fold. The rate of progression, therefore, was nearly twenty times as great in the latter period as in the former." *

These are two instructive Tables. They show that, whilst the imports increased with great rapidity, the exports had far more than kept pace with them, the former having multiplied from a period a little before the dissolution of Arkwright's patent eight-fold, and the latter fifteen and a half fold.

By this foreign export, the manufacturer, in freeing himself from a dead stock of yarns, and in laying the foundation for an enormous trade, ruined the home weaver. The yarn was bought by foreign nations to convert into cloth, and it was soon found that we should become the spinners of the world. But it was overlooked, that although the British spinner got a tolerably fair return for his exported goods, the British weaver, if his produce should ever become superabundant, and

* *Vide* History of the Cotton Manufacture, pp. 215, 216.

z

give rise to the necessity for opening a foreign market, would have to meet his customers on their own ground, and that the price of his labour must therefore depend on the price paid for labour in other countries. Now this is precisely what has happened, and this it is that has perpetually been crushing the hand-weaver. Yarn is produced in such immense quantities, that the makers have always a full market, and it is shipped abroad, till it has become one of the most important items of our export trade, and till our home workers have to compete with the natives of other countries lightly taxed and cheaply fed.

The extent to which the exportation of cotton goods has been carried will be seen from the following Table, extracted from Burn's " Commercial Glance" for 1833, a work of standard authority :—

	lbs.	lbs.
Number of lbs. consumed	282,675,200	
Allowed for loss in spinning	30,917,600	
Total quantity of yarn spun in England, &c.		251,757,600
Total quantity of yarn spun in Scotland		24,474,931
Total yarn spun in England		227,282,669

HOW DISPOSED OF.

Exported in yarn during the year . .	67,760,822	
————— thread	1,187,601	
————— manufactured goods . .	76,246,339	
Estimated quantity of yarn sent to Scotland and Ireland	5,500,000	
Exported in mixed manufactures . .	12,000,000	
Balance left for home consumption . .	64,587,907	227,282,669

Out of the 227,282,669 lbs. of cotton spun during the year 1833, above 145,000,000 lbs. were absolutely sent to the foreign market, and 64,587,907 lbs. retained only for home consumption and stock.

Of the 145,000,000 lbs. of yarn, specified as being sent out of the country, 76,246,339 lbs. were in a manufactured state—and here we find the truth of the foregoing observations, that by exporting twist we condemn the English hand-manufacturer to contend with the foreign weaver on his own ground; and hence the wages paid to the British weaver must assimilate themselves to those paid to the foreigner, although there is no ground of comparison between the cost of living in different countries; a man in Russia, or Germany, supporting himself in comfort, and even affluence, on a sum which will hardly procure the most ordinary necessaries of life in Great Britain.

In the following Table the kinds of exported manufactured goods are marked, as well as the producing agent :—

Manufactured Goods exported from England in 1833, *showing the Kinds, and producing Agent ; the first particulars taken from Burn's " Commercial Glance ;" the second from Baines' " History of the Cotton Manufacture."*

Descriptions.	Yards.	How produced.
Dimities	150,599	. . Hand
Quiltings and ribs	256,127	. . Hand
Lawns and Lenos	7,843	. . Hand
Calicoes, printed . . .	143,573,899	. . Hand chiefly
Calicoes, plain	172,082,093	. . Hand chiefly
Cambrics and Muslins . .	12,754,365	. . Hand
Cotton and Linen mixed .	2,840,687	. . Hand
Ginghams	2,079,896	. . Hand
Imitation Shawls	329,836	. . Hand
Nankeens	17,935,523	. . Hand
Velveteens	8,162,991	. . Hand chiefly
Lace, &c.	79,193,574	. . Hand
Ticks, &c.	431,672	. . Hand

Descriptions.	Yards.	How produced.
Damasks	32,701 . .	Hand
Counterpanes	54,886 . .	Hand
Shawls, &c.	690,514 . .	Hand and power
Tapes, &c.	116,413 . .	Hand and power
Hosiery	468,602 . .	Hand
Unenumerated	137,709	

The yarn consumed in these manufactures, spun entirely by power, we repeat, amounts to 76,246,339 lbs. whilst, at the same time, we send abroad with these manufactures 67,760,822 lbs. of unmanufactured yarn.

Thus we perceive that machinery, in the first place, destroyed domestic spinning; in the second, it has opened up an immense export trade in yarn; and, in the third, it condemns the domestic weaver to clothe the whole world, whilst he himself is working fourteen hours a day in rags and poverty. " Nonfactory processes of art," says Dr. Ure, " which can be condensed into a single frame, or machine movable by hand, come within the reach of operatives in every adjacent country, and will have their profits reduced ere long to the *minimum* consistent with the employment of capital in it, and their wages brought down to the scale of those in the cheapest or meanest living country. The stocking-trade affords a painful illustration of this fact. No manufacturer in this country can afford to make stockings unless he can get labour at as low a rate as in Germany; because a German stockinger may easily have as good a stocking-frame, and work it as well, as an English frame-knitter. In the market of the world, therefore, Great Britain has here no advantage by its machinery and capital over other countries, where the materials of the fabrics can be purchased at nearly the same price. The same reasoning may be applied to the bobbin-net trade, in so far as it is carried on by hand-machines. The wages now made for this most ingenious fabric are deplorably low, in consequence of the competition of the continental handicraftsmen, who are content to live in the poorest manner. Thus, also, the profit on lace, made by power-machines, has been reduced, for a time at least, below its natural level, in consequence of the possessors of hand-machines continuing to work them,* in the vain hope of redeeming their first great cost in some degree, though the wages of their labour meanwhile can hardly keep them alive."†

The commercial part of these observations is strictly true, and applies with equal force to the cotton hand-loom weavers, as to the parties mentioned by the writer. The British manufacturer, to dispose of his productions, must sell at a lower price than the native workman of other countries can produce them ; and he does this even whilst he supplies the foreign manufacturer with the basis of his cloth—namely, yarn ; but to enable him to do this, he has to bring down the wages of the producers to something like a level with the wages earned in other countries, and then his capital and his skill make him a profit, though now a small one. "The sale of our goods depends, in a great measure, on the lowness of their prices.... The more remote the market, the more necessary is it to keep the price low, to guard against contingencies, as the good may otherwise be undersold by the product of the rudest machinery cheaply worked," is the language held in the " Philosophy of Manufactures."† For this purpose, therefore, the operative here is condemned to suffer the extremest privation,

* The real fact of the case is, that the impoverished operatives have sunk under competition, and *cannot* change their condition.

† *Vide* Philosophy of Manufactures, p. 333.

‡ *Vide* pages 313, 314.

and machinery is urged on at a rapid pace in order to keep up some profit, whilst goods, both yarn and cloth, are perpetually cheapening.

The rate of profit, it has just been said, is small : the following evidence was given by Mr. Kirkman Finlay, of Glasgow, an intelligent man, and a very competent witness, before the select Committee of the House of Commons, on Manufactures, Commerce, and Shipping, in 1833.*—" I attribute the low state of profit not to any want of demand—if we compare the demand now with the demand of any former period—*but to an extremely extensive production, with reference to the demand arising out of great competition* .... *A practice has greatly prevailed, of late years, of the manufacturer making large consignments of his productions to foreign countries.*" Many corroborative facts and striking examples of thus pushing away produce upon any terms, may be examined by referring to the Minutes of Evidence, taken before the Select Committee on Hand-loom Weavers, in 1834.

The weight of this perpetual reduction of price falls chiefly upon the hand-producer, and we shall show presently how it will, before long, act upon the power-worker. The fall in the value of goods, and the small profit of the manufacturer, are exhibited in the following Table, which will at once explain the absolute need under which the capitalist lies to turn out an immense quantity with great rapidity.

* *Vide* Report, p. 45.

Years.	Price of one Piece in Warp.		Price of one Piece in Weft.		Expense of sising.	Cost Price.			Selling Price.		
	s.	*d.*	*s.*	*d.*	*d.*	£	*s.*	*d.*	£	*s.*	*d.*
1814	9	5	7	5½	6	1	3	10½	1	4	7
1815	7	10¼	6	3	—	0	18	10½	0	19	8¾
1816	7	0½	5	5¼	—	0	16	4¼	0	16	8½
1817	6	6¾	5	4½	—	0	16	2½	0	16	8½
1818	6	9½	4	2	—	0	13	0¼	0	13	9
1819	5	3¼	3	6	—	0	11	1½	0	12	1½
1820	4	2½	2	6	—	0	9	10½	0	9	8¼
1821	3	9¾	2	3	5	0	8	11	0	9	3½
1822	3	8¼	2	2½	—	0	8	8¼	0	8	11¼
1823	3	8¾	2	2½	—	0	8	5¼	0	8	5¾
1824	3	8¼	2	2	—	0	8	0¼	0	8	5¼
1825	3	4	1	10	—	0	6	2¾	0	6	3¼
1826	2	8	1	9½	—	0	6	3½	0	6	6
1827	2	6½	1	9	—	0	6	4½	0	6	5¼
1828	2	8	1	9	—	0	5	11	0	5	8
1829	2	8	1	10½	—	0	6	5½	0	6	3¾
1830	2	9	1	9½	—	0	6	0¾	0	6	2¼
1831	2	3½	1	9	—	0	5	8¾	0	5	8
1832	2	4	1	9	—	0	5	10¾	0	6	2
1833	2	5	1	9¾	—	0	5	10	0	6	0

PRICE OF COTTON YARN, No. 100, FROM 1786 to 1832.

In the Year	Yarn, No. 100, sold for		In the Year	Yarn, No. 100, sold for	
	s.	d.		s.	d.
1786	38	0	1798	9	10
1787	38	0	1799	10	11
1788	35	0	1800	8	5
1789	34	0	1801		9
1790	30	0	1802		4
1791	29	9	1803		4
1792	16	1	1804		10
1793	15	1	1805		10
1794	15	1	1806		2
1795	19	0	1807		9
1796	19	0	1829*		2
1797	19	0	1832		11

In addition to these Tables, showing the rapid decline of prices, the following statement exhibits the same fact in still more striking colours, because applied to the mass. The enormous export trade which has grown up has filled the minds of many people with the most extraordinary delusions. Let us, however, see how and upon what terms it has grown to its present magnitude.

The terms *official* and *declared* value must be explained before we can make ourselves understood. *Official value* indicates *quantity* only: it is the quantity of any given export, reduced to money by a fixed and unvarying scale, adopted by the Custom House many years ago. Thus, in speaking of the *official* value of an exported article, we say, in 1800 it was 1,000,000*l.*; in 1835, 10,000,000*l.*; that is, a certain number of yards were valued in 1800 at one million, and another certain number of yards at ten millions in 1835, both upon the same scale; and this advance points out at once

* After many fluctuations.

that *ten times* more yards were exported at the last period than the first.

Declared value, on the contrary, is the *real price* of the exported article, according to the declaration of the exporter. This signifies, therefore, the absolute worth of the article; and hence, the *official value* and the *declared value,* when compared, show at a glance the increase or decrease in the worth of the article. If the *official value* rises, whilst the *declared* remains stationary or declines, it is obvious that a greater quantity of goods are disposed of, without any correspondent return in money.

The condition of the export trade connected with our cotton manufactures is singularly instructive as to the effects of machinery upon production and value. In 1814, the *official value* of the cotton exports was 17,655,378*l.*; *the declared value,* 20,033,132*l.* In 1833, the *official value* of cotton exports was 46,337,210*l.* the *declared value,* 18,459,000*l.*

It is worth while to pause a moment, and reflect on this extraordinary statement, founded as it is on Parliamentary Papers and Finance Accounts. The clearest way of showing the depreciation in value to the non-commercial reader, is to call the 1*l.*, in *official* value, yards, when it will stand thus—

1814, sold 17,655,378 yards for 20,033,132*l.*
1833, sold 46,337,210 yards for 18,459,000*l.*

so that, notwithstanding we have almost trebled our export trade since 1814, its absolute return is nearly 2,000,000*l.* less in 1833 than 1814.

Well may profits be small, well may the productive powers of automatic industry be eagerly urged forward, and well may human labour be crushed by a system like this. Steam and mechanism produce yarn, and man hitherto has, in a great measure, produced cloth; but it will require both steam and mechanism to produce cloth, if this enormous trade is to be sustained,—and this they have begun doing to a vast amount.

In twenty years hence we may find, if the system should proceed unchecked, an export trade,—100,000,000*l. official value*, and 10,000,000*l. declared value.* Automatic industry will enable us to do this;—with human labourers it cannot be done; and yet it must be done, if our foreign trade is to be continued on the present system. Any serious interference with it, such as a rise in the value of labour, carried so far as to influence the price of manufactured goods, would lose us a great proportion of our trade, and would give such a spur to foreign production as would for ever deprive us of our markets.

Automatic industry, we again repeat, will enable us to carry on the present system, and to keep in advance of manufacturing nations, where food is cheap, and the necessaries of life untaxed. How far such a system is just to our own labouring community is another question; but we hold the opinion, that the industrious operative, willing and anxious to labour for his sustenance, is subjected to great wrong by this state of things.

It has been said that any serious interference with the price of goods would overthrow a great part of our foreign trade; that, in fact, we undersell other producers, and thus keep our markets. One great cause, therefore, of the perpetual cheapening of production is to be found in foreign as well as in home competition. The United States of America have spinning machinery, energy, and industry, equal to our own, and already the manufacture has acquired a large extent. From a report made to Congress in 1832, it appears that 57,466 hands are employed in spinning, weaving, &c., and that the amount paid for wages was 2,144,780*l.* The growth of this manufacture has been as rapid in America as in England—the number of factories being only fifteen in 1807, producing 300,000 lbs. of yarn. In 1831, there were 795 mills working, which produced 67,862,665 lbs. of yarn. The cotton goods of the United States, chiefly of a coarse quality, are displacing, to some extent, those of Great Britain, in the Mexican, South American, and some of the eastern markets, and have also been introduced into Europe, besides supplying, as far as they go, the wants of her citizens.

The cotton trade in France has also thriven rapidly, and employs a great number of hands, perhaps not fewer than 700,000, and the gross annual produce has been estimated at 24,000,000*l.* This has risen since Napoleon enforced his continental system, and in 1810 the quantity of cotton wool consumed was 25,000,000 lbs.; in 1832, it had risen to 80,000,000 lbs. The interests of this manufacture have been guarded by duties to keep us from the French markets, but the smuggling of yarn is carried on to a large extent.

Switzerland, Prussia, Austria, Saxony, Lombardy, and Belgium, manufacture cottons : the manufacture, however, is upon a small scale compared to our own. Still the seeds are sown ; and any interference with the present *cheapness* of British produce, would at once bring them into close competition with us. We overpower them by machinery—and by machinery alone ; hand-labour being cheaper than with us—having a price indeed nearly the same as that paid to the domestic manufacturer of Britain.

Our immense export trade, therefore, has been

generated by abundant production, cheapened by the
substitution of automatic for human labour ; and if it is
to continue, it must be continued by the same means.
The human labour now expended upon it, as being the
dearest and the least manageable agent, must of necessity
give way ; and as we have been chiefly met by woven
cloths in other countries, and as we were enabling them
to weave plentifully by exporting machinery and yarn,
the great trial has been to beat down the wages of the
hand-weaver.   Now, however, he is on the point of
being quite superseded.   " The usual rate of profit in
England is lower than in any of the countries whose
competition has been feared;. and on this account
English manufactures can be sold cheaper than those of
other countries, especially owing to the extensive
employment of machinery, which causes the price of the
goods to be regulated more according to the wages of
labour.   Since the introduction of the power-loom the
maintenance of English superiority is rendered much
more secure.   This country excels every other in the
making of machines, and in the means of working them
advantageously ; and besides this, for the reason just
mentioned, our manufacturers are interested in having
their goods produced as much as possible by machinery.
The power-loom changes the mode of manufacture,
from that in which we labour under a considerable
advantage, to that in which we possess the greatest
superiority."

We have thus seen,—that since the year 1786, when
cotton yarn was sold for 38s. per lb. and when the hand-
weaver earned liberal and sufficient wages, yarn has fallen
to 2s. 11d. per lb. and the wages of the hand-weaver to
4s. per week ; that whilst the quantity of manufactured
goods has increased enormously in amount, it has in

equal ratio decreased in value, the capitalist making his profit from rapidity of production, and diminution in the price paid for labour, till in the end a state of things has resulted which renders human labour, even at the miserable price paid for it, too expensive; and consequently, that an immense body of operatives are being stranded without any hope or prospect of saving themselves.

Whilst this has been going on, the factory operative has earned a tolerably steady rate of wages, which is still kept up chiefly because those engaged in mills have bound themselves in close and operative unions to keep up their value. So operative are these unions that the masters *dare not* reduce wages below a certain fixed price; and the men, rather than suffer their own surplus body to interfere with wages, ship them off to America * These unions, which have ramified throughout the entire factory labourers, are sources of great embarrassment to the master, whose energy, activity, and capital, are more or less at their mercy. He cannot, however, dissolve them by force; and the knowledge which the men have of the *cheapening* power of machinery keeps them together. If the master cannot overcome them by force, he has another and a sure, though gradual agent of destruction in the workshop of the machinist; and it is this that he is wielding with silent but irresistible force, which will free him from his adult and combined labourers.

It is impossible to deny that the men have accelerated the advance of the mighty agent which is to destroy them. We have expressed our opinion freely and dispassionately on the subject of combinations, and yet no man can wonder that a body of artisans, placed as

* *Vide* Philosophy of Manufactures, p. 327.

these have been, should combine. That combinations, justified in many cases by grasping and tyrannous measures on the part of the masters, have degenerated into violence and assumption on the part of the men, is quite certain. If the present rapid advances of mechanical adaptation are permitted to proceed, the struggle will soon cease between the opposing powers—men on the one side, and masters on the other.

" The masters finding, after many struggles renewed from time to time, that a reduction of wages commensurate with the fall in the price of the goods in the general market could not be effected, had recourse to an expedient which the workmen could not decently oppose, because its direct tendency was to raise or to uphold, at least, the wages of each spinner, *but to diminish the numbers necessary for the same quantity of work.* * * * This necessity of enlarging the spinning-frames created by the union decrees, has recently given an extraordinary stimulus to mechanical science. It is delightful to see from eight hundred to one thousand spindles of polished steel, advancing and receding in a mathematical line, each of them whirling all the time upon its axis with equal velocity and truth, and forming threads of surprising tenuity, uniformity, and strength. In doubling the size of his mule, the owner is enabled to get rid of indifferent or restive spinners, and to become once more master of his mill, which is no small advantage. I am well assured that but for the extra-- vagant pretensions of the ruling committee, this catastrophe would not have happened for many a day to come. * * * * By this marvellous elongation, one spinner comes to manage a pair of mules containing from

* Assuredly not; but it would have come from causes we have already detailed.

fifteen hundred to two thousand spindles, and to supersede the labour of one or two companion spinners.
The men so displaced might easily find employment
upon the power-looms at 15s. per week,* but generally
speaking they will not condescend to this inferior task,
but loiter about in idleness, consuming the funds of
their ' society, and teaching a lesson of moderation.
Meantime mill-owners possess an abundant choice of
good hands, and the power of ensuring their best services, since they can replace them by others in case of
negligence or incapacity."

" During a disastrous (union) turmoil at Hyde, Staley
Bridge, and the adjoining factory townships, several of
the capitalists, afraid of their business, being driven to
France, Belgium, and the United States, had recourse to
the celebrated machinists, Messrs. Sharp, Roberts, and
Co. of Manchester, requesting them to direct the inventive talents of their partner, Mr. Roberts, to the
construction of a *self-acting* mule. * * * To the delight
of the mill-owners, who ceased not to stimulate his
exertions by frequent visitations, he produced, in the
course of a few months, a machine apparently instinct
with the thought, feeling, and tact of the experienced
workman, which, even in its infancy, displayed a new
principle of regulation, ready in its *mature state to fulfil
the functions of a finished spinner.* Thus the *Iron Man,*
as the operatives fitly call it, sprung out of the hands of
our modern Prometheus at the bidding of Minerva—a
creation destined to restore order † among the industrious classes, and to confirm to Great Britain the empire

* This is opposed to the fact.

† " This expression of Dr. Ure's strongly reminds us of the
celebrated expression of the Russian Emperor—' Order reigns in
Warsaw.' "

of art. * * * Several months ago (December, 1834,) the machine was in operation in upwards of sixty mills, working between 300,000 and 400,000 spindles." *

Since this time, the self-actor—the *Iron Man*—has been rapidly introducing into general use, as it is essentially necessary from the closeness of competition amongst manufacturers, that they should stand on equal terms in point of productiveness: hence any improvement of great capabilities must be generally adopted, otherwise those working with *self-actors* would undersell those working with the common mules.

In this single instance we have exhibited the natural and inevitable tendency of mechanical improvement to destroy human labour. Spinning machines, when first introduced by Highs, Kay, and Arkwright, at once destroyed domestic spinning: the *Iron Man* of Roberts will as surely destroy the factory spinner. It is utterly ridiculous to say that the extension of the trade will or can absorb the discharged hands — *it is impossible.* Whether they will consent to be expatriated by such of their brethren as continue to be employed we know not, but we conceive the progress of *automata* will cause them to be dismissed too rapidly ; for, be it remembered, it is not in this department only that these wonderful mechanical adaptations are taking place,—every process is alike passing from the hand to machines. Two-thirds, at least, of the spinners employed will be dismissed by the improvements we have just spoken of ; and these improvements, striking as they are, are but the germs of others still more perfectly automatic.

The same series of improvements are in operation in the other branches of textile manufactures with precisely the same results ; and were it possible to find data, it

* Philosophy of Manufactures, pp. 364—366.

would unquestionably appear that, notwithstanding the extension of these, a diminution is rapidly taking place in the number of hands employed. " The Factories Regulation Act of 1833 has had the effect of causing thousands of young children to be dismissed, whose place it has in many cases been found unnecessary to supply, *as their work can be done by new contrivances with the operatives that are left.*" * This remarkable illustration might be greatly multiplied ; as Mr. Baines observes, " that improvements in machinery are constantly altering the number of workmen employed in each department."

Dr. Ure remarks, that " the factory system, instead of being detrimental to the comfort of the labouring population, is its grand palladium." † ' He however entirely overlooks his own statements. Had he said that the factory system will gradually throw out of employment the greater portion of the hands now employed in it, but that to those it did retain it would secure liberal wages, he would have spoken the truth, and shown that he was acquainted with the bearing and inevitable tendency of the system.

The time is not remote when a coalition will take place between the masters and such hands as they are obliged to retain, and the unions will fall to pieces, or at all events will cease to be supported by the earnings of the employed labourers. Self-interest will overpower the *esprit de corps*, which now binds the employed to the unemployed, a revolution which is already effecting in more than one mill. The question is, will the mass of factory hands sink thus into a condition of absolute destitution without a struggle ? They are on the road to this. All the operations in their peculiar branch of industry are

* History of the Cotton Manufacture, p. 375.
† Philosophy of Manufactures, p. 329.

A A

being withdrawn from them. " The cotton is brought
to the mill in bags just as it is received from America,
Egypt, or India, and is then stowed in warehouses,
being arranged according to the countries from which it
may have come. It is passed through the *willow,* the
scutching machine, and the *spreading machine,* in order
to be opened, cleaned, and evenly spread. By the
carding engine the fibres are combed out, and laid
parallel to each other, and the piece is compressed into
a sliver. The sliver is repeatedly drawn and doubled
in the *drawing-frame,* more perfectly to straighten the
fibres to equalize the grist. The *roving-frame,* by rollers
and spindles, produces a coarse and loose thread,
which the *mule,* or *throstle,* spins into yarn. To
make the warp, the twist is transferred from cops to
bobbins by the *winding-machine,* and from the bobbins
at the *warping-mill* to a cylindrical beam. This beam
being taken to the *dressing-machine,* the warp is sised,
dressed, and wound upon the weaving beam. The latter
is then placed in the *power-loom,* by which machine the
shuttle being supplied with cops of weft, the cloth is
woven.

" Such, without entering into minutiæ, are the processes by which the vegetable wool is converted into a
woven fabric of great beauty and delicacy ; and it will
be perceived that the operations are numerous, and
every one of them is performed by machinery, without the help of human hands, except merely in trans-
ferring the material from one machine to another. It is
by iron fingers, teeth and wheels, moving with exhaust-
less energy and devouring speed, that the cotton is
opened, cleaned, spread, carded, roved, spun, wound,
warped, dressed, and woven. The various machines are
proportioned to each other, in regard to their capability

of work, and they are so placed in the mill as to allow the materials to be carried from stage to stage with the least possible loss of time. All are moving at once— the operations chasing each other—and all derive their motion from the mighty engine, which, firmly seated in the lower part of the building, and constantly fed with water and fuel, toils through the day with the strength of a hundred horses. Men, in the meanwhile, have merely to attend on this wonderful series of mechanism, to supply it with work, to oil its joints, to check its slight and infrequent irregularities; each workman performing, or rather superintending, as much work as could have been done by *two or three hundred men* sixty years since."*

The effects of mechanical production, as far as we have traced them, are, in the first place, to lower the value of human labour, and, in the next, to destroy it altogether, except in so far as the hands engaged in machine making are concerned: and even these are being encroached upon—machines making machines. The intermediate step between the two just mentioned, is its effects upon the higher qualities of the operative, namely, his skill, emulative pride, and respect for his own position.

It is singular to observe how widely apart are the opinions of those who contend that every mechanical improvement must of necessity benefit the workman; and in nothing more is this discrepancy visible than on this point. In a paper on the cotton manufacture, in the Edinburgh Review, No. 91, written by Mr. M'Culloch, the following words occur. To the

* History of the Cotton Manufacture, pp. 342, 343.

A A 2

truth of some of these we have borne ample testimony;
from others we entirely dissent.

"Our master manufacturers, engineers and artisans,
are more intelligent, skilful, and enterprising, than those
of other countries, and the extraordinary inventions they
have already made, and their familiarity with all the principles and details of the business, will not only enable
them to perfect the processes already in use, but can
hardly fail to lead to the discovery of others. Our establishments for spinning, weaving, printing, bleaching,
&c., are infinitely more complete and perfect than any
that exist elsewhere, *the division of labour in them is
carried to an incomparably greater extent, the workmen
are trained from infancy to industrious habits*, and have
attained that peculiar dexterity and sleight of hand in the
performance of their separate tasks, that can only be
acquired by long and unremitting application to the
same employment."

This is the language of Mr. M'Culloch, a leading
authority in that particular school of political economy
to which he belongs. Its variance with the fact is
extraordinary; and here Dr. Ure, in his "Philosophy of
Manufactures," being a skilful *mechanician*, sets right the
abstractions of the theorist.

"It is in fact the constant aim and tendency of every
improvement in machinery to supersede human labour
altogether, or to diminish its cost, by substituting the
industry of women and children for that of men, *or that
of ordinary labourers for trained artisans*."—P. 23.

"This tendency to employ merely children with
watchful eyes and nimble fingers, *instead of journeymen
of long experience*, shows how the scholastic dogma of
the division of labour into degrees of skill has been exploded by our enlightened manufacturers."—*Ibid.*

" Improvements in machinery effect a substitution of labour comparatively unskilled, for that which is more skilful."*—P. 30.

" The principle of the factory system is, to substitute mechanical science for hand-skill, and the partition of a process into its essential constituents, for the division or gradation of labour among artisans. On the handicraft plan, labour, more or less skilled, was usually the most expensive element of production; but on the automatic plan, *skilled* labour gets progressively superseded, and will eventually be *replaced by mere overlookers of machines.*"—P. 20.

" Mr. Anthony Strutt, who conducts the mechanical department of the great cotton factories of Belper and Milford, has so thoroughly departed from the old routine of the schools, *that he will employ no man who has learned his craft by regular apprenticeship.*"—P. 21.

" An eminent mechanician of Manchester told me, that he does not choose to make any steam-engines at present, because, with his existing means, he would be obliged to resort to the old principle of the division of labour, so fruitful of jealousies and strikes among workmen; but he intends to prosecute that branch of business whenever he has prepared suitable arrangements on the equalisation of labour, or automatic plan."—P. 21.

We might multiply these extracts; but they are sufficient to show what is the truth. It is, as Dr. Ure justly remarks, the great aim of machinery to make skill or strength on the part of the workman valueless, and to reduce him to a mere watcher of, and waiter upon,

* The singular discrepancies which characterise Dr. Ure's work—here asserting and there denying positions—may be remarked in comparing these extracts with some observations at p. 311.

automata. The term artisan will shortly be a misnomer as applied to the operative; he will no longer be a man proud of his skill and ingenuity, and conscious that he is a valuable member of society; he will have lost all free agency, and will be as much a part of the machines around him as the wheels or cranks which communicate motion.

This, we repeat, is the intermediate stage between the diminution in the value of human labour, and the entire destruction of it. Already this is far advanced, and the adult operatives are being rapidly ejected by the factories.* These have been principally engaged in the spinning and dressing departments. " The effect of substituting the self-acting mule for the common mule, is to discharge the greater part of the men spinners." The dressers, who have hitherto been the best paid factory labourers, are nearly superseded by a machine.† The same remarks apply to every process of manufacture, whether of cotton, wool, linen, or flax; mechanical adaptations are at work in them all, and in all discharging the skilled and adult workman,‡ and gradually, but steadily, lessening the number of human agents employed. It is the policy of the masters to pay those hands which they retain well, because by so doing, as we have already said, self-interest will lead them to detach themselves from the mass of unemployed and malcontent labourers.

A crisis has, therefore, partly arisen, and it behoves every man, interested in the welfare of his country, to examine into the present means for lessening its inevitable evils. An ingenious and eloquent writer in the

* Philosophy of Manufactures, p. 23.
† Ibid. p. 40, 370.   ‡ *Vide* Ibid. *passim.*

Quarterly Review has said, " So far are we from regarding the increased use of machinery as an evil which requires to be checked, that we hail every such application of the discoveries of science as another step in the steady course by which the Author of Nature pushes forward the improvement of the human race. In our opinion, instead of being an evil to be deprecated; and if possible counteracted and repressed, the application of machinery, as a substitute for labour, serves to disengage a large number of human beings from manufacturing toil, in order that they may be employed in perfecting and extending our tillage, thereby at once increasing their own happiness and the resources of the empire."

He goes on to say, " We have arrived at a great and most important crisis of social arrangement. We are embarrassed with a superfluity of human labour, of animal machines, which cannot be absorbed in manufacturing operations. What is to be done with this superfluous, or rather disposable fund of human, physical power? shall these men be compelled to eke out a miserable existence, with half employment and scanty wages? or shall they be thrown upon their respective parishes for eleemosynary relief?"

In speaking of the crisis which led to the introduction of poor laws, and laid the foundation for the extension of manufactures, and which had resulted from an excess of agricultural labourers, and the breaking up of the monastic institutions, he remarks:—

" The extent to which the employment of machinery has been pushed, as a substitute for human labour, has at length brought on a new crisis: it is one essentially different from that which presented itself to the statesmen of the sixteenth century, and which appears to

demand a different remedy. Then the agricultural
population had become too numerous, whilst a large proportion of the surplus produce of the English land was
exported in exchange for wrought commodities;—now,
the difficulty is of a totally different origin and kind.
So far are our manufactures from requiring an increased
supply of hands, that they overflow with workmen, for
whose industry there is no profitable demand.   The
employment of machinery not only stops up the gap
through which the surplus of our agricultural population
had been used to make its way into manufactories, but
it has likewise thrown out of employment a considerable
portion of the hands, which had been previously occupied in the fabrication of wrought commodities.   From
both these sources, a number of unemployed hands
accumulate; the gradual increase of population produces
a surplus of labourers, who cannot find profitable employment in the tillage of our old lands; and to this
surplus is daily added a crowd of workmen, whom the
extension and improvement of machinery disengages
from manufactories."

But these do not constitute all the elements of the
crisis which is developing itself.   Agriculture is undergoing a transition as great, and almost as remarkable as
manufacture—and these are progressing, step by step, to
one and to the same end.   Mechanical contrivances for
lessening human labour are sought for with as great
avidity in the one case as in the other; and in a single
instance,—that of the use of a peculiarly constructed
plough for hoeing up potatoes,—one man and one horse
get through as much work, as would, a few years ago,
have required at least thirty labourers, and perform the
task much more completely and efficiently: and this is
only one solitary example.   The current of prejudice

has hitherto run strongly against the use of machines
for farming purposes, and has been kept up by the
limited intelligence existing amongst farmers as a class.

The depression which has been gradually but steadily
creeping over them, has at length succeeded in breaking
up the cottier and small farm system, and has thrown agriculture into a new shape and into new hands ; which has
brought all the force of this epoch of mechanism to bear
upon it. The same causes are at work, therefore, upon the
two great divisions of national industry, and their effects
have even been more severely felt by the agricultural than
the manufacturing labourer ; and they have, in a great
measure, already pauperized the whole body, and nearly
extinguished the peasantry, as a moral and independent
class of the community. The present crisis involves
not one particular portion of labourers, or one particular
branch of trade, but the interests and future welfare of
all are intimately connected with it.

The time, indeed, appears rapidly approaching, when
the people, emphatically so called, and which have
hitherto been considered the sinews of a nation's
strength, will be even worse than useless; when the
manufactories will be filled with machinery, impelled
by steam, so admirably constructed as to perform nearly
all the processes required in them ; and when land will
be tilled by the same means. Neither are these
visionary anticipations ; and these include but a frac-
tion of the mighty alterations to which the next century will give birth. Well, then, may the question be
asked—What is to be done? Great calamities must be
suffered. No extensive transition of this nature can be
operated without immense present sacrifices ; but upon
what class, or what division of property or industry,
these must be more especially inflicted, it is impossible

clearly to indicate.   Much should be done—and done
vigorously and resolutely.   Like other great revolutions
in the social arrangement of kingdoms, it is to be feared
that an explosion will be permitted to take place, un-
directed by the guiding hand of any patriotic and
sagacious spirit, that its fragments will be again huddled
together in hurry and confusion, and finally have to
undergo a series of painful gradations, before society
can regain a healthy and permanent tone.

APPENDIX.

NOTE REFERRED TO IN PREFACE.

ANALYSIS *of the* EVIDENCE *taken before the* FACTORY COMMIS-SIONERS, *as far as it relates to the Population of Manchester, and the Vicinity, engaged in the Cotton Trade. Read before the Statistical Society of Manchester, March,* 1834. *Abridged.*

[The contradictory nature of this evidence should be constantly looked at.]

The Evidence may be conveniently arranged under the following heads :—

    I.   The *Health* of the Factory Population.
    II. Alleged *Fatigue* arising from the long hours of labour.
    III. Alleged *Cruelty* towards the Factory Children.
    IV. State of *Education.*
    V. State of *Morality.*
    VI. Wages and Poor Rates.

I.—HEALTH.

The evidence regarding the state of health among those employed in factories, and the effect of their occupation on the constitution, is various and conflicting, but very full. The Medical Commissioner, Dr. Hawkins, on whose examinations we should naturally be most disposed to rely, gives but very few ; and the report which he prefixes to them is too vague and general to supply this deficiency. He states that he examined eight hundred children at two Sunday schools in Manchester, and gives the result as follows :—

Of 400 in factories—	Of 400, *not* in factories—
86 had *bad* health,	22 had *bad* health,
153 — *middling* health,	106 — *middling* health,
161 — *good* health.	272 — *good* health.
———	———
400	400

This table would have been more satisfactory, if Dr. H. had stated on what he founded his classification, and whether or not the pale appearance of the children entered into his estimate. In the same page he gives a similar table, which leads to a very different conclusion. Of 1190 adolescents examined in thirteen factories, 787 had *good* health, 311 had *middling* health, and 92 only had *bad* health. Hence it appears, by the first table, that *one-fifth* of the factory children had bad health, and by the second only *one-twelfth*. Dr. Hawkins imagines the reason 'of this discrepancy to be, that several of these thirteen factories were situated in the country districts, and not in Manchester.

In the third, or supplementary report, Dr. Hawkins fortunately gives a tabular view of the state of health in several *cotton* factories he examined, which we have analyzed, and the result is as follows :—

MALES.	FEMALES.
122 had *good* health,	162 had *good* health,
94 — *middling* health,	82 — *middling* health,
29 — *bad* health.	27 — *bad* health.
———	———
245	271

Thus, only *one-eighth* of the males and *one-tenth* of the females enjoyed bad health in the cotton factories examined by Dr. Hawkins. The examination of these tables presents us with two important results,—*First*, they show that the health of females employed in cotton-mills is better than that of males; and *secondly*, that the proportion of healthy workpeople is always greatest in the largest factories.

Dr. Hawkins seems to have been a good deal struck with the pale and delicate appearance of those engaged in factories. That this impression arose from a want of comparison with *other* inhabitants of large and dirty towns, appears from the following remark of one of his fellow-commissioners:—" In Bennet-street Sunday School I made a comparison of the factory and nonfactory children, by separating each at different sides of the school-room, and contrasting in this way more than one thousand children; but neither myself, nor my colleagues, could detect the smallest difference in their personal appearance. I also made the same comparison, with the same results, in two other schools."

It appears, from Dr. Hawkins's report, (which is confirmed by the other commissioners from all parts of the country,) that those employed in factories enjoyed a singular exemption from the cholera; and it appears, from the evidence of other medical men, that the same exemption extends to the influenza, and to infectious disorders generally.

Dr. Hawkins also states, on the authority of Mr. Roberton, that in Manchester fifty-four out of every hundred die under five years of age, while in country places the proportion is only thirty-two per cent. This, however, is contradicted by two surgeons at Bolton, and partially by a physician at Stayley Bridge.

In concluding his report, Dr. Hawkins seems to state that the defective health which, he conceives, *does* exist amongst the factory population generally, is *not* a necessary result of their occupation; for he states, that in some factories he could see no desire nor necessity for legislation, and no dark shades in the condition of the people.

Thus far the report, though not so definite as could be wished, tends to prove that the population employed in factories is, from some cause or other, inferior in health to that which follows other occupations; but when we come to the evidence of the operatives themselves, and of resident medical practitioners, the statements become more conflicting, and the preponderance is decidedly the other way. Almost all, however, agree that, in general, children employed in factories are paler and less healthy looking than others. This is nothing more than was to have been expected, paleness of complexion being an almost invariable concomitant of in-door occupation in a warm atmosphere.

One question frequently put to the witnesses by different examiners was, " Whether the factory population were dege-nerated in appearance, and stunted in growth?" The answers to this question are somewhat remarkable. Of *six* operative witnesses examined, *three* declare that they can perceive a very distinct deterioration in size and appearance, while *three* others declare positively the contrary. Of *eight* others ex-amined, *three* state that the growth of factory children is greatly stunted by their occupation, and Dr. Hawkins evidently leans to this opinion ; but the remaining *five* assert this to be a total mistake, and declare that factory children are as well grown as any others living in large towns. This last opinion is confirmed by some tables given by Mr. Cowell, who had the patience to try a large and laborious experiment to decide this controverted point. This gentleman actually measured upwards of one thousand children, under eighteen years of age, and carried his calculation to three places of decimals to insure finding some result, and the result was this :—

	Inches.		Inches.
Boys in factories measured	55·28	Girls in factories	54·951
—— *not* in factories . .	55 56	—— not . .	54·976
	·28		·028

Thus it appears that the difference in stature between the factory and the nonfactory population is appreciable only by a species of micrometrical measurement, being in the case of boys $\frac{23}{100}$, and in that of girls $\frac{25}{1000}$ of an inch. One of the witnesses above quoted, declared that the race was degenerating so fast, that in a short time the people "would be absolute dwarfs*."

* These remarks, it must be remembered, refer to *town* la-bourers.

In *weight*, however, the difference between the two classes is more decided, being, in the case of boys, 3·5 lbs. and in that of girls, 0·3lbs. On this one of the Commissioners remarks:— " This result is just what might be expected, inasmuch as factory labour requires no muscular exertion whatever, consequently, many of the muscles are never fully developed, and the additional weight which their development would give to the body is lost. If their employment was more laborious than it is, they would doubtless weigh heavier."

One of the most important questions to be decided was— " Whether the factory population had worse health than those engaged in other occupations?" this being, in fact, the real gist of the whole inquiry. *Twenty-six* witnesses were questioned on this point, and the analysis of their evidence is as follows:—*Fifteen* declare that, to the best of their knowledge and observation, the factory population are as healthy as those engaged in other occupations. One says, " There are other occupations that are better, and some that are worse for the health, than factory labour;" and two qualify their statements, by saying, " factory labour is as healthy as any other occupation *in a large town.*" Of these *fifteen* witnesses, *ten* are operatives, *three* are surgeons, and *two* are resident ministers.

Six witnesses, on the other hand, declare that " factory people are not generally so healthy as others." *Two* of these are recruiting officers, the rest are operatives.

The replies to questions, respecting the alleged deformity induced by factory labour, are contradictory and perplexing. *Thirteen* witnesses speak to this point, of whom *seven* declare, that they have seen others crippled, or been so themselves, in consequence of working in mills; while *six* others, chiefly operatives, affirm that they do not know of any instances of deformity so caused, and cannot perceive that factory labour has any such tendency. The truth most probably is, that instances of deformity have *formerly* been caused when a child has entered, with a weak frame, or at too early an age, into an ill-regulated factory. Mr. Tuffnell remarks, " All the seriously deformed persons sent to me were *adults,* nor did a single instance of a *child badly* deformed by its work, come under my notice. The reason is this; many years ago it was the practice to work much longer hours than at present, and several persons who were injured by over work, *at that time,* are to be met with."

II.—FATIGUE.

Considerable difficulty appears to have been experienced, in ascertaining whether or not the children feel much fatigued in the evening, after twelve hours' work, in factories, a question which at first sight appears to involve no difficulty whatever. Almost all who have been superficially acquainted with factories, or who have heard them described, agree in their opinion that children must be greatly fatigued with so many hours' standing and exertion; but the operatives themselves are by no means so unanimous in their statements of the *fact.* Dr. Hawkins states in his report, that a large number, both of boys and girls, "declared that they had no desire to play about on the Saturday and Sunday, but preferred remaining quiet," in consequence, (we presume him to mean from the context,) of the fatigue of the previous week. Among *forty-three* witnesses, however, who were examined on this point, only *nine* affirm the children to be much fatigued at night; and one of this number, after declaring that the children feel little inclination to attend evening school, owing to having been so long on their legs, qualifies his statement by the remark, "that they are like *wild Irish* when they come out of the mill."

The natural conclusion from all appears to be, that *weakly* children *are* fatigued by twelve hours' labour, but that healthy ones are not.

III.—ALLEGED CRUELTY TO CHILDREN.

On this point, we are glad to say, the evidence is clear, uniform, and explicit; for while all the witnesses, with *four* exceptions, declare that ill-treatment of children in mills is a thing unheard of and unknown, a large majority allow that spinners do not unfrequently beat their piecers; they also declare that this corporal punishment is not more severe— perhaps less so, than what is received at home, and at school that it is never allowed by the master; and that if a spinner is detected in its infliction, he is generally severely reprimanded, or dismissed. Two of the exceptions, we have noticed, are from the same mill; they affirm that they have been beaten " as hard as the spinner could lay it on," one says for five, and the other for ten minutes together, so that they were confined at home in consequence. There is, however, a tone of careless exaggeration which pervades the evidence of both these witnesses, which inclines us to receive it with the greatest caution; and one of them, John Wilson, meets with positive contradiction from three of his fellow-workmen.

In conclusion, we will only give the statements of another Commissioner on this subject.—" To the accusation of cruelty I can give the most decided and unqualified denial. It is not only *not true*, but *cannot* generally be true." *How so?*

IV.—On the Alleged Immorality of those Employed in Factories.

The witnesses whose evidence bears upon this point are the following: — forty-eight operatives, three clergymen, one Unitarian minister, two overseers of the poor, and one clerk· to the Manchester bench of magistrates; in all, fifty-six witnesses.

The substance of the evidence of forty-five of the operatives is this :—

That some of them have heard much improper language among the boys and girls, in the factories in which they have worked, but only two say that they have ever seen any gross· improprieties of conduct; and agree that such conduct, when observed, is always checked by the other hands. That difrent factories, however, differ much in the character, language, and conduct of those engaged in them; that the natural tendency of the boys and girls, working together during the whole day, is much checked by the presence of fathers, brothers, or near relations, and, on the other hand, is vastly aggravated by the practice of night-work in the mills.

Of fifty-three witnesses who are asked their opinion as to the comparative morality of those engaged in factories, with those otherwise employed, forty-six affirm their belief that the character of the factory population is equally good with that of other trades; and seven, that it is worse than others.

With respect to another question that is put to several of the witnesses,—viz. What sort of wives the factory girls make? there is considerable diversity of evidence; some stating that they make very bad wives, can neither sew nor wash, and are entirely ignorant of all domestic duties; while others, and these the greatest number, say that they have time enough to learn these duties, if they are so inclined; that many make up the linen of their fathers and brothers, as well as the whole of their own clothing; and that they are more active and diligent than girls otherwise brought up. The inference from the whole evidence appears to be, that they are too often ignorant of domestic economy, but that otherwise they make very good wives, and that men engaged in mills generally prefer them.

V.—EDUCATION.

Much has been said, in and out of Parliament, about the defective education and consequent ignorance of the children employed in cotton factories. It was therefore very desirable that this point should have been thoroughly examined, and the results founded on extensive inquiries laid before the public. We are sorry, however, that the evidence on this point is very scanty, and we are surprised that it should be so, as there could not have been any difficulty in obtaining abundant information upon the subject in every part of the Lancashire district. The evidence that has been taken, however, as far as it goes, is very favourable on this point.

Three witnesses are examined who are connected with Sunday schools. One witness states, that in the schools under his care there are about one thousand children, of whom *seven-tenths* are factory children. Another states, that out of one thousand children in the schools he superintends, *nine-tenths* work in factories. A third, that out of four thousand children in his schools, *seven-tenths* of those who are employed at all work in factories. In the Sunday schools of Stockport there are 4932 children; of these 584 are too young to be employed any where; of the remaining 4348, 2668 are factory children.

In Mr. Ashton's mill, at Hyde, there are 1175 hands employed. Of these 87 cannot read; 512 can read only; and 576 can read and write.

In Mr. Ashworth's mills, at Turton, there are 532 persons employed, of whom 525 can read, 247 can read and write, and seven, who have been recently engaged from other employments, cannot yet read.

VI.—Poor Rates.

We think that important evidence, upon the state of comfort and general respectability among the population engaged in factory labour, may be afforded by ascertaining how far they are accustomed to depend upon parochial relief. On this point the evidence is short, but most decisive. Two overseers of the poor are examined, one from Salford, another from Gorton, a township near Manchester, containing 2600 inhabitants. Both these witnesses agree that the factory people require less aid from the parish than others, and that they are in all respects in a more comfortable condition. In Gorton, where about seven hundred people are employed in factory labour, only one has applied for relief during three years. The factory that employs these people pays one-fourth of the whole rates, which generally amount to upwards of 800*l.*

In the township of Hyde, in the year 1801, when machinery was first introduced into it, the population was 830; the estimated value of the property assessable to the poor rate, 693*l.*; and the sum levied for the relief of the poor was 533*l.*

In 1830 the population was about seven thousand, the assessable value of property 2727*l.* and the poor rate 550*l.*

In Stockport, in the year ending March 1833, the number of families who received parish relief was 651; and the amount distributed among them was 2447*l.* Of these, sixty-five families were connected with factories, and the sum distributed among them was 297*l*.; leaving 2150*l*. to be divided among 586 families, who had no connexion with factories; and this too in Stockport, which is one of the most exclusively manufacturing towns in the cotton district.

VII.—WAGES.

In the last report, returns are given from 151 mills in different parts of the Lancashire district, in answer to a list of questions sent down by the Central Committee in London, about a year ago, and now first collected and laid before the public; from which it appears that the total number of persons employed in the above mills is 48,645 : of this number, 10,541 are children under fourteen years of age. The average weekly wages of the whole number employed is 10*s*. 5*d*., and the wages of the children, under fourteen, is 3*s*. 10*d*. The total number of persons employed in cotton factories is stated to be 212,800, whose whole yearly wages will amount to 5,777,434*l*.

This then is the evidence given before the Commissioners for the manufacturing district of Lancashire. We believe that those who have received their impressions of the injurious tendency of the factory system, from the reports that were so industriously circulated upon the subject some months ago, will be not a little surprised by the results which this evidence establishes. *We confess that we are so ourselves.* The inapplicability of the Factory Bill to such a state of things must be evident to all who will compare the two; and can only be accounted for by the fact, that the Central Committee in London drew up their first report, and framed the present Bill, in accordance with the statements therein contained, when only a small portion of the evidence had become known to them; that the second volume of evidence appeared several weeks subsequent to this period; and that the third supplementary volume, which contains much important information materially affecting the merits of the whole question, made its appearance at the end of March 1834, *seven months after the Bill had passed into a law.*

It must be obvious that individuals without any previous know-
ledge of the habits, characters, and conditions of the parties
giving the above evidence, which is so contradictory and anoma-
lous, must have been exposed to have their judgment warped by
causes totally foreign to the important subject of factory labour.
In fact, the Bill, founded upon the Reports of the Commissioners,
is in accordance with the first part of the Reports, and at direct
variance with the concluding portions.

Note A. Page 24.

Changes in the Industrial Condition of the Domestic
Manufacturers.

In the year 1770 the land in our township (Mellor,
fourteen miles from Manchester,) was occupied by between
fifty and sixty farmers; rent, to the best of my recollection,
did not exceed 10s. per statute acre; and out of these fifty or
sixty farmers there were only six or seven who raised their
rents directly from the produce of their farms, all the rest got
their rent partly in some branch of trade, such as spinning
and weaving woollen, linen, or cotton. The cottagers were
employed entirely in this manner, except for a few weeks in
the harvest. Being one of those cottagers, and intimately
acquainted with all the rest, as well as the farmers, I am
better able to relate particularly how the change from the
old system of hand-labour to the new one of machinery,
operated in the raising the price of land. Cottage rents, at
that time, with convenient loom-shop, and a small garden
attached, were from one and a half to two guineas per annum.
The father of a family would earn from eight shillings to half
a guinea at his loom, and his sons, if he had one or two, or
three alongside him, six or eight shillings per week each; but
the great sheet-anchor of all cottages and small farms was the

labour attached to the hand-wheel; and when it is considered that it required six or eight hands to prepare and spin
yarn of any of the three materials I have mentioned, sufficient for the consumption of one weaver, this shows clearly the
inexhaustible source there was for labour for every person,
from the age of seven to eighty years (who retained their
sight and could move their hands,) to earn their bread, *say
one to three shillings per week, without going to the parish.*

From the year 1770 to 1778 a complete change had
gradually been effected in the spinning of yarns; that of wool
had disappeared altogether, and that of linen was nearly gone;
cotton, cotton, cotton, had become the universal material for
employment; the hand-wheels were all thrown into lumber-
rooms; the yarn was all spun on common jennies; the carding
for all numbers, up to forty hanks in the pound, was done on
carding engines, but the finer numbers, of sixty to eighty, were
still carded by the hand, it being a general opinion, at that
time, that machine carding would never answer for fine
numbers. In weaving, no great alteration had taken place
during these eighteen years, save the introduction of the fly-
shuttle, a change in the woollen looms to fustians and calico,
and the linen nearly gone, except the few fabrics in which
there was a mixture of cotton. To the best of my recollection,
there was no increase of looms during this period, but rather a
decrease.

The next fifteen years, viz. from 1778 to 1803, I will
call the golden age of this great trade. Water twist and
common jenny yarns had been freely used in Bolton, &c. for
some years prior to 1788; but it was the introduction of the
mule yarns about this time, along with the other yarns, all
assimilating together, and producing every description of
clothing from the finest book muslin, lace, stocking, &c., to
the heaviest fustian, that gave such a preponderance to the
loom.

· The families I have been speaking of, whether as cottagers
or small farmers, had supported themselves by the different
occupations I have mentioned, in spinning and manufacturing,
as their progenitors, from the earliest institutions of society,
had done before them. But the mule twist now coming into

Note C. Page 41.

Present State of Hand-loom Weavers.

EVIDENCE OF JAMES BRENNAN, TAKEN BEFORE THE SELECT
COMMITTEE ON HAND-LOOM WEAVERS, JULY 22, 1834.

Where do you reside? No. 15, Fawcett-street, Hancote-
street, Manchester.

You are a weaver? Yes.

In what branch of manufacture are you employed? Mar-
seilles toilet covers.

What is the rate of wages given in that branch? Ten
shillings a-week they earn generally, with deductions of
2s. 6d. from it, leaving 7s. 6d.

Is yours the worst paid branch of weaving in Manchester?
The best, owing to several inventions that have been usually
put to it, such as the machine they call Jacquard.

Have you been long a weaver? Twenty-three years.

What did you get when you commenced weaver? I was
but a boy then; I could earn 12s. per week then.

Clear profit? No: three shillings taken from it for expenses;
but I could do much more work now than I could do then,
when a boy.

What is the effect of the fall of wages upon persons in your
situation? It deprives me of all the comforts of life entirely:
I can get nothing but the coarsest of food, and less in quantity
than I used to do.

What do you do for clothing? As well as I can; sometimes
I have some, and sometimes very little.

When did you last purchase clothes? It is twelve months
since I bought the trousers I have on, and I never had them
on before.

How do you for shoes? Ever since I was a boy I have
dealt with one man for shoes, and whether I have money or

no he trusts me, and I owe him some trifle for shoes; I always strive to give him something as often as I can.

What do you do for furniture in the house? I have never bought any in my life.

How does your wife do for clothes? Just as I do—quite as bad.

Have your children any stock of clothes? No, they have just enough to shift to put on clean on Sunday: they have one dress on and one off.

What do you do for cooking utensils? I have never bought any since I was born, only pots. I live in the same place where my father and mother occasionally lived; they are dead, and the apparatus they had, when I was young, I have still. I never had it in my power to buy any since I have been married.

Do you belong to any friendly society? No, I do not, I could not pay it; I have all my children, my wife and myself, in a penny club for burial.

How do you pay the doctor when you are ill? I have to work myself well again.

What do you do when your wife lies in? It costs very little when my wife lies in; we get a midwife from the Lying-in-hospital; she has only a little gruel, and perhaps a gill of ale.

What do you pay for your church-seat? I am not prepared to go; I would, if I had got decent clothing. When I was a young man I did get more wages; I had three suits of clothes, and a good watch in my pocket, and two or three pair of shoes, and one or two good hats.

You were better off then? Yes, those were the happiest days of my life.

What does your wife earn? About 5s. per week.

Does she go to a cotton factory? Yes.

Is it not painful to you to have to send your wife to a factory? *Yes, it causes great grief to me.*

Do you not think that a weaver must regret having his wife taken away from his family, and mixed up with people not of the best character? Yes, it is very hurtful.

If you were not residing in Manchester, or a great town where your wife had access to that employment, should you have to live upon that bare 7s. 6d.? Nothing more.

RICHARD NEEDHAM, *examined.* (*July* 18, 1834.)

You have given in a statement of the earnings of journey-men weavers that work at sixty cambric cut per week, that he performs as much labour as any man in the cotton trade per week, and you make his earnings 5s. 6d.; and you have given a statement of the cost of lodging and food, such as is barely sufficient to keep him in existence? Yes.

You make his earnings, when the reductions have been taken from the gross, to be 4s. 1½d. a week? Yes.

And the cost of his lodging and food to be 5s. 5½d. leaving him minus 1s. 4d. to supply himself with those lodgings and proper food; you believe this to be a true statement? I am sure it is true.

The following letter from a teacher, formerly a hand-loom weaver, powerfully illustrates the condition of these artisans:—

" *Woodside, near Holytown, 16th April,* 1833.

" SIR,—In reply to your letter of the 13th inst., I beg leave to inform you that tea, coffee, sugar, soap, ham, and cheese, are articles, which, although formerly deemed essentials, are seldom seen upon a weaver's table. Indeed, how can they be procured by a family whose allowance for food and clothing is so scanty as I described in my last letter to you? That I did not exaggerate the statement of the severe penury the weavers endure, is apparent from the fact, that the weavers' agents in *Airdrie* deponed last week, before the provost there, that the weavers in that town had not earned more than 3s. 9d. a week for the last twelve months on an average, the expense of carriage and starching the web being deducted. I formerly stated to you that the maximum of the best weavers' earnings, after the necessary expenses of rent, fire, light, &c. were deducted, was only 2s. 5½d. per week; without these deductions, carriage and starching excepted, it appears that the average are only 3s. 9d., leaving, after the deductions which I enumerated in my last, only 1s. to support the weaver for four weeks in food and clothing! But as every weaver has not an house of his own, it may be necessary to state. that the deductions of house rent, or lodging, only affects householders or journeymen, and not apprentices, or such of the weaver's own family as may follow the same occupation : consequently, when such exist in a family the average deductions will be less, and thus only is the existence of the vital spark accounted for among the weaving population.

" But this will be best illustrated from the following statements of the earnings of a weaver, of the name of Wm. Russell, and his family, in Airdrie, with whom I conversed the other day minutely upon the subject. William has two of his boys on the loom, the *one is seven and a half, and the other nearly nine years of age!* He has a wife and other three children. The three looms are employed weaving twelve hundred pullicates at 2d. per ell. The boys earn about 6d. a day each, and the father can do no more, as his attention and time is taken up with the boys. The wife contrives to wind a loom's peirns, which yields about 2d. per day, making about 1s. 8d. a day as the earnings of the whole family; but as one of the boys and the father are necessarily off work a day every new web, which among the three occurs almost every week, the average earnings are somewhat less. The family can have thereof no more than 9s. per week of income, from which we must make the following unavoidable weekly deductions :—

	£	s.	d.
For wear of material and rent of shop for three looms	0	3	0
Fire for house and shop	0	1	0
House rent for one apartment	0	1	0
Oil for house and shop	0	1	0
Starching, twisting, and carriage . . .	0	1	0
Amount of deductions	0	7	0

Leaving only 2s. to feed and clothe seven human beings for seven days! 'How in the name of all that's wonderful,' I exclaimed to the individual who told me, 'can you subsist on such a pittance?' 'I dinna ken,' said he, 'if ye call it subsistence, but its a' we hae.' 'But what do you get to eat?' 'Parritch in the morning, and potatoes and salt to dinner, and the same to supper, or sometimes a wee drap brose!' You see, therefore, that to talk about the use of tea, coffee, sugar, soap, ham, and bread, in such a case, is out of the question. When a cup of tea is enjoyed, it is only on Sabbath morning. Where extraordinary industry is exerted, the man and his apprentices toiling sixteen or eighteen hours a day, tea, &c. may be seen more frequently, but their price is a sickening anxiety of mind and emaciation of body.

"I consider the labour of every artisan ought to afford him and his family three substantial meals a day, and comfortable clothing. I shall now state what is necessary to afford these to a man with a wife and four children, under eight years, at the present rate of the markets, and thus show how wofully deficient the earnings of the weaver are to meet the demands of the common necessities of life, for I shall exclude all luxuries. In such a family I shall suppose the children breakfast and sup on *parritch* and milk, that the whole family dine on broth (Scotch kale), beef, and potatoes, that the husband and wife take what is called a tea or coffee breakfast, and a cup of tea in the afternoon. This is the way weavers lived when I was one, and trade was good.

Proper Weekly Expenditure of a Man, Wife, and Four Children.

	£	s.	d.
One peck of Oatmeal for bread . . ·	0	1	0
Two pecks of oatmeal for breakfast and supper to children	0	2	0
Two oz. of tea for breakfast	0	0	9
One lb. of butter	0	1	3
Carried forward	0	5	0

	£	s.	d.
Brought forward . . .	0	5	0
Loaf bread	0	1	0
One lb. sugar	0	0	7
Ham, fish, or cheese	0	1	2
Milk	0	1	0
Butcher's meat, 8 lb.	0	3	4
Barley	0	0	8
Potatoes and other vegetables	0	1	0
House rent, room, and kitchen	0	1	6
Loom rent	0	1	0
Fire	0	0	8
Candle or oil	0	0	6
Soap, 1 lb.	0	0	8
Church-seats, taxes, police money . . .	0	0	4
Shoes	0	1	3
Clothing, including shirts, stockings, &c. &c.	0	3	3
Total . .	1	2	11

"Your obedient servant,

"John Craig."

Result of a Survey made in January, 1833, *of the Condition of the Poor in thirty-five Manufacturing Townships (hand-weaving,) in Lancashire and Yorkshire.*

The population of these townships amounted to 203,349; the families visited were 8362; the persons in these families, 49,294; the number out of work was 2287; the number unfit for work, 23,060; the number of workers, 23,947; the weekly wages earned by the families visited was 4447*l.* 18*s.*: this sum gave for each of the workers a weekly average of 3*s.* 8*d.*, and for each of the whole number visited a weekly average of 1*s.* 9¾*d.* The rent paid by these families was, per annum,

32,693*l.* 17*s.* 5*d.*; this sum gave an average of 3*d.* per week to each individual. Fuel, light, and wear of implements, will average at least 3½*d.* per week for each individual; this and the rent being deducted from the weekly income of each person, leaves for food and clothing 1*s.* 3¼*d.* a week.

The whole parish relief given weekly to the families visited was 139*l.* 7*s.* 6*d.*, or for each, of a penny. The average income of each individual per day, including relief, was 2⅜*d.* This was the entire fund for their subsistence.

Note D. Page 45.

The Report and Resolutions of a Meeting of Deputies from the Hand-Loom Worsted Weavers, residing in and near Bradford, Leeds, Halifax, &c. Yorkshire.

GENERAL REMARKS.

The difficulty of making a very accurate report arises from the following causes among others:—

1st. There are always a considerable number of employers who are endeavouring to screw down wages without any reasonable cause, for their own profit; and there are, on the other hand, others who resist as long as they can these reductions; but as all go to one market, the generous are at last forced to follow the selfish.

2d. There are some employers, in the worsted trade especially (which trade has many peculiar advantages *at present* in the manufacturing market), which are enabled from their connexions, or from their abundant capital, or from local advantages, to afford better wages than others. But the power-loom is the great "SCREW" both to hand-loom employers and weavers. The power-loom masters can undersell the hand-loom masters three or four shillings in a piece. How can they stand against this?

3d. The difference of the work is very great. The same nominal *sets* are sometimes from five to ten per cent. better or worse to the weaver, by reason of tender material or short wool, which occasions the warp to require constantly piecing, and hinders the work. Sometimes the lessening of the width of the pieces is no gain, but a loss to the weaver, who has so many more picks to put in. At other times the distance from the place of putting out work is very considerable, and is not only harassing, but also expensive, and wastes much time and strength.

· 4th. The very fine quality of the yarn, which improved spin-ning machinery produces from a comparatively coarse and short kind of wool, occasions much more labour than sounder or longer wool would do. The object of many spinners is, not to manufacture a good article, but " to make something out of nothing."

5th. Much caution is necessary in those who wish to arrive at truth as to the earnings of weavers. Employers may give (not necessarily with intention) a false statement. The *taker in* is desired to make an extract from his book of the sums paid per week, or per fortnight, to individuals, and it will thus appear that A. B. receives (say 30*s.* per week.) Upon inquiry, however, it would probably be found, that three or four per-sons are working for this sum, and that they are arrived, or part of them, at an age which entitles them to dispose of their own earnings; or, it may often happen, that a family of ten or twelve persons have to subsist upon the sum thus earned ; or it might be found that one or two of the parties was accustomed to work for an unusual length of time (for instance at rent-days.) It is therefore quite certain that no safe conclusions can be drawn from statements thus furnished, unless the *number of workers who produce*, the *hours* they *work*, and the number of *consumers* dependent on the wages, are clearly specified.

6th. Those who are not intimately acquainted with the weaver's affairs, may easily be deceived by statements of his *gross* wages, and by neglecting to take into account his *out-goings* for the following particulars :—1. Sizing, &c.; 2. Looming in the warp or twirling; 3. Winding the weft; 4. Wear and tear—repairs; 5. Lights, the year round. When these are reckoned off, and house rent, fire, and washing, are added, the remainder applicable for food, clothing, furniture and education, will be ascertained, and if fairly averaged and stated, it will be seen that industry has to struggle with great discouragements and gradually increasing depreciation.

Having made these general remarks, we now come to a statement of the progressive depreciation of worsted weaving during the last seven years. By thus commencing with 1828, we pass over the distressing years of the panic, 1826 and 1827, but we would have it borne in mind, that the effects of those years were felt by the working classes for several years afterwards.

By tables of prices which have been prepared, it appears that in 1828 there was 1s. 5d. (average) generally given for weaving *twenty hanks.* In 1830, the price per score banks was lowered to an average of 1s. per score. In 1832 it remained stationary. In 1833 it advanced on most sets to 1s. 3d. per score. In 1834, power looms having greatly increased, prices fell to 1s. 0½d. per score. In 1835, (at present) they are reduced to 10d. per score on average. Comparing the different *sets* of six-quarter pieces, there will be found a general reduction of 40 per cent. in the actual wages.

The three-quarter pieces will exhibit a somewhat greater deduction from 1s. 6½d. to 1s., and from 1s. 3d. to 9½d. That which is now 1s. a score is a sort very small in quality.

The tables are not now given, but will be ready for presentation when a fuller account of the whole worsted district has been obtained. When that is done, it is apprehended that prices of more remote parts will exhibit a worse picture. To the 40 per cent. reduction it is only right to add a further depreciation of from 5 to 10 per cent. for worse work, more tender warp, and worse (that is, more slender) spinning. In many cases, the increased number of *picks* will be one in every twelve or fourteen, by reason of the narrowing of the piece, and will reduce the profit of the weaver (or increase his labour) 5 per cent. more. But wishing to put the best face upon matters we pass this over, and will take the actual depreciation to be 45 per cent. since 1828.

It may also be here noticed, that in many cases a great

disparity of wages is given in the same township or immediate neighbourhood. In Bradford, the prices of broad weaving (six quarters) varies from sixpence to two shillings and sixpence per piece : three-quarters, sixpence to ninepence : and yards, or four-quarters, sixpence to one shilling. Such a disproportion clearly shows the necessity of some authoritative regulations for honesty's sake. It should also be remarked that by this long hour system, a scarcity of work is occasioned in a part of every year (in some years more than others), which averages under two-thirds employment during three months in winter, whilst the power looms are all nearly, if not fully employed.

The steam loom will produce, as far as can be learned, two pieces and a half a week (six days) of that sort which takes an able weaver six days to do one piece, working twelve hours ; thus throwing at least three weavers out of employment for every two steam looms, and giving not more than a man's wages, and in some cases not more than half, to the tenter of the power loom. The impossibility of fair competition by hand labour is thus manifest. Add to this, that all the best work, and all the new patterns, which used to be an encouragement to good hands, are now taken to the power looms, and thus proficiency in "the mystery of weaving" is discouraged, though the hand loom could perform it equally well.

We may here remark, that worsted weavers are subject to many impositions, viz. in some cases a false set is given to weave, forty-six is given for forty-four, and yet, if done by a good hand, is sold for forty-eight. Again, the weaver is sometimes told—" you must put in a few more hanks *this time*, it's too thin." Remonstrance would be vain. Had there been a board of trade, all these cases would have been referred. Many other impositions might be mentioned. There is, however, one harassing system adopted by some employers which requires notice, viz. keeping a weaver on the run several hours in every week, in slack-time, for his material.

A part of the tenderness of the work already noticed, may also be fairly attributed to the increased quantity and undue length of the work of the factory children. If they were not worked so long, their attention to the piecing would be more vigorous, and it would be much better for the weaver.

We have now to notice the weaver's expenditure. It will be seen that six-quarters have considerably lowered in price, during twelve months past. Blame has been laid upon the high price of wool; but the power loom and *over production* have been the chief causes. Taking the average earnings of broad and narrow weavers, six-quarters, three-quarters, and eighteen to twenty-one inches, we shall find about nine shillings and sixpence a week, gross wages, or, to be at the fullest average, ten shillings, gross wages.

The outlays from the work are, per week :—

	s.	d.
Sizing	0	4
Looming, or twirling	0	3
Winding the weft	0	$9\frac{1}{2}$
Light, year round	0	$3\frac{1}{2}$
Wear and tear, repair outlay of loom, or loom stand	0	4
Outgoings on the work.	2	0
Rent, average	1	9
Fire and washing	1	6
	5	3
Leaving but	4	9

applicable to food, clothing, furniture, education, &c. Let this be considered as the very frequently occurring case of a man with from three to five children. If the woman, in this case, employs herself at the loom, it is generally to a loss, and not to any advantage, whilst the family wardrobe is neglected. The utmost she can do *profitably* is to earn the ninepence halfpenny for winding, which will make five shillings and sixpence to fill the stomachs, and clothe the backs, and furnish the beds, of six persons, or perhaps seven,—tenpence or eleven pence per head per week.

Then take the case of a family of eight persons, and three workers.

	s.	d.
1st worker's wages.	10	0
2d ditto	7	0
3d ditto	3	0
	20	0

Deductions for outgoings of work, and for rent, fire, and washing :—

	s.	d.
For 1st weaver	5	3
2d ditto	1	6
3 ditto	1	0
	7	9
	12	3

This sum, 12s. 3d. is but a poor provision for food, clothes, furniture, and education, for eight persons—1s. 6d. per head per week. We have not mentioned work in slack times—we never suppose them to be ill—we allow no holidays—nothing for the wedding ring, nor the day of sickness, nor the funeral day. What a struggle for a bare subsistence! And yet Mr. Baring is reported to say that this case ought not to be considered, and that there is no hope even for the amendment of a worse case than this! Surely if it be so, Britain's death-knell will soon be heard.

As to this branch there has been a great expense in altering the three-quarters looms for six-quarters during three or four years past, which all have some difficulty to pay, and some have never paid to this day.

Thus, we have given the very best account of the hand-loom weavers which truth and honesty will allow. We wish well to our masters—we rejoice to see their prosperity, *by fair means*, but we do not relish to labour in vain, and spend our own strength for nought.

The lowness of wages, as common sense teaches, is a cause

of increased production to make up the deficiency, and this again reacts to glut the market and lower the wages; so that the longer a man works, the worse it is for him, and yet his mouth craves it of him, and the mouths of his children, and he cannot forbear.

If the worsted weavers have been overlooked in the estimated 800,000 hand-loom men, we are sure they ought not to be left out, and we hope they will have their case considered *this time.*

Our wish is, to see men and their masters inspired with mutual confidence and good will, and both of them delivered from that degrading system of *competition*, which may, for a time, enrich a few, but which is sure ultimately to prove a great and bitter national curse. Wealth is the accumulation of labour, and the very life's blood of our idolized " capital," and those who expect to eat the honey, should be the last to pine the bees.

Resolutions adopted unanimously at a Meeting of Deputies from the Hand-Loom Worsted Weavers of Bradford, Leeds, and Halifax, and of several Townships in those Parishes and others adjoining, at Bradford, on Saturday, March 21st, 1835.

The Report having been discussed and adopted, it was—

Resolved, I. That it is desirable to form a *Central Committee* of five persons, to keep up communications between John Maxwell, Esq. M.P., Chairman of the Hand-Loom Weavers' Committee, and the Worsted Weavers, to furnish him with information, and to communicate with the weavers. (Five persons were accordingly appointed.) That in case any of the five shall be absent, a worsted weaver shall be called in to represent the absent party, or each of them, for the transaction of business.

Resolved, II. That each township be requested to contribute to the expenses of obtaining and circulating information in the manner above proposed. That the sums thus raised shall be disbursed by the Central Committee, and accounted for to a Deputies' meeting, when the proceedings are closed.

Resolved, III. That this meeting is actuated by no unkind feeling towards the employers in general, and that its proceedings and resolutions shall be made public, excepting as to the names of individuals who may not be willing to be known, for fear of losing their employment.

Resolved, IV. That a Public Meeting is desirable, to bring forward the subject of the unequal competition between steam-looms and hand-looms, and for devising and recommending some legislative and effective protection for the hand-loom weavers and their employers (who do not use steam-looms), from the steam-looms and their proprietors; and that both parties, and especially the employers, be respectfully invited to attend, and that the arrangement of such a meeting be left to the Central Committee.

Resolved, V. That this Meeting attributes the depressed state of the working classes in general, and of the worsted and other hand-loom weavers in particular, to the following general causes among others :—

1st. To home competition and over production, beyond the profitable demands of the market.

2d. To a ruinous foreign trade.

3d. To the unrestricted use (or rather abuse) of improved and continually improving machinery, especially of steam or power-looms, as well as combing machines.

4th. To the *inequality* of taxation, which lies most unfairly upon the working classes. To its unjust *amount*, inasmuch as the public creditor is receiving *more than his due ;* and many unprofitable salaries, pensions, and retiring salaries, ought to be abolished.

5th. The neglect of providing for the employment and maintenance of the Irish poor, who are compelled to crowd the English labour market for a piece of bread.

6th. The adaptation of machines, in every improvement, *to children, and youth, and women,* to the exclusion of those who ought to labour—THE MEN.

Resolved, VI. That to fill a country with inanimate and

nonconsuming machines, and to drive away the cultivators of
the soil, and the consumers of produce, to foreign climes, when
there are seventeen millions of acres of uncultivated land in
Great Britain and Ireland, for the most part capable of being
made productive, is a species of combined political folly and
cruelty—of folly, which a worsted weaver ought to be ashamed
of—and of cruelty, which barbarians would not, and Christians
ought not to practise.

Resolved, VII. That this meeting is convinced that no re-
mission of taxes, no reduction of provisions, and no enlargement of political privileges, however desirable, will suffice to
uphold the just interests of the labouring classes, in manufacturing parts especially, unless a due and wholesome legislative
restraint be placed upon the time of working machinery, so as
to prevent the ruinous glutting of home and foreign markets,
and so as to keep the human machines in profitable employment. And also, that MANY OF OUR MASTERS REQUIRE THIS
PROTECTION AS MUCH AS OURSELVES.

*Answer of the Hand-loom Weavers to Mr. SCROPE, as to
Emigration.*

" And now, Sir, we come to your magnificent ' cure all,'
for all our many woes—emigration. Some of us have a
mortal hatred of this emigration, and such an invincible an-
tipathy, that we have all but sworn that we will die at the
cannon's mouth before we will go: perhaps it's all disease.
We have read of the poor Africans who, when on the ' middle
passage ' from their native coast to a country, as the slave
merchants said, far superior to their own, often sought opportunity to jump overboard into the sea rather than encounter
the horrors of that European mercy which awaited them in
the West Indian plantations. And we have heard that the
French physicians and physiologists (who are very knowing),
discovered that this was all disease, and they actually coined

a new name for it, which being interpreted is,. ' A strong passion to return to one's own country,' the nearest way to which the poor blacks supposed to be by water. Now, Sir, be it known unto you, and to the Emigration Committee, that we are afflicted with a malady somewhat similar in effect, though rather different in its symptoms; we will not leave our country— we resolve to die on its shores. ' The land we live in' is our motto; and whilst there are seventeen millions of reclaimable and uncultivated land, and whilst the land now under the plough is not half so productive as a good demand and remunerating price for corn and meat would render it, we will stay by it, and on no condition but one will we consent to emigration.

"Really, Sir, you do write with marvellous coolness of transporting ' every distressed labourer,' now ' a burden and discredit' to society; and about the 'transfer of indigent labourers from the British islands to the British colonies,' and yet labour without capital is declared to be worth nothing! We are to sail, — we, the 'indigent, distressed,'—we that are the ' burden and discredit' of our country, (and pray who made us so?) and when we get over the great salt pond, what are we to have? ' Abundance of rich land to be had for asking there!' In other words, 'live, horse, and thou shalt eat grass.' We are to sit down beside an impenetrable forest, to teach the art of emigration to its present four-footed possessors, to fell its firs and pines, and to ' tear from the soil' those magnificent stumps which now encumber it: and when all this is done (ah! 'when' indeed,) we are to have four shillings a day, if — if wages do not drop fifteen per cent. several times over before then, by reason of competition and increased ' immigration!' as they recently did in Van Dieman's Land.—See Governor Arthur's Dispatch, dated January, 1834.

" And for a share in this lottery we are to go down upon our knees to parliament, and most humbly crave their cle_mency and charity, to grant to us, out of those taxes which have been wrung from our very sinews and bones, and which have been paid from an ' excise' of almost every morsel we have eaten; we are to implore that the 'Atlantic may be bridged over,' ' a free passage' in some of his Majesty's 'rotting frigates' to the delightful regions of the 'outlying counties!'

"Build the 'bridge,' if you like, we will not go — we'll die here where we were born. You may twitch the Amended Poor Laws tighter, if you can, round the throats and bellies of the poor; and you may send your grenadiers to 'dragoon' the conscripts for emigration; but our native shores we leave not, though bullets fly, and bayonets bristle all around us. Here we will die, here we will live."

The Extent of Foreign Competition in the Cotton Trade at present, is shown by the following Data.

It appears that in 1821 the exportation of raw cotton from the United States of America to France, and the European continent, was somewhat more than *one-sixth* of the quantity sent to Great Britain. In 1832 it amounted to more than *one-half*.

In 1831 France produced 63,000,000 lbs. of cotton yarn, which will have required a consumption of nearly 80,000,000 lbs. of the raw material. In the same year the *export* of cotton goods from that country amounted to 2,192,240 francs.

In Switzerland the consumption of cotton in 1831 amounted to 19,000,000 lbs. Only a few years have elapsed since that country received the greatest part of her supplies of yarn from England; she now not only receives very little below seventy shillings, but she has herself become an exporter to other countries.

The manufacture of cotton is rapidly increasing in Prussia, throughout the Rhenish provinces, in Silesia, in Saxony, and in both the German and Italian provinces belonging to the crown of Austria.

From information obtained on the spot, or replies to questions which were sent to manufacturers on the continent, it appears that they can compete successfully with England in coarse numbers, some say as high as 40*s*., others as high as

70s. and 80s. It must be kept in mind, the quantity of yarn spun in England above 80s. is very small, about the proportion of 100 or 120 lbs. of coarse for one pound of fine.

The wages paid per week in England and the continent are as follows:—

	England.		Continent.	
For spinners . .	20s. to 35s.	. .	8s. to 10s.	
Piecers	4s.	8s.	. . 2s.	3s.
Card-room hands .	6s.	14s.	. . 4s.	5s.
Reelers	7s.	13s.	. . 4s.	6s.

There is no cotton twist of low numbers now exported from England to France or Switzerland. Last year there were several orders came for yarns from Germany, restricted to a certain price, but stating that this fixed price was what it could be spun for in that country; these prices were $\frac{1}{4}d.$ per pound lower than they could possibly be produced here.

In America the official report of the Committee of the New York Convention shows a consumption in 1831 of 77,516,316 lbs. of cotton, which equals the quantity consumed in Great Britain twenty years ago. American fabrics are rapidly superseding those of this country in Mexico, the Brazils, and, in fact, throughout all the markets of the South American continent, and have been brought of late in much larger quantities than heretofore into the ports of the Mediterranean, which can only be accounted for by the success which has attended their previous transactions.

It will also be kept in mind that two very important items, in the cost of a piece of cotton cloth, are raw cotton and food. How much greater, therefore, must be the advantages of these rivals, who obtain both these articles free from taxation, pay no poor rates, and negotiate for manufacturing labour free from time bills, &c.

The superiority of machinery and trade details, possessed by Great Britain, are abundantly obvious from the above data. They enable her to compete with manufacturers who have the opportunity of paying one-fourth the price for the raw material, although she pays her workmen a fourfold price for their labour.

AGE, SEX, AND NUMBER OF FACTORY ARTISANS.

District.	AGES OF OPERATIVES.						TOTAL OPERATIVES.	
	Under 11.		From 11 to 18.		Above 18.			
	Male.	Female.	Male.	Female.	Male.	Female.	Male.	Female.
Scotland	285	343	6,629	14,902	8,904	19,113	15,818	40,358
North of England	39	34	542	1,021	685	1,261	1,266	2,316
...land, including Kendall.	27	23	146	196	203	115	376	334
Lancashire	1,109	1,086	27,898	31,271	36,789	37,063	65,796	69,420
West Riding of Yorkshire	1,093	856	14,981	17,631	16,419	12,276	32,493	30,763
Cheshire	879	1,008	7,537	9,698	11,849	12,513	20,265	22,219
...ire			202	241	250	458	452	699
Derbyshire	28	28	938	1,287	2,825	2,863	2,841	2,885
Staffordshire	101	150	370	695	521	617	992	1,462
Leicestershire, &c.	1,055	1,563	2,938	6,951	3,274	8,516	7,267	17,030
West of England and Wales	181	193	3,646	3,009	5,017	4,905		
South of ...	6	11	483	832	1,153	1,062	1,642	1,907
North of Ditto	8	13	893	2,088	970	2,050	1,871	4,151
	4,811	5,308	67,203	89,822	88,859	102,812	151,079	193,544

AMOUNT OF IRISH POPULATION AS INDICATED BY THE POOR RATE.

Parochial Relief administered in eight months of the year 1831, *in the Township of Manchester.*

	NUMBER OF CASES.			
1831.	Newtown.	Ancoats.	Central.	Portland-street.
March . . .	English . . 2,037	1,943	2,430	1,764
	Irish 1,099	804	226	236
April	English . . 2,022	1,917	2,879	1,769
	Irish 984	806	202	230
May	English. . . 1,931	1,961	2,285	1,735
	Irish . . . 902	841	180	214
June	English . . 1,968	1,980	2,380	1,782
	Irish 911	882	207	217
	11,854	11,134	10,789	7,947
July	English . . 1,986	1,969	2,378	1,730
	Irish 888	856	199	220
August . . .	English . . 1,987	2,024	2,324	1,687
	Irish 856	813	. 175	227
September .	English . . 2,086	2,023	2,284	1,754
	Irish 856	823	152	205
October . .	English . . 1,937	2,091	2,301	1,732
	Irish 809	788	169	211
	11,405	11,387	9,982	7,766

PROGRESS OF CRIME IN ENGLAND AND WALES.

(Prepared from Returns to Parliament.)

Years	Total Commitments in England & Wales, County Assizes.	No Bill found.	Acquitted.	Convicted.	Murder. Committed.	Murder. Intent to commit.	Larceny. In a Dwelling-house.	Larceny. From the Person.	Larceny. Not otherwise described.	Burglary.	Breaking into a Dwelling-house.	Highway Robbery.
1811	5,337	940	1,234	3,163	87	29	177	194	3,689	140	53	96
1812	6,576	1,169	1,494	3,913	66	35	215	214	4,363	156	66	157
1813	7,164	1,291	1,451	4,422	87	18	235	272	4,623	287	97	119
1814	6,390	992	1,373	4,025	80	51	216	311	4,259	163	50	109
1815	7,818	1,287	1,648	4,883	61	31	222	277	5,409	204	84	128
1816	9,091	1,410	1,884	5,797	85	66	277	402	6,123	360	109	246
1817	13,932	2,198	2,678	9,056	80	64	283	519	9,396	627	220	276
1818	13,567	1,987	2,622	8,958	51	42	315	551	9,303	568	207	222
1819	14,254	2,109	2,635	9,510	69	41	286	646	9,653	545	211	240
1820	13,710	1,881	2,511	9,318	49	45	302	776	9,160	466	222	244
1821	13,115	1,826	2,502	8,788	71	60	223	639	8,725	467	210	311
1822	12,241	1,684	2,348	8,209	85	74	196	625	8,445	496	142	278
1823	12,263	1,579	2,480	8,204	60	63	213	550	8,477	402	170	301
1824	13,698	1,662	2,611	9,425	73	71	277	695	9,554	460	176	258
1825	14,437	1,685	2,788	9,964	94	57	265	835	10,087	428	150	189
1826	16,164	1,786	3,271	11,007	57	47	301	1,055	11,122	478	168	307
1827	17,921	1,950	3,407	12,564	65	82	295	1,081	12,014	572	300	381
1828	16,564	1,672	3,169	11,723	83	72	122	1,079	16,989	249	491	314
1829	18,675	1,820	3,614	13,261	47	115	119	1,138	12,628	171	781	299
1830	18,107	1,832	3,470	12,805	65	80	134	1,234	12,031	155	726	301
1831	19,647	2,094	3,723	13,830	57	104	169	1,421	12,118	152	665	573
1832	20,829	2,066	3,706	14,947	66	132	180	1,718	13,469	175	759	382

GIN AND WHISKEY

Consumed in England, Scotland, and Ireland, on two Periods of Three Years Each.

Years.	FIRST PERIOD.			Total First Period.
	England.	Scotland.	Ireland.	
	Gallons.	Gallons.	Gallons.	Gallons.
1821	3,820,050	2,229,435	2,649,170	8,798,655
1822	4,346,348	2,079,556	2,328,387	8,754,281
1823	3,521,586	2,232,728	3,348,505	9,102,819
Total..	11,687,984	6,541,719	8,326,062	26,655,755

Years.	SECOND PERIOD.			Total Second Period.
	England.	Scotland.	Ireland.	
	Gallons.	Gallons.	Gallons.	Gallons.
1831	7,434,047	5,700,689	8,710,672	21,845,309
1832	7,259,287	4,861,515	8,657,756	21,778,559
1833	7,717,303	5,988,556	8,168,596	21,874,458
Total..	22,410,637	16,550,760	25,537,024	65,498,326

Gallons.

Total First Period 26,655,755

Ditto Second ditto 65,498,326

TABLE

Showing the relation existing between Crime, Pauperism, Drunkenness, and the State of the Industrious Classes, as viewed connectedly with the Progress of Mechanical Substitutes for Human Labour.

YEAR.	CRIME. Commitments.	PAUPERISM. Poor Rates.	DRUNKENNESS. Spirits Consumed.	COTTON TRADE EXPORTS.	
				Official Value.	Declared Value.
		£	Gallons.	£	£
1821	13,155	6,674,938	8,798,655	22,522,079	16,516,758
1822	12,242	6,102,253	8,754,281	23,541,615	16,094,807
1831	19,647	7,929,608	21,845,309	33,682,400	17,182,936
1832	20,829	8,255,315	21,778,559	37,060,750	17,344,676

LONDON:
R. CLAY, PRINTER, BREAD-STREET-HILL,
DOCTORS' COMMONS.

LONDON.

LIST No. I.

Price 1s.,

NEWTON and FLAMSTEED.—REMARKS on an ARTICLE in No. CIX. of the QUARTERLY REVIEW. By the Rev. W. WHEWELL, M.A., Fellow and Tutor of Trinity College, Cambridge.

I shall conclude, leaving it to the reader to decide, whether the blame of intemperate virulence of feeling, and irrational violence of conduct, does not rest solely with Flamsteed; whether Newton's philosophical and moral character do not come out from this examination blameless, and admirable as they have always been esteemed by thinking men; and whether the Reviewer has not shown extraordinary ignorance of that part of scientific history which he has attempted to elucidate, and unaccountable blindness and perverseness in his use even of the *ex parte* evidence which he had before him.

In the Press. Two Volumes Post Octavo, with Maps,

SKETCHES of the COASTS and ISLANDS of SCOTLAND, and of the ISLE of MAN. By LORD TEIGNMOUTH.

Preparing for Publication, in One Volume, Octavo,

AN ANALYSIS of the ROMAN CIVIL LAW, in which a Comparison is occasionally made between the ROMAN LAWS and those of ENGLAND. By the late SAMUEL HALLIFAX, LL.D., LORD BISHOP of ST. ASAPH. A NEW EDITION, with ADDITIONS, in the TEXT and NOTES. By JAMES WILLIAM GELDART, D.C.L., And Regius Professor of Civil Law in the University of Cambridge

Nearly Ready. One Volume.

CONVERSATIONS AT CAMBRIDGE; including, among others, the following :

S. T. COLERIDGE at Trinity, with unpublished SPECIMENS of his Table-Talk.
The Poet WORDSWORTH and PROFESSOR SMYTH.
KIRKE WHITE and the Johnians.
One Hour with HENRY MARTYN, the Missionary.
The History of a LOST STUDENT, taken down from his own lips.

The Poet COWPER and his BROTHER. of Benet.
GRAY and MASON — a Day with the Muses.
COWLEY and his Friend WILLIAM HERVEY.
MILTON, MORE, and HENRY HOWE.
The DESTRUCTIVES in 1642;
OLIVER CROMWELL at Cambridge.

1

CLERGYMAN.

Edited by the Rev. J. HOBART CAUNTER, B.D.,
Author of the *Oriental Annual*.

THE object of this work is to enforce some of the sublime truths of Christianity, by showing, in the way of practical illustration, the issues of moral good and of moral evil. Punishment in this world, in some shape or other, sooner or later, hidden or overt, positive or indirect, bodily or mental, is the never-failing consequence of guilt,—Reward, of innocence. Trace how we may the course of human events, the tendency of human actions, the same results follow,—they all operate to the same end; the former to promote virtue and discourage vice; the latter to produce happiness and ensure misery, according as men incline to the one or to the other.

Price 3s. 6d.,

LIGHT in DARKNESS ; or the RECORDS of a VILLAGE RECTORY.

Happy the man that sees a God employed
In all the good and ill that chequer life.—-COWPER.

THE VILLAGE.	THE VILLAGE SCHOOLMASTER.
THE RETIRED TRADESMAN.	THE VILLAGE APOTHECARY.
THE GOOD AUNT.	THE DESERTED WIFE.
THE FAMILY AT THE HALL.	

Price 7s. 6d.,

MUSICAL HISTORY, BIOGRAPHY, and CRITICISM; being a General Survey of Music from the earliest period to the present time. By GEORGE HOGARTH.

AT a period when Music is more and more extensively cultivated as a branch of polite knowledge, as a powerful aid in the exercises of devotion, and as a rational and elegant recreation in social and domestic life, a work like the present appears to be called for. The Author's object is, to give in an original and attractive form, that information respecting the progress of Music, the personal history of the most eminent Musicians, and the present state of the art in this and other countries, which is now looked upon as indispensable to every person of liberal attainments; he has accordingly treated Music, not as an intricate science, but as one of the most beautiful of the Fine Arts.

In Two Pocket Volumes, price 9s., THE

BRITISH MONTHS, a POEM, in TWELVE PARTS. By RICHARD MANT, D.D., M.R.I.A., LORD BISHOP OF DOWN AND CONNOR.

IT has been the Author's endeavour, to give in this Poem a pleasing representation of the principal natural appearances, especially with respect to our native plants and birds, which invite attention in their monthly succession; with such reflections as those appearances are calculated to suggest to a contemplative mind

---

Demy Octavo, price 9s. 6d.,

DISSERTATIONS on the EUMENIDES of ÆSCHYLUS, with the Greek Text, and Critical Remarks. Translated from the German of C. O. MULLER.

MULLER'S Work on the EUMENIDES has deservedly obtained the approbation of some of the first scholars of the day; it is an admirable specimen of the Author's searching and comprehensive spirit of inquiry, and claims the attention of every person who would fully understand the Dramas of Æschylus in general, as well as have a thorough perception of the peculiar beauties and train of ideas which characterize the Tragedy of the Eumenides.

3

Complete in Five Volumes, at 6*s.* 6*d.* each, or in Parts at 1*s.* each,

ORIGINAL FAMILY SERMONS;
comprising upwards of One Hundred and Sixty Discourses,

By CONTEMPORARY DIVINES OF THE ESTABLISHED CHURCH.

THESE Sermons are printed from the Manuscripts of the respective Authors, among whom are many of the dignitaries of the Church, contributed exclusively to this collection. The series is completed in Thirty Numbers, forming Five Volumes, either of which may be had separately. In the Fifth Volume is given a GENERAL INDEX of the Contributors, and of the subjects of the various Discourses.

Price 2*s.* 6*d.*,

THE IMAGERY and POETICAL ORNAMENTS of the BOOK of PSALMS; its Prophetic Language, and Apocalyptic Character, and the Modes of using the Psalter, from the earliest to the present Time.
By the Rev. GEORGE HENRY STODDART, A.M.,
Of Queen's College, Oxford.

I HAVE rather compiled from the researches of others, than depended on my own powers; and the principal observations are selected from the writings of Bishops Horsley, Lowth, Patrick, Horne, and Jebb; Dr. Lightfoot, Dr. Allix, and Mr. Boys. I still claim, however, the credit of having most carefully examined their conflicting opinions on many important topics. I have advanced no remarks but such as appeared to me to rest on most substantial grounds, and to be fully accordant to Gospel principles; and I have used much diligence in the effort to arrange and simplify the stores of erudition of the above distinguished critics, and to commend, in a popular form, the information thence derived for general readers.

Fine Paper, Gilt Edges, 2*s.*; Cheap Edition, 1*s.*

PSALMS and HYMNS, for PUBLIC WORSHIP;
Selected and Revised by the Rev. J. E. RIDDLE, M.A.,
Assistant Minister of Brunswick Chapel, Upper Berkeley Street.

GREAT care has been bestowed on this selection, in order to make it, in every respect, a valuable manual of Congregational Psalmody The Psalms have been adopted from various versions, and the Hymns from numerous writers :—all the best, but the best only, have been taken : —and the compiler has endeavoured to present *uniform* simplicity and gracefulness of style, together with the purity and fervour of CHRISTIAN devotion. The Psalms and Hymns amount to about a hundred and fifty, including every variety: and it is hoped that both sweetness and fulness of tone, will be found in this harp of Zion.

Complete in Two Handsome Folio Volumes, price £2 2*s.*, Half-bound, or in Nos , I to XXIV., at 1*s* 6*d.* each,

SACRED MINSTRELSY; a COLLECTION of the FINEST SACRED MUSIC, by the best Masters,
arranged as Solos, Duets, Trios, &c., and Choruses; and with Accompaniments for the Piano-Forte or Organ.

THE exclusive nature of nearly all existing collections of sacred music, and the high price at which novelties are in general produced, renders this work particularly desirable. Many fine productions, at present comparatively unknown, would be hailed with delight as additions to the stores of Sacred Harmony, could they be procured in a familiar form and on reasonable terms. The design of the present work, therefore, is to place within the reach of families, and of persons unaccustomed to playing from score, really good practical music; classical, yet not laboriously and uselessly learned; and thus to attract towards Sacred Music a portion of that patronage which is too generally bestowed, in so disproportionate a degree, upon works of a secular kind.

5

MISCELLANEOUS WORKS,

Two Volumes, with Portraits, price 10s. 6d.,

THE LIFE of SIR WILLIAM JONES, by the late LORD TEIGNMOUTH; with Notes, Selections from his Works, and a Memoir of his Noble Biographer,
By the Rev. SAMUEL CHARLES WILKS, M.A.

SIR WILLIAM JONES was not only the most eminent linguist, but in many respects one of the most remarkable men of the last century; and LORD TEIGNMOUTH'S Memoir of him has been justly accounted one of the most interesting, instructive, and entertaining pieces of modern biography. To the present edition of this popular Memoir is prefixed a notice of its lately-deceased author; who, though highly respected as an Oriental scholar, and raised to the peerage for his meritorious services as Governor-general of India, was yet better known for the Christian virtues which adorned his character, and rendered him a public benefactor to mankind.

Two Volumes, with Portraits, 9s.,

LIVES of EMINENT CHRISTIANS; containing the Lives of BISHOP WILSON; ARCHBISHOP USHER; DR. HAMMOND; JOHN EVELYN; BERNARD GILPIN; PHILIP DE MORNAY; BISHOP BEDELL; and DR. HORNECK.
By the Rev. R. B. HONE, M.A.

THE paths of good men are commonly so full of peace, and the sorrows which befall them, so mercifully softened and blessed by a sacred influence, that few more pleasing or successful ways of recommending the fear and love of God have been found, than the publication of religious biography.

Foolscap Octavo, with Portraits by Engleheart, price 4s. 6d.

LIVES of SACRED POETS. Containing INTRODUCTORY SKETCH of SACRED POETRY.
GEORGE WITHER, FRANCIS QUARLES, GILES FLETCHER, GEORGE HERBERT, RICHARD CRASHAW.
By R. A. WILLMOTT, Esq., Trin, Coll. Camb.

THE writer of these Lives has endeavoured to present as ample a view as the limits of a volume would permit, of the state of Sacred Poetry in the reigns of Elizabeth, James the First, and Charles the First. Among the poets and distinguished individuals, of whom Biographical and Critical Sketches are given, may be enumerated R. Southwell; H. Constable; B. Barnes; Francis Davison, the author of some exquisite Versions from the Psalms; Donne; W. Browne, the sweetest disciple of Spenser's Pastoral School; Sir John Denham; Heywood, the author of the *Hierarchie of the Blessed Angels*; G. Sandys; Lord Bacon, the friend of Herbert; Hobbes, the philosopher, and Ben Jonson, his associate in the translation of the *Advancement of Learning;* the celebrated Lord Herbert, of Cherbury; the accomplished and learned Selden; Archbishops Williams and Laud; Lord Pembroke, the lover and loved of poets; Cowley, the affectionate friend of Crashaw, &c.

Foolscap Octavo, with Engravings, 5s. 6d., cloth, lettered,

THE HISTORY of MOHAMMEDANISM, and the principal MOHAMMEDAN SECTS.
By W. C. TAYLOR, LL.D., T.C.D.

THIS work contains a full account of the Mohammedan traditions respecting the origin of their faith, an account of the 1.. ical religious and social s... med's life, mainly derived from his own autobiographical notices in the Koran; an original Mohammedan Creed; and the ... h... neared

THE MILITARY PASTOR; a Series of PRAC TICAL DISCOURSES, addressed to SOLDIERS; wit PRAYERS for Patients in Military Hospitals.

By the Rev. JOHN PARKER LAWSON, M.A.,
Author of the *Life and Times of Archbishop Laud.*

As no manual of this description has been published, the Author trusts that it will not be unacceptable to those of his brethren among the clergy, who, either by express official appointment, or from local situation, act as chaplains to the army. But his object has chiefly been to produce a Manual which may find its way into barracks and other military esta blishments, not only for private perusal but for the use of those officers who, in the absence of chaplains, are necessitate by authority to read prayers and a ser mon to the troops under their com mand.

SECOND EDITION, price 1s. 6d. in Black Cloth, lettered,

A DAILY PRAYER BOOK, for the Use o Families and Schools.

By J. T. BARRETT, D.D., Rector of Beauchamp, Essex.

THIS Book of Family Devotion is not only drawn up in the language of the Church, but agreeably to her Form and Order for Morning and Evening Service, throughout the year; and hence is ca culated to lead and confirm her member in her edifying mode of worship at Co mon Prayer.

Price 1s. 6d.,

OFFICE for the VISITATION of the SICK with Notes and Explanations.

By WILLIAM COXE, M.A., Archdeacon of Wilts.

THIS little work contains the office for the Sick, with Notes and Explanations founded on the Doctrine and Discipline of the Church of England. It avoids all points unsuited to a season of bodily affliction, and whilst it suppresses the presumption of enthusiasm on the one hand, and the forebodings of despondency o the other, and goes only to plain an practical questions of primary and vit interest, it will, it is hoped, both facilita the labours of those who visit the Sic and be conducive to the best spiritu benefit of those who are visited.

Price 4s.,

A DISCOURSE on DEATH; with APPLIC TIONS of CHRISTIAN DOCTRINE.

By the Rev. HENRY STEBBING, M.A.

No man will deny that whatever can be said of death is applicable to himself. The bell which he hears tolled may never toll for him; there may be no friend or children left to lament him; he may not have to lie through long and anxious days, looking for the coming of the expected terror: but he knows he must die: he knows that in whatever quarter of the world he abides—whatever may be his circumstances—however strong his pre sent hold of life—however unlike th piey of death he looks—that it is h doom, beyond reverse, to die But if be thus certain that death is the comn lot of all—the great result of lif must surely be the part of a ration creature like man to inquire, what death? and having answered this que tion, to consider what kind of prepar tion should be made for its approach.

7

ARTISANS AND MACHINERY; the Moral, Social, and Physical Condition of the Industrious Classes of Great Britain, connected with Manufactures, considered, with reference to Mechanical Substitutes for Human Labour.

THE absence of a work devoted to an examination of the Moral, Social, and Physical condition of more than three millions of our fellow subjects, men, women, and children, engaged in the arts, manufactures, and trade of the country, has been long deemed a serious evil. The vast importance of the subject, and the numerous interests connected with it, render a dispassionate inquiry not only highly desirable, but, with a view to its influence upon the community at large, absolutely necessary. No apology, therefore, it is thought, will be required, for bringing the matter before the public, in a work which is the result of practical observation, made in the course of long professional attendance among the class of persons to whom it particularly relates.

THE OLD and NEW POOR LAW: Who Gains? and Who Loses? Explained by Conversations on Facts of Daily Occurrence.

THIS little work is addressed to the Working Classes, and to their Friends. Among the latter, the writer would rank himself; and he feels assured that he cannot prove his title to the name better than by endeavouring to make that clear to others, which is established in his own mind,—namely, that the late alterations in the Poor Law are founded in wisdom and benevolence, and that the honest and industrious labourer will be the very first who will feel the advantages resulting from the change.

NATIONAL EDUCATION, and the MEANS of IMPROVING IT.

By the Rev. T. V. SHORT, B.D., Rector of Bloomsbury.

THE question of National Education, is one of vital importance to all who feel concerned for the temporal interests of England. The degree of power which has, of late years, been distributed to the people, cannot be safely intrusted to all orders in the state, unless principles of religion and justice influence their minds; and it is in vain to hope for the diffusion of these principles, except through the blessing of God, bestowed on Religious as well as general Education. Christian principles will teach the rich that they are benefiting themselves while they ameliorate the condition of the poor, and convince the poor that their own interests are best consulted, when the well-being of the rich is advanced; and how can these objects be more effectually advanced, than when the upper orders provide for the education of the children of the lower.

THE INFLUENCES of DEMOCRACY on Liberty, Property, and the Happiness of Society, considered; By an AMERICAN, formerly Member of Congress: With an INTRODUCTION, by HENRY EWBANK, Esq.

I BRING before my reader a living picture of Democracy by the hand of a master. And if the testimony of an eye-witness—an American Republican—and a most ardent lover of liberty—is entitled to any attention, thinking men will perhaps pause before they sacrifice themselves to the Juggernaut of self-government, or give way to the specious, but false opinion, that the transfer of political power to the people is necessarily attended by an increase of liberty.

9

Foolscap Octavo, price 6*d*.

CHURCH AND STATE INSEPARABLE.
By A LAYMAN.

ASSUMING it established by the opinions and practice of ages, that some general principles of Religion, pervading the public councils, and influencing the public conduct, are inseparable from the well-being of every community, let us inquire whether the connexion which has so long subsisted between the Church of England and the Civil Government of these Realms, is in reality essential to our prosperity as a people.

In a large Octavo Volume, price 13*s* 6*d*.,

ARCHBISHOP USHER'S ANSWER to a JESUIT; with other Tracts on Popery.

THE principal treatise in this volume is the learned Archbishop's *Answer to a Jesuit's Challenge*, in which all the augmentations and emendations of the early editions have been adopted, and the gross errors of the edition printed after the author's death corrected. The volume further contains—*The Discourse of the* *Religion anciently professed by the Irish and British; the Speech on the Oath of Supremacy; the Sermon before the House of Commons;* and *The Declaration of the Universality of the Church of Christ.* Copious Indices of Texts, of Authorities, and of Subjects, are appended to this edition

---

FOURTH EDITION, Post Octavo, price 4*s*. in cloth, lettered, A

DISCOURSE on the STUDIES of the UNIVERSITY of CAMBRIDGE.
By PROFESSOR SEDGWICK, M.A., F.R.S., &c.

THE recent attacks on physical science, and the gross misapprehension of its moral tendency, have been singularly wanton and ill-timed. * * * A sceptic may, indeed, think that the whole system of things, moral and physical, has no principle of continued rest,—that it has only been jostled into a condition of unstable equilibrium, which may be destroyed by the first movement of any of the component elements. Such a one may reasonably fear the progress of discovery, for his system wants the essential principles of cohesion; but a sincere believer in the word of God has no fear of this kind.

Second Edition, in Post Octavo, price 9*s*., cloth, lettered.

OATHS; their ORIGIN, NATURE, and HISTORY;
By JAMES ENDELL TYLER, B.D.,
Rector of St. Giles' in the Fields, and late Fellow of Oriel College.

Royal Quarto, with FORTY-EIGHT Plates, price 1*l*. 11*s*. 6*d*,

ESSAY on the ARCHITECTURE of the HINDUS.
By RÁM RÁZ, Native Judge and Magistrate at Bangalore; Cor. Mem. of the Royal Asiatic Society.

THIS work is published from the original manuscript and drawings of the Author, under the direction of the ROYAL ASIATIC SOCIETY of GREAT BRITAIN AND IRELAND.

BOOKS,

In SHEETS, and in PLAIN and ELEGANT BINDING, *Wholesale* and *Retail.*

In a Pocket Volume, bound in cloth, lettered, 8s. 6d., THE

CAMBRIDGE GREEK and ENGLISH NEW TESTAMENT. The Greek, (from the THIRD EDITION of STEPHENS,) 1550, and the English, from the Authorised Version, being given in Parallel Columns on the same Page.

SECOND EDITION, Corrected and Enlarged, 3s. 6d.,

THE TEXT of the ENGLISH BIBLE, as now printed by the Universities, considered with reference to a REPORT by a SUB-COMMITTEE of DISSENTING MINISTERS.
By THOMAS TURTON, D.D.,
Regius Professor of Divinity, Cambridge, and Dean of Peterborough.

Octavo, 4s,

A REVIEW of the PRINCIPAL DISSENTING COL-LEGES in ENGLAND during the last Century; being a Second and enlarged Edition of the Author's Work on the ADMISSION of PERSONS, without regard to their Religious Opinions, to certain Degrees in the UNIVERSITIES of ENGLAND.
By THOMAS TURTON, D.D.

Royal Quarto, 25s.,

AN HISTORICAL ACCOUNT of the THIRTY-NINE ARTICLES, from the First Promulgation of them in 1553, to their Final Establishment, 1571, with exact copies of the Latin and English MSS., and Fac-similes of the Signatures of the Archbishops and Bishops, &c.
By JOHN LAMB, D.D., Master of Corpus Christi College, Cambridge.

Octavo, 8s. 6d ,

HEBREW CHARACTERS derived from HIEROGLY-PHICS. The original Pictures applied to the Interpretation of various Words and Passages in the Sacred Writings.
By JOHN LAMB, D.D., Master of Corpus Christi College, Cambridge.

Quarto, price 25s.,

ASTRONOMICAL OBSERVATIONS, for the Year MDCCCXXXIV., made at the Observatory at Cambridge.
By GEORGE BIDDELL AIRY, Esq., M.A.,
Late Fellow of Trin. Col. and Plumian Prof. of Astron. and Ex. Phil. in the University of Cambridge.

PERIODICAL WORKS.

On the 1st of February, (and continued Monthly,) price 1s. 6d., THE

MAGAZINE OF POPULAR SCIENCE, and JOURNAL OF THE USEFUL ARTS.

Edited under the Direction of the Society for the Illustration and Encouragement of Practical Science, at the Adelaide-Street Gallery, London.

The respective Numbers will in general comprise more or less of the following subjects.

I. Leading Article.—General Remarks on the Claims, Objects, and Results of Science; Popular Sketches of its present condition, recent progress, &c.

II. Intelligence.—New Discoveries, Experiments, Inventions and Improvements in
1. Mathematical and Physical Science; Mechanics, Optics, Hydrostatics, Astronomy, Magnetism, Meteorology, &c
2. Chemistry, Galvanism, Electricity, Heat, Mineralogy, Geology, &c.

3. Natural History, Botany, Physiology, Comparative Anatomy, Conchology, &c.
4. Manufactures; Processes in the Arts; Civil Engineering; Practical Mechanics; Domestic Economy, &c.
III. Review.—Notices of New Works on Science, English and Foreign.
IV. Miscellaneous Intelligence.—Proceedings of Societies. Obituary Novelties in the Gallery of Practical Science.

Numbers I. to IV., continued Quarterly, price 6s.,

JOURNAL of the ROYAL ASIATIC SOCIETY of GREAT BRITAIN and IRELAND;

Containing original Papers, relative to the History, Manners and Customs, Laws, Religion, Natural History, Arts, Commerce, Manufactures, and Productions of THE ORIENTAL WORLD.

Contributed by Members and Correspondents of the Society at Home and Abroad.

In Weekly Numbers, price One Penny; and in Monthly Parts, price Sixpence each.

THE SATURDAY MAGAZINE.

Printed under the Direction of the Committee of General Literature and Education, appointed by the Society for Promoting Christian Knowledge.

Great care and attention are bestowed in adapting this cheap and popular Magazine to all classes of Readers, so that it may with propriety be introduced into Families and Schools, and among Young People in general. Its contents are at once instructive and entertaining. Religious, Moral, and Social Principles, are combined with Useful Information; and a Christian Character and tendency is given to Popular Knowledge. It is most extensively illustrated by Engravings on Wood, which comprise Portraits, Views, remarkable Objects, in Antiquities, Science, and Manufactures, the various branches of Natural History, and indeed whatever is curious and interesting in Nature and in Art.

The Saturday Magazine is also published in Half-Yearly Volumes, at 4s. 6d., and in Annual Volumes, at 7s. 6d.

WS - #0034 - 040325 - C0 - 229/152/23 - PB - 9781330772904 - Gloss Lamination